VIOLENT FATHERING AND THE RISKS TO C

The need for change

Lynne Harne

First published in Great Britain in 2011 by

The Policy Press
University of Bristol
Fourth Floor
Beacon House
Queen's Road
Bristol BS8 1QU
UK

t: +44 (0)117 331 4054
f: +44 (0)117 331 4093
tpp-info@bristol.ac.uk
www.policypress.co.uk

North American office:
The Policy Press
c/o International Specialized Books Services
920 NE 58th Avenue, Suite 300
Portland, OR 97213-3786, USA
t: +1 503 287 3093
f: +1 503 280 8832
info@isbs.com

British Library Cataloguing in Publication Data
A catalogue record for this book is available from the British Library.

Library of Congress Cataloging-in-Publication Data
A catalog record for this book has been requested.

ISBN 978 1 84742 211 8 paperback
ISBN 978 1 84742 917 9 hardcover

Cover design by Robin Hawes.
Front cover: image kindly supplied by www.stockxchang.com
Printed and bound in Great Britain by TJ International, Padstow.
The Policy Press uses environmentally responsible print partners.

Contents

About the author

Lynne Harne PhD is currently a research associate and hononary research member of the Centre for Gender and Violence Research in the School for Policy Studies, University of Bristol. She also teaches on women, family and social policy at the University of Westminster. She has previously worked as a senior lecturer in criminology at the universities of Sunderland and Roehampton and taught on domestic violence courses for professionals at the University of Teesside. She has been working around issues of men's violence towards children and women for the last 25 years and has recently given evidence to the parliamentary justice committee on child contact and issues of violence to children and mothers. Other relevant research and publications include Harne, L. (2009) *Domestic violence and safeguarding children: The use of systematic risk identification and assessment in private law proceedings by family court advisors: A pilot study*, University of Bristol, and Harne, L. and Radford, J. (2008) *Tackling domestic violence: Theories, policies and practice*, Open University Press.

Introduction

In recent years there has been considerable policy emphasis on the benefits of increased father involvement with children. However, these discourses have assumed that all father engagement is good for children, rather than acknowledging differences between fathers and recognising that, as with some mothers, there are those who pose considerable risks to children's safety and their long-term development and welfare. Despite legislation that recognises that child maltreatment includes observing harm towards others, there has been a strange silence in government policies in identifying and naming such fathers as abusers or in questioning their parenting. Rather, in policies to safeguard children in the context of fathers' domestic violence, the focus has tended to remain on abused mothers' parenting and their failure or inability to protect, while in family policies, it has been assumed that violent fathers are still 'good enough' parents on separation, providing that their ongoing relationships with children can be organised 'safely'.

This context has been informed by specifically gendered discourses of parenting, where fathering has been accorded far more social value and status than mothering in relation to children's wellbeing, reflecting the continuing gendered inequalities between men and women in wider society, where men have more social, economic and political power. At the same time, gender-neutral policy definitions of domestic violence have obscured the significant role of violent fathers and father figures in harming children through their parenting practices. Such discourses have, as Hearn has noted, involved 'an implicit coalition between the state and fathers' (Hearn, 2001, p 88) that, despite initiatives to criminalise aspects of domestic violence in the UK as in many other western states, has been limited to not interfering with fathers' familial relationships.

The aim of this book is therefore to look at the harmful impacts of domestically violent fathering in heterosexual relationships and underline the urgent need for changes in policy and practice to improve the safety and wellbeing of the children concerned. Within this, it discusses the findings from original qualitative research with violent fathers on their parenting practices and examines the impact of perpetrator programmes on violent fathers' discourses of parenting and their motivations to change.

Children's rights

Under the United Nations Convention on the Rights of the Child (UNCRC), ratified by the UK, children have the right to be protected from maltreatment by their parents (article 19) and their best interests are paramount (that is, above parental rights; article 3). Children also have the right to express their own views freely in any procedures affecting them and to have these taken into account (article 12). However, the latter right is qualified by consideration of children's 'age and maturity' and children may be seen as not competent enough to judge their own best interests, leading to ambiguity in the ways their views are interpreted by adults who have the power to make decisions about their lives. Nevertheless, children's views are now recognised as increasingly significant in understandings of the impact of parental domestic violence on them and their own needs and perspectives frame the analysis and discussion on violent fathering throughout this book.

The scale of the problem

The extent and impact of fathers' domestic violence indicate that it is not a minor problem, committed only by a few men in familial relationships, as is suggested in some policy discourses. In Sweden, one in 10 children are known to be affected by a father's violence (Eriksson and Nasman, 2008) and UK figures are likely to be similar, although there has been a significant lack of investigation in this area (see Chapter One). While children's perspectives suggest that they experience such violence in different ways, extensive research reviews indicate that overall, they are more likely to be anxious and fearful and fare less well in terms of their developmental outcomes than children who have not lived with such violence (Kolbo et al, 1996; Kitzmann et al, 2003). Research also indicates that there is significant overlap between fathers' domestic violence towards mothers and their direct abuse of children, with many experiencing multiple forms of abuse (Edleson, 1999; Brown, 2006; Hester et al, 2007).

This is highlighted at the extreme end of the scale of harm to children, by the large number of violent fathers and father figures perpetrating child homicides (Brandon et al, 2006; Cavanagh et al, 2007; Ferguson, 2009). In one recent study that looked at 163 child homicides between 2004 and 2008, biological fathers, father figures or male carers were held responsible for these deaths either singly or jointly with mothers in 70 per cent of cases, with biological fathers being responsible for the majority of deaths. Domestic violence was known to be a significant factor in 42 per cent of these cases, but rose to 69 per cent where biological fathers had killed children post-separation (Ferguson, 2009). These figures alone should warrant more policy attention to the high risks of violent fathering, even though such killings are relatively infrequent.

Defining domestic violence

Definitions of domestic violence, sometimes also referred to as domestic abuse, have been highly contested in the UK, with many agencies using different definitions and varying in their recognition of such violence as a gendered phenomenon. One development in government policy has been the use of broader definitions including a range of behaviours, rather than just physical acts. There has also been recognition of differences in forms of domestic violence between ethnic communities, with forced marriage and so-called 'honour' crimes being defined as domestic violence. But over the past decades there has been a shift towards viewing domestic violence in a more gender-neutral way, albeit with the recognition that women are the most heavily victimised group. Radford (2001) has argued that this move is partially a consequence of the growth in men's and fathers' rights groups, which have drawn on equal opportunities discourses and family violence perspectives from the US (Straus and Gelles, 1986) to support perspectives of equal or mutual violence between men and women in heterosexual relationships. Thus the current government definition defines domestic violence as follows:

> 'Any incident of threatening behaviour, violence or abuse (psychological, physical, sexual, financial or emotional) between adults who are or have been intimate partners or family members, regardless of gender or sexuality.' This includes issues of concern to black and minority ethnic communities such as so called 'honour based violence', female genital mutilation (FGM) and forced marriage. (Home Office, 2009)

One consequence of this gender-neutral, incident-based approach is that it has made it much harder for professionals to understand the impact of fathers' domestic violence on children and to assess their safety in different contexts, since the violence may be perceived as a *mutual* problem between the parents, and defined merely as a 'volatile relationship'. In this way, attention then shifts from the violent father to the equal welfare responsibilities of both parents (Macdonald, 2009).

This is not to suggest that mothers are never violent, but as Nazroo's (1995) ground-breaking qualitative study on domestic violence between 100 heterosexual couples demonstrated, women's violence towards male partners usually consists of one-off acts such as a slap or throwing an object and is mainly undertaken in self-defence. On the other hand, men used 'threatening violence', which is based on a combination of repeated physical attacks, intimidation and humiliation of their partners and is intended to inflict both physical and psychological harm. Such findings have been repeated in larger-scale studies and in British Crime Surveys, where women victims have been found to experience much greater fear and anxiety and more physical injuries than men (Walby and Allen, 2004; Hester, 2009).

Another problematic aspect of the government definition is that it only applies to adults (in the UK defined as aged 18) and therefore omits intimate violence in teenage relationships. Yet the first UK prevalence study of young people's experiences of intimate violence between the ages of 13 and 17 found that one in three girls experienced sexual violence and one in four physical violence from a male partner (Barter et al, 2009). Such findings have particular policy implications in relation to the safety of teenage mothers and their children and the involvement of young violent fathers in their lives, since these fathers are most likely to pose severe and lethal risks to children (Cavanagh et al, 2007; Ferguson, 2009).

It is also noteworthy that the Welsh Assembly has included harm to children in its formal definition, stating that:

> The wide adverse effects of living with domestic abuse for children must be recognised as a child protection issue. The effects can be linked to poor educational achievement, social exclusion and to juvenile crime, substance abuse, mental health problems and homelessness to running away. Domestic violence is not a one off occurrence; it is frequent and persistent. (Welsh Assembly Government, 2005:5)

Domestic violence as gendered violence and coercive control

In contrast to gender-neutral perspectives are those that recognise the gendered[1] power dynamics of domestic violence and the different motivating factors that usually distinguish men's violence from that of women in heterosexual relationships and, rather than being viewed as individual incidents, are seen to form an ongoing *pattern* of coercive and controlling behaviours. This is illustrated in the following statement from Women's Aid Federation of England:

> In Women's Aid's view domestic violence is physical, sexual, psychological or financial violence that takes place within an intimate or family-type relationship and that forms a pattern of coercive and controlling behaviour. This can include forced marriage and so-called 'honour crimes'. Domestic violence may include a range of abusive behaviours, not all of which are in themselves inherently 'violent'. Crime statistics and research both show that domestic violence is gender specific (i.e. most commonly experienced by women and perpetrated by men) and that any woman can experience domestic violence regardless of race, ethnic or religious group, class, disability or lifestyle. Domestic violence is repetitive, life-threatening, and can destroy the lives of women and children. (Women's Aid, 2007)

As seen above, the nature of this pattern, often defined as 'coercive control', involves a range of behaviours that can vary cross-culturally and may include not only physical violence, but also sexual coercion and intimidation (involving threats to harm or kill, banging walls, the destruction of family property, harming pets, surveillance and stalking); humiliation, degradation and shaming; isolating women from their own friendship and family support networks; and control over family resources and the 'micro-management' of everyday life (Stark, 2007). Regan and colleagues (2007) have argued that jealous surveillance is a central aspect of coercive control and includes violent men's 'sense of entitlement' to 'police' the boundaries of women's behaviour, 'attempts to isolate women from family and friends and limit their inter-actions with other men' (Regan et al, 2007, p 23). Thus, this concept is broader than mere sexual jealousy, because it involves a sense of ownership of women partners, where all their attention and time is expected to be focused on the needs and wishes of the male partner.

Bancroft and Silverman (2002) have indicated that such a sense of entitlement is not limited to men's expectations and control of women, and in familial settings also influences violent fathers' perceptions of their relationships with their children. It thus has considerable implications for their parenting of children and children's own safety. The extent of violent fathers' coercive control has been shown to be highly significant in identifying their harmful risks to children as well as to mothers, and is therefore used as a key concept in the analysis of their fathering undertaken in this book.

Defining fatherhood

Both fatherhood and motherhood are defined by the social meanings attached to them. At the broad social level, fatherhood can be seen as a changing social construction that has varied historically and cross-culturally. Yet fatherhood and fathering – the social practice of being fathers either individually or collectively – continue to be constructed through discourses of dominant (hegemonic) masculinity, despite some shifts in the division of labour in the home, and such gendering has intensified over recent years. Thus fatherhood is defined in relation and in contrast to motherhood as well as to children as a specifically privileged masculine social status and social identity. Fathers can, for example, act or take on the role of mothers, particularly in terms of childcare and nurturing, but it is never considered that mothers can take on the role of fathers, since motherhood is not accorded the same social status.

The current social and legal status accorded to biological, or, more precisely, genetic fathers over social fathers is a relatively recent development, since fatherhood status was previously defined through marriage (Collier, 1995). In the latter decades of the 20th century, the decline in marriage resulted in changes to the means through which men make legal claims to children and to fatherhood status and identities, primarily through genetic connection. Thus, even where men have had no social relationships with children, these claims are legitimised on the basis of biology alone and are strengthened by policy discourses articulating the view that children need fathers not only for the higher economic support they are presumed to provide, but in terms of their specifically masculinised care (DCSF, 2010). This, it is argued, is particularly so in the case of boys, where father involvement is considered essential to constructing dominant masculinities, with some longitudinal studies suggesting that fathers encourage assertive behaviours in sons but compliant behaviours in daughters (Flouri, 2005). Further, the evidence from such studies are equivocal and contradictory about the benefits of father involvement overall for children, particularly in terms of whether it contributes to children's mental health outcomes – a claim that has consistently been made by the government over recent years (DfES 2007; DCSF, 2010).

Regardless of such findings, however, it is clear that fathering has become significant to *men* in terms of practising masculine identities, not only in relation to demonstrating 'virility' (Smart, 1989) but also through the development of specifically masculinised discourses of emotional connection to children and through seeking control over post-separation families (Beck, 1992; Collier, 2005). Moreover, although for some individual fathers increased involvement in the *care* of children may be a means of constructing more nurturing and less dominant masculinities, for others it can be a way to practise dominant, violent and abusive fathering (Pringle, 1998).

When looking at the parenting practices of violent fathers, therefore, it is necessary to view them on one end of a continuum of social constructions of masculinity, where fathering itself at an individual level is a varying and diverse social practice that includes not only what fathers do with children, but also their perspectives on their relationships with children, their perceptions of their roles as fathers and their social relationships with children's mothers. Fathering does, however, interconnect with its wider social context and the continuing gendered inequalities between men and women, and this book therefore argues that violent fathering needs to be understood in terms of gendered power relations between men and women, as well as power relationships with children.

Violent fathering and its impact on mothering

Fathering as seen above is defined in relation not only to children but also to mothers in heterosexual relationships and often involves conflict over the children. In terms of violent fathering, strategies of coercive control frequently include repeated physical and sexual violence against mothers in front of the children as well as deliberate humiliation and attempts to undermining their parenting and alienate the children from them (Jaffe et al, 2003). Such behaviour can have a profound impact on some abused mothers' own parenting and this needs to be acknowledged as one of the outcomes of violent fathering, as it has significant impacts for children themselves. The impact on mothering is not addressed in detail in this book, as this has been done elsewhere[2]. However, the interconnections between fathers' coercive control of mothers and its impact on children are illustrated in an adapted version of the power and control wheel (Pence, 1987; Pence and Paymar, 1993) shown below.

The power and control wheel (Adapted from Pence, 1987)

Structure of the book

Reflecting the themes outlined above, Chapter One summarises the research on the impact of fathers' violence on children and children's own perspectives of their violent fathers. Chapter Two takes a historical approach to fatherhood policy, locating violent fathering within this wider context. It discusses the influence of fathers' rights movements on policy formation and the contradictions created for practitioners in trying to negotiate between two different policy discourses: that of safeguarding children and involving violent and abusive fathers in children's lives. Chapter Three looks at explanations for men's violence against women in intimate and familial relationships and discusses other research on violent fathers and the beginnings of changing practice to address their harm to children including the use of risk assessment and specific programmes to address their parenting.

Chapter Four discusses the findings from the author's own qualitative research looking at violent fathers' perspectives on their parenting practices while living with children and post-separation during child contact. It contrasts these to those of abused mothers who were also interviewed and whose children were subjected to their fathers' violence. Since all the fathers interviewed were drawn from perpetrator programmes, Chapter Five discusses the impacts of these programmes on fathers' own views and whether they indicated that such fathers had changed enough to have safe contact with children. Finally Chapter Six discusses the policy and practice changes that are needed in order to safeguard children and protect their welfare, locating the discussion within a social justice approach.

Notes

[1] Gender as used here refers to the socially constructed differences between men and women, rather than anatomical sex differences.

[2] See, for example, Harne and Radford (2008) and Radford and Hester (2006).

ONE

Fathers' violence and children's perspectives

Introduction

This chapter looks at the extent and impact of fathers' violence on children and children's own perspectives on their violent fathers. The first section summarises some of the key findings from the research on the varying ways children are harmed through this violence and its interconnections with abusive parental practice. The second section focuses on research on children's own views of living with paternal domestic violence and their feelings towards these fathers. The importance of children's perspectives on their own lives has been highlighted in sociological studies of childhood and indicates that they are active participants in socialisation processes rather than merely passive objects (James and Prout, 1990; Qvortrup et al, 1994). Yet children's perceptions of domestic violence from fathers and their feelings and views have frequently been marginalised and ignored in policy and practice responses (McGee, 2000; Mullender et al, 2002). In this regard even very young children are usually competent to describe their experiences either verbally or through visual representation, as seen in the drawing on page 26.

The extent of fathers' violence

A problem with assessing the prevalence of fathers' violence and its impact on children is that research in this area has not usually asked questions about perpetrators' parental relationships and government policy has defined fathers as non-abusers (Scourfield and Drakeford, 2002; DCSF, 2010). As seen in the introduction, a gender-neutral approach to defining domestic violence has contributed to this invisibility, alongside professional assumptions that violence between parents is often mutual (Hester et al, 2007). Nevertheless, some data is available, with the Department of Health (DH, 2002) estimating that nearly a million children are affected by fathers' violence towards women. This estimate is supported by victim information in British

Crime Survey data where half of the 10 per cent of women in the general population who on average experience domestic violence each year are known to have children (Mirrlees-Black, 1999). It is also known that the presence of children is associated with double the risk of domestic violence towards women (Walby and Allen, 2004). Other information has come from the only UK retrospective study to date that has looked at the prevalence of child maltreatment with nearly 3,000 young adults (Cawson et al, 2000). While taking a gender-neutral approach, this study found that a quarter had witnessed physical violence towards a parent at least once and a fifth were really afraid of their fathers. These figures are much higher than current government estimates, which consider that only 200,000 children are affected (DCSF, 2010) and themselves may be underestimates because of the methods used and victims' unwillingness to disclose the abuse.

Further information on the extent and impact of fathers' domestic violence has come from studies looking at what happens to abused mothers and children when they separate from fathers and are subjected to family law policies that promote child contact with the separated parent in nearly all circumstances (DfES, 2004). While this is discussed below and in the next chapter, studies indicated that between 40 and 60 per cent of cases that came before the family courts and used in-court mediation involved cases where mothers and children had experienced domestic violence from fathers (NAPO, 2002; Trinder et al, 2006). These figures are also likely to be underestimates, since they do not involve cases where abused mothers have agreed child contact arrangements through solicitors (Masson, 2006).

There are also assumptions that biological fathers are less likely to be violent and abusive in families than stepfathers or other father figures, who may be seen as only having transitory relationships with women. Yet UK qualitative studies indicate that between two thirds and four fifths of domestic violence is perpetrated by biological fathers rather than stepfathers and other father figures (Abrahams, 1994; McGee, 2000; Mullender et al, 2002). However, at the same time it needs to be recognised that contemporary fatherhood is frequently fragmented across families, since on separation a violent father may obtain a second family where he is both a biological father and stepfather to some of the children. As a consequence of this fragmentation, the extent and impact of fathers' violence is likely to be more far-reaching as these fathers move from one family to the next and retain contact with children from previous families.

The impact of fathers' domestic violence on children

There is now considerable research evidence that confirms that children are distressed by living with domestic violence from fathers, even though children's experiences may differ according to the frequency, duration and severity of the violence and other factors such as their age, place in the family, disability and ethnicity (Jaffe et al, 2003). For example, children from South Asian families, the largest ethnic minority in the UK, are affected by domestic violence in similar ways to other children but also face 'additional issues and pressures that compound their situations' (Thiara, 2010, p 158). These include institutional barriers such as racism and the way collectivist patriarchal family and community values such as honour, shame and reputation may prevent mothers and children from seeking help (Izzidien, 2008; Thiara, 2010).

While children's experiences vary, the evidence of the distress incurred through living with violent fathers is overwhelming and is based on information from a number of sources including psycho-social research, studies of child protection and health records, research with practitioners and professionals, and mothers' and children's accounts. Thus, research reviews indicate that in general children of any age are more likely to be fearful and anxious, have their developmental needs disrupted and experience worse outcomes than other children (Kolbo et al, 1996; Rossman, 2001; Kitzmann et al, 2003).

This research also indicates three overlapping areas in which children are affected – the emotional abuse inflicted on children through having to observe fathers' violence towards their mothers directly or indirectly; fathers deliberately using or involving children in the abuse of mothers; and fathers directly abusing children. At times these three areas can overlap so profoundly that the abuse of mother and child should be regarded as simultaneous and recognition given to the fact that both are equally affected (Kelly, 1994; Hester et al, 2007).

Pregnancy and the unborn and newborn child

The initial negative impacts on children commence when fathers perpetrate domestic violence during pregnancy and thus pose considerable risks to the unborn child as well as to the health of the mother. Existing research suggests that between 15 and 30 per cent of mothers experience violence during pregnancy, which involves physical and/or sexual abuse (McWilliams and McKiernan, 1993; Coid, 2000). These mothers are at increased risk of miscarriage or still-birth (Mezey and Bewley, 1997) and maternal deaths during childbirth (Lewis and

Drife, 2001, 2005). They are also more likely to experience inadequate weight gain, anaemia, infections, premature birth or haemorrhage and have low birth-weight babies (Parker et al, 1994; BMA, 1997; WHO, 2005). Their children are therefore at increased risk of experiencing ill health or being born with physical impairments (Hester et al, 2007). According to Australian research (Quinlivan and Evans, 2001), teenage mothers and their unborn children are at particular risk, with up to 30 per cent experiencing violence from a boyfriend/partner during pregnancy and having a much higher incidence of puerperal and neonatal mortality as a consequence. Teenage pregnant mothers experiencing intimate violence are also more likely to smoke, drink alcohol and use illegal drugs as a means of coping with the abuse compared to those teenage mothers without such experiences (Quinlivan and Evans, 2001).

Age-related impacts

Following birth, infants can be affected by an increase in the violence (Mezey and Bewley, 1997) and fathers may prevent mothers from attending post-natal care, which itself can lead to further health risks for both mother and child (McGee, 2000). Babies as young as six weeks old are known to have learnt to stay quiet in reaction to hearing the violence; can fail to thrive and frequently experience problems with sleeping and eating (Radford et al, 1999; Sudermann and Jaffe, 1999).

In older infants and pre-school children, fear and anxiety are the most common impacts, which can be manifested through sleep disturbance, bedwetting, withdrawal or aggression, clinginess and refusal to speak, although these problems can also be found with children of primary school age. When these children start school they may have difficulties relating to other children and some may be diagnosed with attention deficit disorder, which, alongside other factors, is associated with the fear generated from living with domestic violence (Jaffe et al, 2003). Clinical depression has also been found among five-year-olds in this situation (McGee, 2000). Some boys of early primary school age may begin to disrespect women teachers and girl pupils, copying the disrespect they see from their fathers towards women in the home and older children in this age group can start worrying about what is happening at home and their educational achievement can begin to be affected (Connell, 1995; McGee, 2000; Jaffe et al, 2003). Adolescents may start to truant from school and engage in antisocial behaviour, while others may use school and educational achievement as a means of escaping from the violence. Low self-esteem, depression, substance misuse, self-harm, running away from home and early marriage can also be found among young people as a consequence of their experiences (Jaffe et al, 2003; Hester et al, 2007; Izzidien, 2008).

While age-related impacts are not fixed and may vary according to children's own individual characteristics and the presence of protective factors, infants and pre-school age children are considered to be at highest risk of harm because they are more likely to be present when the violence occurs, spend longer in the home and have less support from others outside the family. In addition, neuro-scientific studies, although controversial, are beginning to suggest that prolonged exposure to domestic violence from very early on in children's lives may affect brain development and cause post-traumatic stress disorder as children get older (Hester et al, 2007).

Using children in the abuse of their mothers

Close relationships between mothers and children can be a protective factor in violent situations. Many mothers make a considerable effort to protect their children and are able to have effective parenting relationships despite the violence they are experiencing (Radford and Hester, 2006). Yet some violent fathers may deliberately set out to undermine these relationships through specifically humiliating mothers in front of the children, disparaging their parenting and encouraging the children to participate in verbal and or physical abuse. Although some children resist such tactics, others lose confidence in their mothers and their relationships with them can be destroyed (McGee, 2000; Mullender, 2002; Jaffe et al, 2003). Some fathers deliberately abuse mothers in front of their children, including raping them in order to damage the mother child relationship, and using rape as a form of control (McGee, 2000). In addition, in some South Asian families, children may be systematically kept from their mothers, as they may be regarded as the property of the father and the fathers' family (Thiara, 2010).

At other times, fathers may deliberately abuse children or threaten to harm them in order to control mothers' behaviour. These kinds of manipulative strategy are prime examples of the double intentionality used by violent fathers where both mothers and children are controlled and harmed (Kelly, 1994) and need to be acknowledged by professionals as emotional abuse and neglect of children, discussed in more detail below.

Violent fathers' harm of children through direct abuse

Physical abuse

A significant number of fathers use physical violence towards both mothers and children, with 30 to 60 per cent of fathers abusing both (Ross, 1996; Edleson, 1999; McGee, 2000). McGee's UK study found that 52 per cent of children had experienced physical violence from fathers, ranging from 'extreme punishment' such as hitting children around the head with a fist or a weapon, to throwing things at them, hanging them out of windows and pushing their heads in a dishwasher. Children could also be thrown across the room, often when they were in the way of fathers' attacks on mothers. In one Childline study, children reporting physical abuse mainly from biological fathers described being hit with pokers, bottles and furniture and often being 'banged against walls and stairs'. In many of these cases, children had called the helpline because the abuse was so severe they were too frightened to return home and did not know where to turn to for help (Epstein and Keep, 1995, p 53). In later studies, children's accounts indicate that violent fathers may target particular siblings for abuse and that there can be differences between violence directed towards biological and non-biological children (McGee, 2000; Mullender et al, 2002).

Radford and colleagues' (1999) child contact study of 129 abused mothers found frequent physical abuse of very young children as a form of inappropriate punishment when children did not conform to fathers' expectations of how they should behave, as illustrated below:

> 'She would be shouted at and smacked hard for missing the potty and wetting the floor. He asked her to spell a word. When she made a mistake he grabbed her by the back of the neck and repeatedly banged her head down on the table calling her a stupid little shit.' (Radford et al, 1999, p 15)

In its most severe form, fathers' physical abuse can result in the killing of very young children. This is discussed further in Chapter Three.

Sexual abuse

In addition, studies of child protection records indicate that a significant minority of children are at risk of being sexually abused by violent fathers or stepfathers (Farmer and Pollock, 1998; Hester and Pearson, 1998; Brown et al, 2000). While a common misconception is that only stepfathers sexually abuse children, Farmer and Pollock's study of child protection records found that children were sexually abused by biological fathers in 16 per cent of cases, by stepfathers in 14 per cent of cases and by other perpetrators in the remainder of cases. In McGee's (2000) study, 11 per cent of children revealed that they had been sexually abused by their biological father even though they were not specifically asked about this. Radford and colleagues (1999) reported that 14 per cent of children had been sexually abused and groomed by biological fathers, such abuse including making children watch pornography or sexual acts, as well as direct sexual touching and penetration. However, one problem of identifying children at risk of sexual abuse in the domestic violence context is the fact that some children may feel it is not safe to disclose the abuse until they are separated from the abuser. Threats from violent fathers including killing their mothers can prevent such disclosure and in some cases the violence towards mothers can be used to conceal the sexual abuse of children (Forman, 1995; McGee, 2000). In this context, professionals may not recognise that children can be too fearful to disclose abuse before separation and often claim that their mothers' allegations are false, despite most allegations of this nature eventually being substantiated (Brown et al, 2000).

Mental cruelty and violent fathers' neglect and extreme control of children

While domestic violence is now recognised as a form of emotional abuse of children, children may also experience direct psychological and emotional abuse from violent fathers. This may take the form of deliberately harming pets, destroying children's possessions, belittling them and calling them names, frightening or threatening them, or ignoring them in a manner similar to violent fathers' treatment of mothers (Radford et al, 1999; McGee, 2000).

Child neglect is regarded as the ongoing failure to meet a child's basic physical and psychological needs, resulting in impaired health and development (Turner and Tanner, 2005). It is the most common form of child maltreatment registered in child protection practice and the boundaries of neglect can be blurred with other forms of child maltreatment, such as physical or emotional abuse of the type as highlighted above, and can lead to serious harm. Yet its causes are often misunderstood and it is frequently viewed as a failure in mothers' rather than fathers' parenting, even where fathers are perpetrators of domestic violence, since mothers continue to be regarded as the main carers in child protection practice (Daniel and Taylor, 2006) . However, research studies indicate that violent fathers can be directly or indirectly responsible for the neglect of children in various ways, including harming an unborn child during pregnancy through violence towards the mother. Further, violent fathers' neglect of very young children's developmental needs is reflected in the persistent abuse of mothers in the presence of children, as the following example shows:

> 'He started speaking very late, only when he was five years old, he understood but he didn't speak. My husband used to hit me in front of him. He used to cry and get upset.' (Thiara, 2010, p 166)

They may also directly neglect very young children's physical and psychological needs by depriving children of sleep, movement, speech or play, or deliberately encouraging inappropriate behaviour, as illustrated in the following accounts.

> 'It would be 11 o'clock at night … he wouldn't let my daughter go to bed. He made her just sit there all evening, and I kept on saying to her go to bed, and he'd say, 'She's not f★★★ing well going anywhere … she will go when I tell her.' (Abrahams, 1994, p 32)
>
> 'They were never allowed to talk, they were never allowed to play – they had to be quiet. My son did not talk until a year after we left the refuge, because that's what they did at home....' (Mullender et al, 2002, p 159)
>
> 'He never hit K, but, every time he cried or anything, he used to put him in his pushchair and make him sit there all day long. So he wasn't allowed to walk around. He was very quiet … he never used to bother playing, he just used to sit. (Hague et al, 1996, p 44)
>
> 'He would beat me while I was holding the baby ... he went to prison when my son was two years old but he got worse in prison. He used to give my son cigarette lighters and had no boundaries. He didn't send him to school but didn't allow him to play outside either.' (Thiara, 2010, p 166)

Violent fathers' neglectful parenting can also affect older children and young peoples' social and educational development. This is examined below through young people's own accounts.

Fathers' violence and abuse post-separation

It is often believed that children are no longer affected by a father's violence after separation, yet studies to date indicate that most children continue to be very fearful of violent fathers for some time afterwards (Humphreys and Thiara, 2002). Further, over a third of these fathers continue and escalate their violence post-separation, although the abuse may take a different form (Kelly, 1999; Mirrlees-Black, 1999; Walby and Allen, 2004). For example, mothers and children can be subjected to dangerous post-separation harassment or severe attacks in the home, as illustrated in the following survivor's account.

> 'My ex-partner asked a friend of his to come to my home and beat me up because I left him. I did not know this man. I opened the door to a knock one night, a man asked my name. I told him and basically he kicked and punched the hell out of me. He got hold of my three year old son and literally threw him into the glass door which smashed. My son needed his head injuries glued at hospital. I had a fractured skull and extensive bruising to my body and a couple of broken ribs.... All this because I wouldn't go back to my husband.' (Humphreys and Thiara, 2002, p 13)

Since 1992, when the legal principle of contact with fathers was established in nearly all circumstances, much post-separation violence has been connected with child contact arrangements and has become a key context in which children and their mothers continue to experience serious abuse and occasionally lethal harm (Hester and Radford, 1996; Radford et al, 1999; Aris et al, 2002; Humphreys and Thiara, 2002). Separation and child contact are now recognised as very high risk factors in the potential killing of mothers and/or children by previously violent fathers (ACPO/Home Office, 2006). Thus, at least 54 children are known to have been killed between 1992-2008 by fathers during child contact visits, most of whom were identified as perpetrators of domestic violence against mothers when still living with the family (Saunders, 2004; Ferguson, 2009). Children are also at increased risk of abduction during contact visits, more so from minority ethnic violent fathers who have families living abroad (Hester and Radford, 1996; Aris et al, 2002).

Studies with mothers have also indicated that children most frequently witness fathers' domestic violence during contact handover times. This can occur even when the children are handed over at supported or supervised contact centres, or when grandparents informally supervise contact. In Radford and colleagues' child contact study (1999), 66 per cent of children were reported as witnessing violence towards their mothers during contact handover and 14 per cent during handover at centres. While improved protection at supervised centres has reduced some of this violence and the incidence of fathers' abduction of children, it should be recognised that such contact is usually only authorised by the family courts for six months at the most. Further, the professionals involved often place considerable pressure on mothers to move children's supervised contact on more quickly, to open and longer visits, often in response to demands from violent fathers (Aris et al, 2002). Another key issue of concern for children and their mothers in these circumstances is that family law policy and practice increasingly views shared parenting arrangements post-separation as the ideal arrangement for children, so a violent father may end up fairly quickly having the children in his care for half the week, with a corresponding increase in their risk of harm, as seen below (Thiara, 2010).

Violent fathers' direct abuse of children during contact visits

In studies where violent fathers have been identified as directly abusing children prior to separation, there is evidence of the continuation of such abuse during contact visits, and a significant concern has been the failure of child protection agencies to intervene in these circumstances (Saunders, 2001, 2003a, 2003b; Humphreys and Thiara, 2002). In this regard, some mothers viewed social workers as helpful when violent fathers were still living with the family, but disinterested when problems arose through child contact, as illustrated in one mother's views below:

> 'They were the first people I spoke to and they believed me. Putting the children on the "at risk" register helped. Not supporting me when contact was abusive.' (Shaiza) (Humphreys and Thiara, 2002, p 95)

Radford and colleagues' (1999) study found that 76 per cent of children who had experienced direct abuse prior to separation (many of whom were under the age of five) continued to be abused following court-ordered contact. This included 10 per cent who were sexually abused, 15 per cent who experienced physical abuse, 62 per cent who were directly emotionally harmed and 36 per cent who were neglected, with a number of children experiencing multiple forms of abuse. In terms of emotional/psychological abuse, the research shows that as well as the forms of such abuse outlined above, this could include direct threats to kill the children, making threats to harm mothers through the children, using the children to gain information about mothers and deliberate attempts to undermine children's relationships with mothers, often informed by motives of using children as a weapon against their ex-partners (Radford et al, 1999; Jaffe et al, 2003; Thiara, 2010). For example, Thiara's research with South Asian mothers on child contact found that some children (particularly boys) were encouraged by their fathers to perpetrate violence towards their mothers, as well as engage in other inappropriate behaviour in order to undermine mothers' parenting capacities to professionals:

> 'He was telling them to hit Mummy and call the police, run away from home, don't go to school. All so that my record would be bad, even after the divorce.' (Thiara, 2010, p 172)

Radford and colleagues' study indicated that fathers' neglect of children during open visiting contact included a failure to pay attention to their basic health needs, for example not changing nappies or leaving very young children alone for several hours, and, in a quarter of cases, getting drunk. Violent fathers who were alcohol or drug users were particularly likely to neglect children. One mother whose child's father was a drug user described such a situation as follows:

> 'He had our child overnight and locked [her] in a bedroom with a bucket to wee in. All this because he was using heroin downstairs with his partner and friends.' (Radford et al, 1999, p 22)

The child contact studies discussed above also identified discriminatory professional and legal practices towards abused mothers and these practices contributed significantly to professional failures to protect the children. In Radford and colleagues' study, over half of mothers had initially tried to set up informal contact arrangements, with many being pressurised by solicitors to do so. Most of these arrangements broke down, because of fathers' further violence and direct abuse of children and 121 cases involving 178 children proceeded to court, usually on the father's application. However, mothers consistently felt that court welfare professionals did not believe them when they raised concerns about the safety of their children and some were regarded as making false allegations of child abuse. Where mothers continued to oppose children's contact with their fathers on the grounds of the children' safety, 63 per cent were threatened in some way, with 39 per cent being told they would be sent to prison if they did not comply with contact orders by judges and with children being ordered to live with the abusive father in 11 cases.

The view of mothers making false allegations of abuse was reinforced in Aris and colleagues' child contact centre study (2002), where some child contact centre workers and coordinators believed that when mothers raised safety concerns about their children they were regarded as being deliberately obstructive merely because they did not want fathers to have contact. Some of these workers demonstrated no understanding of the impact of domestic violence on children, nor of the risk of direct abuse. Over and beyond this, these professionals tended to accept fathers' counter-allegations of abuse against mothers and showed a preference for the fathers' point of view. The study concluded that children frequently continued to be put at risk, as even supervised centres did not always provide enough vigilance to prevent children from being harmed. There were also a number of cases where contact should never have been permitted, because it was clear that some violent fathers would never be safe enough for contact outside the centres.

A further issue identified was that even though most cases involved court-ordered contact, there were limited efforts to seek and foreground children's views. Children's views were usually only sought through a court welfare report, but in Radford and colleagues' 1999 study no court welfare report was undertaken in 35 per cent of cases. Further, where a court welfare report was prepared, a fifth of children were not consulted. While the young age of children (under five) was frequently given as a reason for this, a third of children were older than this. Where children's views were sought, 83 per cent stated they did not want contact, but, as in other research, their views were usually only taken into account where they stated they wanted contact, suggesting that while children have the right to have contact, they appear to have no right to oppose it (Smart and Neale, 1999; Bretherton, 2002).

Impact of violent fathering on children

Unsurprisingly, the studies that addressed children's contact with violent fathers found that those young children who were afraid of their fathers and/or experienced abusive parenting during contact visits continued to be harmed. For example, mothers in one study reported very young children displaying increased behavioural problems such as aggression or withdrawal, inappropriate sexual behaviour (where children were being sexually abused), delayed speech or other developmental problems, and continuing anxiety problems such as nightmares and clinginess. Mothers also described physical symptoms such as hair loss and skin disorders in some cases. Twenty per cent of children would hide themselves away in order to avoid contact visits and older siblings who could not be forced to have contact were affected by the ongoing harm experienced by younger brothers or sisters (Radford et al, 1999). Later research with 100 mothers found that although all children who had lived with violent fathers had emotional and behavioural problems during the first six months following parental separation, children who had continuing contact with abusive fathers were more likely to demonstrate ongoing problems at six months at a 'statistically significant level' (Humphreys and Thiara, 2002, p 93). These findings reflect other earlier international research. For example, one Australian psychological study that interviewed children aged 8-12 years (Mertin, 1995) noted that 31 children who were afraid of violent fathers on separation experienced a significant reduction in fear and anxiety after a 10-month period of no contact, suggesting that, as seen in some of the accounts above, fearful children may recover from some of the negative impact of living with a violent father once he is removed from their lives. A much earlier New Zealand study, where 51 mothers reported the views of six- to 12-year-olds on contact one year after separation, found that:

> ... the children who recovered most rapidly tended to be those who had no further contact with their violent fathers ... the children who showed the least improvement following separation were the children who although frightened of their father, were forced to regularly visit him regardless of their own fears. (Church, 1984, p 79)

Children's perspectives

Research that specifically seeks children's perspectives has increased understanding of the impact of domestic violence and suggests a broader, more diverse picture than that based only on professional and adult observations. For example, children's accounts indicate that most are aware of domestic violence even when mothers believe it has been hidden from them (Jaffe et al, 1990; McGee, 2000). They also highlight more complex experiences due to gender or sibling position within families and because some domestically violent fathers target specific children for direct abuse. Their experiences are framed by ethnicity and racism and can vary as a result of family structure or disability, and a number of children experience domestic violence from both biological fathers and stepfathers or other father figures (Mullender et al, 2002; Izzidien, 2008;Thiara, 2010). Further, such research indicates that even very young children will attempt to develop coping strategies to protect themselves from harm and while many feel powerless, some will try to protect mothers from violent fathers. Much has also been made of some children's resilience to abusive experiences; this can be due not only to individual characteristics but also to the amount of support they gain from others, including siblings, friends, mothers and other relatives (Mullender et al, 2002; Hester et al, 2007).

Moreover, children's accounts have decimated a number of myths, including the claim that their relationship with their father is usually unaffected by the latter's violence. Nevertheless, it is also known that children's willingness to express their views is affected by the context in which they are sought and some children still living with violent fathers or having contact with them post-separation may be unwilling to express their views through fear of what the father or other family members might do (Abrahams, 1994; Aris et al, 2002; Mullender et al, 2002; Izzidien, 2008). Most of the research in this area reflects the views of children who are no longer living with violent fathers, although some helpline studies do include children's perspectives in cases where the violent parent is still living with the family (Epstein and Keep, 1995; Izzidien, 2008), and one Swedish study (Weinehall, 2005) which focuses on teenage perspectives where violent fathers or father figures are still present in the home. Other research indicates that some children avoid or are reluctant or unable to articulate any views about violent biological fathers, perhaps because of their own traumatisation or confusion and inability to come to terms with his behaviour at the time the study took place (Mullender et al, 2002).

Early research on children's experiences by US researchers Jaffe and colleagues (1990) noted that they included a range of observations from directly witnessing violence and threats made towards their mothers, to hearing it when they in other parts of the house, seeing mothers' physical injuries or 'observing the emotional consequences of fear, hurt and intimidation which may be very apparent to them' (Jaffe et al, 1990, p 17). Significantly, this research demonstrated that children do not have to witness fathers' violence directly in order to be harmed by it and this has been confirmed by later, more in-depth, UK studies, as seen in the following children's accounts:

''Cause when I wake up in the night there was always fighting, sometimes I hear Mum crying and sometimes I hear her getting smacked and John shouting at her. So I start screaming myself.' (Sabrina, aged 10)

Paul and Tracey were crying ... we was all crying, because we could just hear our mum crying and screaming. And our Dad shouting at her. (Glenda, aged 9) (McGee, 2000, pp 64, 73)

Further research has stressed that the physical violence does not have to be repeated very often for it to 'engender fear and distress in children', since it is 'the atmosphere of threats and intimidation' in the home that can mean children's lives are lived 'in constant dread' (Mullender et al, 2002, p 206). This is illustrated in accounts of children who have witnessed specific verbal abuse such as threats to kill, where children may fear for their own or their mother's safety or that of other family members:

'He used to always say that he was going to kill my mum, he used to always say that he was going to kill all my family ... and he really sounded serious like he would do it....' (Mona, aged 17) (McGee, 2000, p 62)

'He used to say he was going to put petrol in the house and burn it whilst we were asleep we were always frightened he was going to do that.' (Eight-year-old South Asian girl) (Mullender et al, 2002, p 183)

Mona (cited above) described how it made her feel to hear such threats as a young child:

'... constantly on edge, never free, never safe. It was like there was no safe [place] ... being at home wasn't safe at all, it was just that is the place where you are and you are constantly alert. You don't sleep properly – you just sit there and wait for something to happen.' (McGee, 2000, p 72)

The same study described very young children's continuing fears of violent fathers' attacks even when they had left the family home. One five-year-old child, who had blocked up the windows and doors of a doll's house in a refuge playroom, stated that it was his mother's new house and he had done this to prevent his daddy from getting in. Young children also described the nightmares they had as a result of hearing this type of threat:

> 'Well one [nightmare] I had was that when I was asleep [my father] got a knife and stabbed me, that was the other one I had. I had some more but I've forgotten them.' (Gerard, aged 5) (McGee, 2000, p 71)

These studies emphasise that observing fathers' constant belittling and humiliation of their mothers, and fathers' attempts to involve children in such behaviour, could be just as disturbing for children as witnessing other forms of violence, as the following accounts show:

> 'He was just hitting her with his hands and shouting and swearing at her – saying that she's horrible, she's wicked and that she's not a very good mummy. Just saying all horrible things to her and really hurting her making her cry and Mum couldn't do anything. I called the police.' (Mullender et al, 2002, p 183)

> 'One night he was proper bugging me, asking me all these questions about her: "Was she this? Did she that?" And he got really angry and jumped out of bed and slapped my mum really badly. I was crying and crying….' (16-year-old white boy) (Mullender et al, 2002, p 163).

These studies demonstrate that fathers may try to implicate different siblings in emotional abuse in order to create alliances against mothers, with the consequence that some younger children were left feeling emotionally confused or guilty that they were to blame for the abuse. McGee's research indicated that, even where young people had never witnessed the fathers' violence or been implicated in the emotional abuse of the mother, seeing it happen to other children in the family could still have a lasting effect on them, as illustrated in the following example:

> 'I mean I had experienced verbal things he was saying to [my younger sister] like "Call your mum a slut. Your mum's a f★★★★★★ c★★★." I witnessed all that, but not actually any violence towards her.' (Hannah, aged 15) (McGee, 2000, p 63).

While some children were able to stand up to their violent fathers and call the police, as seen above, others were constrained from doing so or felt powerless to prevent the abuse:

> 'I got in the way and pushed my dad. My dad just walked out.' (Seamus, aged 10) (McGee, 2000, p 76)

'I tried to stop him but he pushed me away.' (Paul, aged 6) (McGee, 2000, p 101)

'When my dad started all this, right, I would get really angry and start shouting at him, telling him off.' (12 year-old mixed race girl) (Mullender, 2002, p 188)

Children's perceptions of fathers' parenting

While it is accepted that the physical and sexual abuse of children causes significant harm, a less acknowledged area is the extent to which children's development and wellbeing are affected by violent fathers' extreme control. This can result in children's activities and movements being severely restricted, as seen in the accounts below from older children:

'I wasn't very happy and we [my sister and I] wasn't allowed down in the front room at all, we had to stay in our bedrooms. We had to stay, the only time we could come out was when we eat.' (Ralph, aged 9)

'It was like everyone had to do everything he says, otherwise he goes mad.' (Aaron, aged 13) (McGee, 2000, pp 54, 100)

Children may also be controlled by threats of violence towards their mothers. Ten-year-old Kara, for example, was not allowed to play but was forced to do household chores instead:

'He said "If you don't do them I'll hit your mother." I felt so scared I thought I had better do them.' (McGee, 2000, p 54)

This research records children and young people describing a catalogue of fathers' cruel and emotionally abusive behaviour towards them, such as destroying school work, school reports and toys, harming pets, not allowing children out of the house, not allowing them to speak to their mothers and not allowing friends to phone or come to the house. Some fathers are shown to deliberately emotionally abuse children and young people, insulting and humiliating them in a similar way to their mothers (McGee, 2000; Mullender et al, 2002). Older girls in particular experience being called 'sluts' and 'slags' by violent fathers and for South Asian young women this may have very specific impacts, as seen in the following example:

'He has never liked me. He has always threatened me and said I will do badnaami [get a bad name] – bring shame on the family. He used to say I slept around. Really Auntie [to the researcher] my own father! He also called my mum names….' (16-year-old South Asian girl) (Mullender et al, 2002, p 141)

Children's views of violent fathers

Lack of respect, shame, embarrassment and hatred of fathers

Fear and anxiety are common childhood responses towards violent fathers, but as children get older, they may also lose respect for them and become more aware of the social consequences of having a violent father:

'I didn't talk to him much after that [witnessing my father's violence]. I felt he wasn't worth talking to.' (Tracey, aged 15) (McGee, 2000, p 85)

'I am ashamed of him – I can't tell anyone because then they will know I haven't got a proper father.' (Epstein and Keep, 1995, p 48)

'I used to think to myself what's my friends at school going to say with my mother with all marks on her face.… I remember it was my tenth birthday party. I just remember being in the kitchen, crying my eyes out that he had embarrassed me so much in front of my friends.' (Abrahams, 1994, p 39)

'I have really good friends at school. But they couldn't come round when he was here. He would be so violent to everyone. He drove everyone away. I'd be too embarrassed.' (14-year-old white girl) (Mullender et al, 2002, p 10)

Children from the Childline study (Epstein and Keep, 1995) who had experienced severe abuse and still lived with their violent fathers frequently expressed extreme hatred towards them:

'I hate my dad and I want to leave home.'

'My dad is a power maniac.'

'My dad behaves like a mad dog.' (Epstein and Keep, 1995, p 52)

Others felt that their fathers had paid no attention to them and favoured another sibling:

> 'I didn't like it ... it just felt like I wasn't there at all ... I don't know why but he wasn't really interested in anything I done good. Whereas Oliver [my brother] he would have a lot of interest in and I think it's probably because he was a boy. When we weren't seeing him I didn't feel that I missed him a lot, because he didn't show much appreciation of anything I did or show that he loved me or that he cared or anything like that. So I didn't actually miss him.' (Regina, aged 9) (McGee, 2000, p 87)

Feelings of powerlessness

The kind of feelings towards fathers identified above were echoed in Weinehall's (2005) Swedish study with 15 teenagers (aged 15 to 16) who were still living at home. While at times they chose to stay away from home, on other occasions they chose to stay to protect their mothers or other siblings. One teenager said:

> 'I had to check it out. I stayed at home to watch out for my mother ... and it was necessary because my father acted like a f***king idiot. It's almost like having a killer living in the house. You have to watch him so that he won't do anything.' (Weinehall, 2005, p 142)

As in the Childline study, these young people's views of their fathers were affected by their own sense of powerlessness to end the violence, or obtain support from other adults. Most had endured the violence for a long time and had been physically assaulted by their fathers, and half of the 10 girls interviewed had been subjected to sexual violence. It was therefore not surprising that most stated that they hated their fathers and harboured feelings of revenge – with some wishing that they could kill them. While they were sometimes able to keep these feelings in check, they often coped through adopting harmful strategies, such as alcohol or drug abuse, cutting themselves or making suicide attempts.

A more recent Childline study involving South Asian young women found that their fathers' violence could also produce a sense of powerlessness, since by reporting the abuse or seeking help, they risked bringing shame on their wider family and community that could have punitive consequences. As one young woman said:

> 'I have spent my whole life watching my dad hit my mum. I was scared and never felt I could speak to my family. I'm too frightened to do something like call the police.' (Izzidien, 2008, p 23)

Other research has found that some South Asian young people experiencing domestic violence gain support from paternal and maternal extended family members (Mullender et al, 2002), indicating that South Asian families are not homogenous in their responses. However, where these young people seek help from professionals such as teachers or statutory services, lack of confidentiality and inadequate or inappropriate responses (for example to teenage young women at risk of forced marriage) may compound their experiences of abuse (Izzidien, 2008).

Holding violent fathers responsible for loss of education and other social consequences

Some children and young people clearly blamed their fathers for lack of educational achievement at school:

> 'When I went to school it affected me a lot because all day I was thinking about what would happen when I got home. So at school my work level dropped for quite a bit.' (Regina, aged 9)

> 'I failed all my exams – I put it down to him, what happened at home.' (Karina aged 16)

> 'I would keep getting letters coming home saying I hadn't done the course work and it was just all down to him ... I used to just sit there and cry and shake because I couldn't do my homework.' (Jackie, aged 19)

Jackie also described the impact of witnessing her father's violence on her younger siblings, who became aggressive at school:

'At the time I was sorry for Terry and Karina because they were younger, they couldn't get out of it.... Obviously they grew up with the violence all the time so they used to go and beat up the kids at school 'cause they thought that was the right thing to do....' (Jackie aged 19) (McGee, 2000, pp 79-81)

While some young people view school as a refuge from violent fathers, for others observing their fathers' violence towards their mothers, as seen above, can produce aggressive behaviour, lack of concentration on school work and even school exclusion (McGee,2000). All of which contradicts government policies that argue fathers' presence is essential to children's educational achievement (DfES, 2007b).

The wider social implications for children having to leave home with their mothers to get away from violent fathers not only means disruption to their school education but also leaving behind friends, pets and possessions. As one nine-year-old girl said:

'He made me leave my home. He made me leave all my best friends. He made me leave all my things behind.' (Mullender et al, 2002, p 108)

Young people who experience post-separation harassment and have to flee from their home may also feel extreme resentment towards their fathers:

'I hate him. We've been in three refuges. When I was in the second one I liked it. One day, when I was coming home from school – he knew which school I was at – I turned round and saw him following me....' (12-year-old white girl) (Mullender et al, 2002)

Having to flee their own communities to get away from fathers' violence may have particular consequences for South Asian children, because it means that they may have to move to areas where they will experience racism, as illustrated in the following account:

'Sometimes people tease me and call me names, especially white people in the area.... Mum is trying to get me a transfer to another school. I am just worried about being teased by white people – they do it because they don't like black people and can cause problems and be violent so you can feel really unsafe.' (10-year-old Asian boy) (Mullender et al, 2002, p 139)

Children's views on contact with violent fathers

Given the views expressed above, it is not surprising that many children feel extreme resentment towards their fathers and want nothing to do with them after separation. Early limited qualitative research in this area argued that children are usually ambivalent or conflicted in their feelings towards violent fathers on separation (Saunders, 1995; Peled, 2000). However, as more research into children's perspectives on violent fathers is undertaken, it becomes clear that children's views and feelings about having contact with fathers post-separation are widely variable (Higgins, 1994; McGee, 2000; Mullender et al, 2002).

Children wanting no contact with fathers

In the studies cited above, there were large groups of children who had no affectionate bonds with fathers and these were mainly children who had lived with a violent father for most of their lives and had experienced nothing but fear and control. Children who had witnessed severe violence by fathers or experienced threats such as threats to kill also fell into this group. Some expressed happiness at having finally left fathers and wanted to cut off from them completely. Others expressed extreme hatred towards their fathers, which could be combined with continuing fears of post-separation violence and harassment, and, for a few younger children, fantasies about killing their fathers. One 11-year-old white boy's advice to violent fathers was 'to go and die in the gutter' (Mullender et al, 2002, pp 187-8). These findings frequently echoed an earlier study with children who had fled to refuges with their mothers (Higgins, 1994) as illustrated below:

> 'My Dad cut my Mum with a knife; children left and went to Auntie. I was there – I used to hear arguments and shouting and drinking ("Alcoholic!"). Unhappy I felt – I'd go to my room and play, I was 10 years. Domestic violence is horrible – not worth it, people getting hurt. I never see my Dad – I saw him once a year ago, walking down the street; we just walked on. I don't feel anything for my Dad.' (14-year-old Asian/Caribbean boy, ex-refuge resident, Higgins, 1994, p 20)

'My Dad really wants to kill us and shoot us. He will lock us in a room and we will never get out and have nothing to eat. I must look after my Mum, my Dad is really bad. When I am big, I could be Batman and go and kill my Dad and throw him in a dustbin.... I am scared when I have to see my Dad sometimes, that he will hurt me and shoot me. He said lots of times he would do that to all of us.' (6-year-old Asian boy, refuge resident, Higgins, 1994, p 20)

'I am happy now – I have a few problems now, but only little ones. I hope that when I am older, I won't let a man push me around. My Mam is happy now and so are we. We never see my Da now. I like it.' (15-year-old white girl, ex-refuge resident) (Higgins, 1994, p 22)

'Complete pig.... And I just, I don't want to even to be in the same country as him, I think he is a complete psycho.' (Hannah, aged 15)

'Can't stand him. Can't stand him at all. I'm scared though, because he's everywhere.' (Mona, aged 17) (McGee, 2000, pp 84-5)

'I'm happier.' (8-year-old African girl)

'No. What he did to my mum – I don't really want to see him. I don't forgive him.' (9-year-old white boy)

'We don't see my dad now and don't want to see him. I am happy about not seeing him.' (8-year-old South Asian girl)

'I don't want to see him because he makes me upset.' (9-year-old South Asian boy) (Mullender et al, 2002, p 195)

'I feel really different. I can sleep without any fear. I can really live like any other young person in the community.... Now he is not around to terrorise me I can get on with my studies.' (16-year-old South Asian girl) (Mullender et al, 2002, p 196)

The feelings of children and young people who were forced to have contact, however, could be very different. Very few of the children cited above who refused contact had been through the family court system, but a small number had been forced to have contact with a violent father against their wishes, often through a court order. Thiara (2010), for example, relates how one young teenage South Asian boy was extremely angry about the violence he had suffered and about being forcing to have contact with his abusive father:

> 'I can't forgive him for putting my mother and us through all that and now he expects me to see him and talk to him.' (Thiara, 2010, p 170)

> 'I don't want to go, always, but I have to go because the law people said we had to.... I like to stay with my mum.' (8 year-old white boy) (Mullender et al, 2002, p 201)

In another case considerable pressure by family court welfare professionals was placed on a young person to agree contact, with the assumption that he had been influenced by his mother.

> 'To be honest, I used to not know what to say. I used to think I was saying the wrong thing.... The worst thing I could think of was actually having to see him again.... I don't think most of them believed me. I thought that after saying it once, that would be it. But it happened about six times. Each time the main question was if I wanted to see him again.... Maybe it's just because I'm a child and they probably think my mum got me to say whatever.... One of them asked if it was my own views or not.' (15-year-old mixed race boy) (Mullender et al, 2003, p 33)

Similarly, a Swedish study found that children are often pressurised into contact by family court welfare investigators because of fathers' 'rights', although the children themselves theoretically have a right to have their own views considered (Eriksson and Nasman, 2008). One child talked about his experiences of such coercion to have contact with a violent father whom he had not seen for several years:

> 'When they came the first time, [and] should talk to me and they said it was about me, that I should feel safe and that it should all be about me [pause] and not about him [pause] and then they came several times and said but [he] has said he wants to see you and he has the right to see you

because he is your daddy, he is your biological daddy, but then I told them that you said that it was I who should feel safe because I do not want to see him at home. Okay. But you can try a little. Then I said No. Then they said okay we will come another time. [They] came another time, said he wants to see you and he has the right to see you. Then they started … they came so many times, so I said okay, I can see him but I do not want to.' (Bill, aged 10) (Eriksson and Nasman, 2008, pp 268-9)

Other experiences of pressure being placed on children by court welfare officers were highlighted in the UK television programme 'Dispatches' (Ferguson, 1999) looking at children's views where they were compelled to have contact with a violent father against their wishes as part of wider survey on the issue of harm to children during contact with a violent father (Radford et al, 1999). In one case, the family court originally acknowledged that a five-year-old boy's father was too dangerous to have contact with him, but three years later the court ordered contact although his mother had remarried and he considered his stepfather to be his real father. The boy, then aged eight, said:

> "I didn't want to see him, because he was nasty and horrible.... I was angry they didn't listen – I just wanted him to leave me alone."

Later, however, when the father was admitted to hospital for psychiatric treatment and contact ceased, the child said:

> "I am happy I don't have to see my first father anymore."

Some children participating in the programme were not so fortunate and two young sisters who were compelled to have ongoing weekly contact with their father made the following comments:

> "They made me go and visit and I didn't want to go. It was really frightening."
> "I feel very scared I didn't want to see my dad. I said I didn't want to see my dad, because he might hit us again, but they didn't listen."
> "If someone said I didn't have to see him I would be very happy."

Other research has focused on children's experiences of court welfare investigations in cases where parents cannot agree about contact arrangements (Bretherton, 2002). This study interviewed 30 children and 56 mothers, 78 per cent of whom reported that they had experienced domestic violence. It found that less than half the children interviewed felt that their views had been taken on board in decisions about contact. It also emphasised the pointlessness of children's participation where welfare officers 'had already decided that the best outcome will be one that includes direct contact' (Bretherton, 2002, p 455).

Children's views of contact with violent fathers at contact centres

Research with 21 children aged from 5 to 13 at supervised and supported contact centres (Aris et al, 2002; Harrison, 2006) found that a third who had contact with violent fathers felt that it was neither positive nor safe for them, while others were at best ambivalent, as seen in the accounts below:

'I don't like seeing him.' (Girl, aged 5)

'I wish it [contact] never happened.' (Girl, aged 11)

'I wouldn't change it, because I don't want to see him outside of the centre.' (Girl, aged 7)

'Sometimes I feel safe and sometimes I don't know.' (Girl, aged 11)

'I like it when he is nice to me.' (Boy, aged 6)

'When he behaves.' (Girl, aged 8) (Aris et al, 2002, pp 107-8)

The researchers also observed some child contact interactions with violent fathers, with the following result:

In some instances, children were observed clearly expressing their views and stating their distress, but were ignored. A supervised centre co-ordinator commented about a 12 year old young man who had been objecting to contact for sometime: 'we really must start listening to what he is saying'. (Harrison, 2006, p 148)

Ambivalence, conflict and changing views of children

While the existing research suggests that there are clearly benefits for fearful children in relinquishing an ongoing relationship with their fathers, other children may be more ambivalent about contact and may have conflicting feelings of craving safety for themselves and their mothers while still loving their fathers. A child in Abrahams' (1994) study described her conflicted feelings about her father but expressed concern that her siblings should not have to live with his violence:

> 'I love him in a way because he's my Dad ... he's what I've always lived with all my life, but I mean I hate him for what he's done to my mother and put me through and I just don't want him to put my brother and sister through that.' (Abrahams, 1994, p 42)

Mullender and colleagues' (2002) study indicated that, for some South Asian young people, it was difficult to adhere to collectivist family values that required them to retain respect for their violent fathers. This is illustrated by the following account of a 14-year-old South Asian boy, who talked about seeing his father occasionally following separation:

> 'We go to his shop sometimes, go to the movies. He is okay with us, Dad. I have to respect him, not for the violence [but] because he is my dad. It is against my religion [not to]. I have to respect my parents. If I was gora [white], I don't think I would have [to].' (Mullender et al, 2002, p 148)

Again, however, this study indicated that divided loyalties could change over time in cases where fathers' violence escalated, as indicated by this 13-year-old African girl who was having continuing contact with her father post-separation:

> 'I had no idea it was going to be this bad.... Up until then ... from when I was a little baby, I always wanted my dad. Then when I started to go with mum he started getting angry....M [her 12-year-old brother] preferred my mum to dad, and my dad would beat him for no reason.' (Mullender et al, 2002, p 192)

Other older children stopped contact when fathers resumed violence towards themselves or their mothers:

'We used to [see him.] Up until 10 months ago. He started getting violent with me and my sister which he'd never done before.... He started doing that and it was getting worrying because he was quite violent so we haven't really seen him since.' (16-year-old white boy, speaking about himself and his 11-year-old sister) (Mullender et al, 2002, p 197)

'I used to visit a lot but then my mum just ran into my dad not long ago and he hit her and that. He tried to smash a bottle round her face or something....' (12-year-old white girl, who said she now hated her father and was afraid of seeing him) (Mullender et al, 2002, p 197)

Other young people stopped contact when fathers put them in dangerous situations, including one 14 year-old girl whose father offered her drugs on a contact visit. A few children who had wanted ongoing face-to-face or telephone contact found it a strain when fathers put pressure on them to find out information about their mothers:

'Yes, I see him every week. It's alright now, but I get upset if he pumps me for information ... it worries me if he keeps on about Mum.' (12-year-old white girl) (Mullender et al, 2002, p 198)

Significantly, this study indicated that only one child stated that she missed her father and was sorry to leave him and that some children's willingness to contemplate seeing their fathers in the future was based on their own feelings of safety not only for themselves but also for their mothers. In this regard, fathers needed to demonstrate that they had ceased their violent behaviour towards mothers before the children would contemplate contact.

Gender and the cycle of violence

As Hester and colleagues (2007) have noted, there is no commonality in the ways girls and boys deal with their experiences of domestic violence. Yet one concern about the impact of domestic violence on children, particularly on boys, is that they will grow up to be violent abusers themselves. Nonetheless, children and young people interpret their experiences in different ways and, as seen in the studies discussed above, a number of boys were protective of their mothers and siblings and were concerned not to end up like their fathers.

There is some evidence, however, that a minority of adolescent boys who have lived with a father's chronic violence and coercive control and been directly physically abused themselves become violent and aggressive in their relationships with others, including their peers and sometimes their mothers. A background of chronic domestic violence has also been found to be a key factor, among others, in young men sexually abusing other children and young people. Nevertheless, these associations are complex and there is no simple inevitability to young men's later behaviour (Farmer, 2006). Gender does, however, appear to be significant in attitudes towards domestic violence in adolescence, where boys and young men appear to be more tolerant or condoning of violence against women than girls and young women (Burton et al, 1998; Mullender et al, 2002). Further, some boys lose respect for mothers and girls as a consequence of their fathers' behaviour, while some girls and young women may become more fearful of boys and men (McGee, 2000). A few of both genders, however, may ally themselves with violent and abusive fathers as a means of coping and survival and often because violent fathers have successfully undermined the mother–child relationship (Mullender et al, 2002).

Conclusion

This chapter challenges the proposition that violent fathers can still be good enough parents since their violence is harmful to infants, children and young people in a number of different ways, both in the short and long term. Further, many children reject relationships with violent fathers because of the harm they and their mothers experience and fear they will continue to experience in the future. These children and young people are clear that they have no affectionate bonds with such fathers and want no more to do with them. Others are only prepared to consider continuing a relationship in cases where fathers can demonstrate that they have ceased their violent and abusive behaviour. In the face of such evidence, and given the potential for further harm, it is difficult to comprehend that family and child welfare policies still promote the idea that children 'need' and will benefit from continuing relationships with abusive fathers through spurious psychological discourses that they will be damaged without such 'attachments' or that their sense of identity will suffer.[1] Nevertheless, the power of such discourses continues to influence family policies and these are discussed in more detail in Chapter Two.

Note

[1] The research in relation to attachment theory demonstrates that it is the quality of the children's attachment to their parents that is significant, not that any attachment is better than none. There is no research evidence that demonstrates that children benefit from fathers who are violent and abusive; rather the evidence is in the opposite direction (see, for example, Flouri, 115-16).

TWO

Changing discourses of fatherhood in family policies

Introduction

This chapter looks at the way fatherhood has been constructed through social policy and law and how this relates to discourses of domestic violence. Domestic violence and related child abuse are frequently regarded as minor issues, if they are mentioned at all, in the context of how fatherhood is viewed, but in this chapter, I argue that they should be regarded as central to family policy formulation if children's safety and wellbeing are to be taken seriously and dealt with effectively in safeguarding children from harm. Collier (1995) has indicated that there are continuities as well as changes to the way fatherhood has been constructed in law and this chapter therefore takes a historical approach. Further, since fatherhood is usually constituted in relation to motherhood, it is necessary to consider changing constructions of mothers in families, as well as those of children and children's welfare and how far these have been affected by gendered social power relationships, where fathers as men, in general retain more social power than women and dominant masculinities continue to be supported through government policies in families (Hearn and Pringle, 2006).

Traditional private patriarchy: absolute father right

First, it is important to recognise that historically fatherhood has been constructed and institutionalised through marriage in western societies as a hierarchical social relationship, where women and children are regarded as the property of their husbands and fathers (Davidoff et al, 1999). In England for much of the 18th and 19th centuries both wives and children could, under common law, 'within reason' be legally beaten and physically imprisoned and neither had their own legal status or could own property or money (Blackstone, 1765). Furthermore, although fathers were obliged to protect and maintain their families, mothers had few means of redress if they failed to do so since they lacked legal status. On separation, mothers had no parental rights to access to, or custody of, their children and until they reached the age of 21 (the age of majority) young people were forced to comply with father rule (Holcombe, 1983).

The position of unmarried mothers was different and was affected by the degraded social status attributed to them and their children during this period. The poor laws of 1834 removed the duty of fathers to maintain children of unmarried women, who were defined as the 'undeserving poor', and these mothers were regarded as having responsibility for their children's maintenance. But for much of the century unmarried mothers' children were regarded as the children of 'no-one' under common law, because only fathers could confer status of legal ownership and it was not until 1891 that the law recognised that unmarried mothers had custody rights to their children on the basis that they had responsibility for maintaining them.

In marriage, mothers and children were expected to obey the father's wishes, however unreasonable. This was highlighted in the much-cited Chancery case of *Agar-Ellis v Lascelles*, which began in 1878 and was only completed in 1883. It concerned the fate of three daughters, whose father, Leopold, had originally agreed that the children could be brought up in his wife's catholic religion in a pre-nuptial agreement. He later changed his mind and sought to have his daughters, then aged nine, 11 and 12, made wards of court and to send them to be brought up by a protestant clergyman, away from the influence of their mother. While the mother opposed the application, the court ruled that the father as 'head of his household *must* have the control of his family; that 'the children must be brought up in the religion of the father' and that 'the father must say how and by whom they are educated' (in *Re Agar-Ellis* [1878]: 55).

In 1883, the second daughter, then aged 16, asked the appeal court to allow her to go on holiday and be able to visit her mother rather than 'always being with strangers', and Leopold again refused. Although unhappy with the father's behaviour, the court ruled in his favour, stating that 'the court must not be tempted to interfere with the natural order and course of family life, the very basis of which is the authority of the father' (Brett MR [1883] 24 ChD:317). Further, while the court attempted to remind Leopold of 'his duties towards his children' as separate from his dispute with his wife, they acceded to the father's view that his wife had influenced the children's attitudes and did not see their wishes and welfare as significant enough to affect their judgement (Davidoff et al, 1999).

As Davidoff and colleagues (1999) noted, this case set legal precedent for dominant father right well into the 20th century whenever fathers and mothers disagreed about the upbringing of their children in marriage. Indeed, mothers did not get equal parental rights in this regard until the 1973 Guardianship of Minors Act. Moreover, the 'superior' rights of the father as the 'natural' guardian of his children were not finally abolished until the 1989 Children Act. There are also other aspects of this case that continue to resonate in claims made by fathers in legal disputes over children post-separation, particularly when fathers continue to argue that children have been unduly influenced by their mothers in certain contexts.

Divorce, separation and child custody

It was virtually impossible for women to divorce their husbands for much of the 19th century, and, alongside women's property rights, this became one of the first areas targeted for reform by the emerging 19th-century women's movement. However, the first civil divorce Act in 1857 created a sexual double standard, where men could divorce wives on the grounds of adultery alone, but women could only divorce husbands where there was aggravated adultery, which included incest, bigamy, desertion or cruelty. It did, however, allow women to obtain a judicial separation and keep their own earnings in cases where they had been deserted. They were also allowed to keep custody of their children where aggravated adultery could be proved. But in practice most women could not afford the costs of divorce and were not allowed to give evidence against their husbands in court. In effect, the new law only benefited wealthy husbands who wished to divorce their wives. Davidoff and colleagues (1999) noted that the refusal to make it easier for married mothers to divorce and gain custody of their children was based on the fear that the institution of marriage was very precarious and that large numbers of women would desert their husbands if they could easily obtain child custody.

Changes to the law on domestic violence

As discussed above, domestic violence and abuse of children were an acceptable and legal means of fathers and husbands exerting their authority and this included forcibly taking wives' earnings and denying them child access. This was initially highlighted in England by Caroline Norton, a society woman, who having returned to her own family because of her husband's violence was deprived of her own earnings from writing and denied access to her young children. Later, the emerging 19th-century feminist movement campaigned for women to be able to keep their own earnings and property on the grounds that when they were deserted or had to escape violence, they would still have the means of supporting themselves and their offspring. Cobbe (1868) cited the well-publicised case of a father repeatedly imprisoned for aggravated assault against his wife who, once released, would return to smash up the family home and take his wife's earnings.

In *Wife Torture in England*, Cobbe (1878) cited numerous cases that had come before the criminal courts in support of the need for legislation to protect women from aggravated assault by violent husbands that could end in murder, arguing that English law was more concerned about cruelty to animals than protecting wives against the domestic cruelty of husbands. She also raised concerns about the welfare of children in such cases.

> Alfred Roberts felled his wife to the floor, with a child in her arms; knelt on her and grasped her throat. She had previously taken out three summonses against him, but [he] never attended.

> Alfred Etherington, shoe maker, kicked his wife in dangerous way and a week later dragged his wife out of bed, jumped on her and struck her. He said he would have her life and the lives of all her children. He gave no money for the support of his family (6 children) and he prevented her from keeping the situations she had obtained for their maintenance. She had summoned him seven times. (Cobbe, 1878, cited in Radford and Russell, 1992, pp 50-1)

Subsequently, the 1878 Matrimonial Causes Act, which was the first law specifically to address domestic violence allowed women who had experienced life-threatening aggravated assault from husbands to be granted a separation order and obtain maintenance from husbands, as well as to gain custody of young children. However, magistrates were reluctant to implement the law and tried to persuade mothers not to break up the family, highlighting the gap between formal legal gains that were meant to protect mothers and children and the implementation of the law in practice (Hammerton, 1992).

Caroline Norton's individual campaign and later feminist campaigns in the late 19th and early 20th centuries gradually enabled mothers to gain custody of infants on the welfare grounds that children of 'tender years' should be in the care of their mothers, providing that they had behaved appropriately as women (that is, they had not committed adultery and had fulfilled their duties as good wives). In contrast to the rights of fathers, married women's parental rights on separation were therefore tied for much of the 20th century to the way the law defined mothers in relation to the welfare of the child as well as to their own behaviour as women, thus allowing their claims as parents 'to be side-stepped' until the 1989 Children Act gave them equal parental rights (Barnett, 2009b).

Separate spheres: fathers as breadwinners and public figures

With the increase in industrialisation and changes in households to more familial nuclear forms, alongside emerging discourses of child welfare, fathers were constructed as family breadwinners and providers in the 19th century, with the home and the care of young children being defined as the 'dependent' mother's sphere. While this was the ideal for middle- and upper-class families, in working-class families mothers' paid labour was frequently the major, and sometimes the only, contribution to family income. This was despite working-class women being forced out of major occupations through the male trade union movement and subsequent legislation that defined certain occupations as specifically masculine. Further, where they could afford it, middle-class women rarely looked after their own young children and employed nursery maids to do this work, while older children were often sent away to boarding school. Although, based on Christian doctrine, mothers were regarded as responsible for the moral upbringing of children under five, fathers were still viewed as being morally responsible for older children, and particularly boys, in terms of discipline. Fathers also retained all the major decisions about children's lives in families, as seen in the Agar-Ellis case. In reality, not all fathers were distant from their children and some engaged in 'manly nurture', instilling 'masculine' virtues in boys, communicating information about the world and enjoying children's company (Tosch, 1999). However, fathers' 'successful exercise of authority over women and children' has remained an important part of the construction of fathering identities alongside that of provider, in late modern discourses (Davidoff et al, 1999, p 157).

The development of public discourses of child welfare

The 19th century is also significant for a particular construction of childhood that retains some relevance for contemporary child welfare policies. At the beginning of the century, children in lower-class families were frequently sent to work in other households to learn trades at the age of seven. In upper-class families, the practice of sending infants out to be cared for and fed by wet-nurses until the age of three or four was also common (Gittens, 1985). By the middle of the century, emerging discourses of children's 'moral welfare' began to call for the exclusion of young children from work in some factories and mines alongside their mothers and by the end of the century concerns about children's health, neglect and abandonment, physical abuse, incest and the prostitution of young girls and children's elementary education became major concerns within discourses of children's moral welfare. Concerns also began to emerge about the health of the race in terms of fighting for empire, drawing on naturalised discourses based on Darwinism (Williams, 1989). While late 19th-century and early 20th-century feminists focused on the sexual exploitation and sexual abuse of girls by men in the public sphere as well as the private sphere of households and families, working-class mothers were increasingly being held responsible for their children's welfare by the early 20th century whatever the form of abuse, a notion that was accompanied by naturalised discourses of mothers' maternal duties (Jeffreys, 1985; Gordon, 1988). The role of inspector for the National Society for the Prevention of Cruelty to Children, created as a result of the 1889 Prevention of Cruelty and Protection Act, focused on mothers' care of children in the home and in the early 20th century emerging child welfare measures were targeted at working-class mothers. Education also reflected the increased gendering of fathers and mothers, with the emphasis on boys being trained to become breadwinners and to acquire manly skills, including those required in wartime, and on women (whether middle or working class) being encouraged to anticipate their maternal duties. This continued for much of the 20th century despite feminist concerns. By the 1920s, feminist discourses concerning fathers' violence and abuse of children in families had largely become lost in the UK, and domestic violence disappeared off the public policy agenda until the emergence of second-wave feminism in the 1970s (Jeffreys, 1985; Hague and Wilson, 1996).

During the two world wars, women took on work previously defined as only suitable for men, demonstrating once more that gender differences in the labour market were socially constructed. But with the emergence of the welfare state in the 1940s and functionalist sociology (Parsons, 1951), naturalised discourses of masculinity and femininity were once again used to define fathers as providers and breadwinners and mothers as dependents and carers of children. The shortage of work for men and the closure of state nurseries combined with ideologies of mother care being essential to children's development and wellbeing, through the utilisation of emerging theories of maternal deprivation and children's attachment theories, to return mothers to the home (Bowlby, 1953). Welfare policies in this area, however, were differentially applied and did not include Black women from Commonwealth countries who were being encouraged to emigrate to the UK to provide cheap labour for the new state health service (Williams, 1989).

With the growth of second-wave feminism, women began to challenge these highly gendered discourses. They began demanding equal pay and arguing against the sexual division of labour in paid work and for the right to legal and financial independence. The Equal Pay (1972) and Sex Discrimination Acts (1975), were limited responses to these pressures. Women were also analysing the way motherhood was controlled and defined by patriarchal discourses and institutions (Rich, 1977) and highlighting the exploitation of women's labour in the home (see, for example, Oakley 1976). Some women were also demanding that men should share childcare in the home, although as Williams (1998) noted, women's demands at this time were more frequently for collective childcare to be provided in the public sphere. Women's collective and individual agency during this period, although not unitary, was represented through discourses not only of equality, but also of autonomy and independence. However, these challenges produced resistance from men and the state and family policy became a major area of contestation throughout the rest of the 20th century and beyond.

Family law policies

By the mid-1970s, women had achieved a number of formal legal rights affecting familial social relations, including equal rights to divorce supported by legal aid and simplified divorce procedures, more equal rights as parents within marriage and new civil laws on domestic violence.[1] The latter, however, despite including new orders for non-molestation and exclusion of perpetrators from the family home, remained largely ineffective in practice, as it had been in the 19th century (Barron, 1990). Custody decisions supported the principle of child stability, known as maintaining the 'status quo', on divorce. Thus children usually stayed with their mothers on the basis that they had been the main carers of children, allowing fathers reasonable access, and it was assumed that women would remarry and children would be provided with new social stepfathers. Neale and Smart suggest that this was supported by psychological discourses (see, for example, Goldstein et al, 1979) that defined the welfare of the child in terms of continuity of care and emotional security with their psychological parent (usually their mothers) and the 'restabilisation through remarriage and the creation of a step family' (Neale and Smart, 1998, p 7). Within these discourses, the emphasis was on social rather than biological fatherhood, where the new husband would take on the fatherhood role in the second family. It is interesting to note that in some court decisions over access to children, social (married) fatherhood continued to take precedence over biological fatherhood into the early 1990s (Smart and Neale, 1997). However, such discourses were complicated by maintenance issues and men's resistance to paying maintenance to their ex-wives (Brophy, 1985).

The importance of fathers' presence in families was underlined by the courts' opposition during the 1970s and 1980s to granting custody to lesbian mothers. In this context, decisions often focused on the 'inability' of the lesbian mother to provide a 'normal' family with a father and mother and the absence of male role models, as much as on her 'deviant sexuality' (Rights of Women, 1984; Harne and Rights of Women, 1997). Furthermore there was an increase in the number of lone unmarried mothers, who were challenging the previous social stigma attached to illegitimacy and arguing for their rights of autonomy in social welfare policies. Legally, never-married mothers retained sole legal rights to custody and care and control of their children.

The New Right and father absence

By the early 1980s, increasing concern was being expressed about women's 'flight from marriage', the growing number of lone-mother families and the undermining of fathers' authority and roles in social welfare and legal discourses. There was also resistance from newly emerging fathers' movements, discussed further below. The development of New Right policy under Thatcherism involved a number of discourses that aimed to put fathers back at the head of the table and ensure that they performed their provider responsibilities, reduce welfare to the 'undeserving poor,' and, within this, specifically target and stigmatise lone, unmarried mothers. Another aspect of this approach, which was also supported in some Christian socialist discourses (Dennis and Erdos, 1992), was that poor lone mothers were viewed as producing an underclass of unruly, uncivilised young men, who failed to fulfil their provider responsibilities and became engaged in criminality (Murray, 1990). At an ideological level, the New Right thesis posed a 'crisis of masculinity' in which it was argued that men had lost their rightful place as the heads of families through women's selfish bids for autonomy and independence. At the same time, young men's criminal behaviour in areas of high unemployment was attributed to a lack of 'proper patriarchal control in the family', and women were viewed as 'being inherently incapable of exerting parental authority' (Laws, 1996, p 65). The second strand of this thesis was that fatherhood, defined as providing for families, civilised men and gave them a sense of masculine identity. For example, Murray argued:

> Supporting a family is a central means for a man to prove he is a mensch [man]. Men who do not support families find other ways to prove that they are men which tend to take various destructive forms. As many have commented through the centuries, young males are essentially barbarians for whom marriage – meaning not just the wedding vows, but the act of taking responsibility for a wife and children – is an indispensible civilising force. (Murray, 1990, pp 20-2)

In this blatantly ahistorical analysis, Murray failed to acknowledge that for a significant proportion of fathers neither marriage nor the role of provider had 'civilised' them but rather had institutionalised forms of male dominance and oppression of women and children. Nevertheless, these discourses helped to obscure the impact of Thatcherite economic policies, which had produced massive unemployment for both men and women during the 1980s (Abbott and Wallace, 1992). Eventually they resulted in the 1991 Child Support Act, which aimed to compel unmarried, lone mothers on social security benefits to name absent fathers and enforce the payment of child support on all fathers who had either left the family home or were not living with mothers. New Right policies have continued to have significant influence on family policy today, with aspects of traditional fatherhood having been absorbed into New Labour 'third way' approaches (Giddens, 1998) and the continuing stigmatisation of lone motherhood. This is discussed further below.

Father deprivation and father involvement discourses

From the 1980s onwards, contestation and debates about the significance of father presence and fathers' involvement in the care of their children have characterised the family policy child welfare agenda. These were informed by discourses about whether fathers provide different or similar care of children, sexual division of labour analyses and their impact on gendered social relations in families.

In the 1980s, there was a plethora of new sociological and small-scale psychological studies on fatherhood from a number of different perspectives that focused on the emergence of the 'involved father'. Such studies indicated that 'fatherhood had become a distinctive and prestigious substantive issue' and 'mother-focused research programmes had become increasingly outmoded and criticised' (McKee and O'Brien, 1982, p 3). While a few studies emphasised the similarities in the care of young infants provided by mothers and fathers, others stressed the differences (Beail, 1982; Lewis, 1982). These latter studies began to argue that father involvement was important to children's emotional and cognitive development, particularly that of boys, emphasising discourses of the effect of father deprivation on children (Richards, 1982). Moreover, although the early studies demonstrated differences in their theoretical perspectives, methods and findings, they were used to support the discourse of the 'new nurturing father' who increasingly participates in the care of infants (Beail and Mcguire, 1982). These were accompanied by popular representations of the caring new man holding a baby or toddler, which, by the late 1980s, had become a style accessory for fashionable young men (Rutherford, 1988) and, as Smart noted, signified virility and the 'proprietorial relationship between men and their offspring' (Smart, 1989, p 14). These images further related to the increasing cultural significance given to biological fathers, rather than social fathers.

Discourses of blaming mothers

There were also emerging arguments that mothers 'power' in the home was preventing father involvement, with Backett (1987) suggesting that mothers' main responsibility for childcare gave them a 'hidden power' in the choice of children's activities and routines, based on her research about how parenting was negotiated in 22 families. In contrast, other studies of parenting in two-earner families (Brannen and Moss, 1987) were describing the difficulties for women in trying to get fathers to take more responsibility for childcare when they wanted to return to work and indicated that the research evidence for the new caring and nurturant father was less than convincing (Lewis and O'Brien, 1987). They also argued that 'accounts of fatherhood should be understood in the context of women's continuing domination by men in the public sphere' and 'in certain respects within the family itself' (Lewis and O'Brien, 1987, p 2). However discourses of blaming mothers for fathers' lack of involvement in childcare increased throughout the 1990s (see, for example, Burgess and Ruxton, 1996) and were adopted by some influential New Labour feminists (Williams, 1998).

Reconstruction of discourses of gender difference

Large-scale surveys in the 1990s continued to emphasise that shifts in the sexual division of labour in the home were small, with mothers still shouldering most of the labour of childcaring, although father involvement was greater where mothers worked outside the home (Gilbert, 1993; Ferri and Smith, 1996; Burghes et al, 1997). These also suggested some gendered differences in the caring duties undertaken, where core activities such as cooking and washing were more likely to be undertaken by mothers and fathers were more involved in leisure and play activities (see, for example, Warin et al, 1999). Other research had looked at how father care continued to reinforce gendered inequalities between boys and girls, more so than that of mothers (Sharpe, 1994; Mann, 1996). This was supported by evidence from comparative research in developing countries indicating that boys brought up in woman-headed households where fathers were absent learnt greater respect for women and showed a greater willingness to share household tasks, previously regarded as women's work (Chant, 1997). By the end of the 1990s, some qualitative empirical studies on father involvement in heterosexual relationships (Lupton and Barclay, 1997) found that although most fathers undertook some care of infants, this was characterised by conflicts with their partners over the division of labour in the home and the way fathers constructed discourses of masculinity in their parenting. Thus, parenting for these fathers meant 'being there' for their child and contained idealised notions of love and affection in how they wanted to father children, with some demonstrating disappointment when parental bonds were not immediately established. They regarded themselves as being ideally positioned to be the children's permanent 'guardians and guides' and viewed this as giving them a 'sense of strength and mastery' in their practices as fathers, where their main fathering roles were as protectors and providers (Lupton and Barclay, 1997, pp 144-5).

Fatherhood as resources and social capital

Studies in the 1990s also placed an increasing emphasis on the differences in father 'involvement' with children in fatherhood studies and less emphasis on equality discourses that were initially a part of some of the early 'men against sexism' and feminist approaches in arguing that men should share childcare (Pringle, 1998). This emphasis on difference is indicated in a review of the evidence by Burghes and colleagues (1997) referred to above, where it is suggested that the paucity of evidence for increased father involvement 'may reflect the [different] nature of paternal care rather than the lack of it' (Burghes et al, 1997, p 3). Others emphasised the different and, by implication, superior ethical values involved in father care. For example, the US researchers Hawkins and Dollahite (1997), drawing on feminist discourses of domestic labour as work, argued that father involvement was about 'generative father work', in which fathers had an ethical responsibility for future generations. They stated that 'fathers are not mothers and shouldn't try to be' and that fathers' most significant role is in their physical presence, the intellectual stimulation they give to children through play and the material sources they provide. There are some parallels to this approach in Maclean and Eekelaar's UK socio-legal study (1997), which focused mainly on absent fathers' perceived social obligations towards children and child support and the connection between the two. In its analysis of the latter, the study drew heavily on the authors' own definition of social capital, which encompassed fathers' level of commitment to the child and the provision of material resources.

However, such ethical discourses circumvented and submerged gendered social power relations, returning more to the notion of essential biological differences between mothers and fathers developed in the 19th century and accepting the economic social inequalities between men and women, including that of pay and mothers' earnings being further reduced because of the need to work part time to fit around childcare commitments. At the same time, US psychological research was challenging the rhetoric of father deprivation and its supposed impact on children, particularly boys (Marsiglio, 1995; Lamb, 1997). Lamb (1997) in reviewing the research evidence found similar influences on their children by non-violent fathers and mothers and that parental characteristics such as warmth and nurturance were more significant to children's development than gender differences. He also noted that the studies of children growing up in father-absent families demonstrated that boys grew up 'normally' as far as their gendered identities and 'achievement' were concerned (Lamb, 1997, p 11). This is a finding that has been confirmed by studies of lesbian families where boys have grown up without fathers from birth (Tasker and Golombok, 1997). Other research has looked specifically at the claim that fathers provide more or 'better' intellectual stimulation to their children and found that this is not related to father involvement 'but the presence of caring individuals and the extent to which they are willing to work with or stimulate their children' (Mott, 1993, p 213). Further, both Marsiglio (1995) and Lamb (1997) found that father hostility and violence towards mothers could worsen the outcomes for children. As Marsiglio stated:

> Although greater father involvement with their resident or non-resident children does not necessarily enhance children's well-being at the aggregate level, this pattern may be sustained to some extent by fathers who are abusive and/ or intensify friction within their children's home through negative interactions with their mother. (Marsiglio, 1995, p 10)

Discourses of father absence post-separation

Discourses of father absence and deprivation were also informed by emerging discourses of children's welfare post-separation in 'private' family law through psychological studies looking at the impact of divorce on children during the 1980s. One of these studies, by US researchers Wallerstein and Kelly (1980), was interpreted as meaning that children's emotional development was invariably negatively affected by father absence and therefore the principle of ongoing contact with the 'non-custodial parent' should be applied unless there were 'exceptional circumstances' (Latey, in *Re B (A Minor) (Access)* [1984] FLR 649). However, as Barnett (2009a) notes, this research actually rejected 'any presumptive pattern' and pointed to a number of 'potentially detrimental consequences of contact in certain circumstances,' (Barnett, 2009a, p 2). Subsequently, a growing body of research evidence has challenged this discourse, arguing that the evidence is ambiguous and contradictory. For example, Hunt and Roberts (2004) in their examination of the small number of UK studies available found that one (Dunn, 2003) reported 'unequivocal' findings of the benefits of contact to child adjustment and the other (Smith et al, 2003) showed 'no effects' (Hunt and Roberts, 2004:2) Moreover, alongside other researchers, they found that such benefits did not apply where there had been excessive conflict and hostility between parents, including domestic violence, *prior to separation* and that this was a more significant factor in affecting child adjustment than contact with the absent parent per se. Further, if the quality of contact with the non-residential parent was poor, there were unlikely to be any benefits to the child (Rogers and Pryor, 1998, Pryor and Rodgers 2001; Harold and Murch, 2005). Research reviews have also emphasised the need to take children's views into account in considering contact and post–separation parenting and the harm inflicted when reluctant children are forced to enter into contact arrangements against their wishes (Sturge and Glaser, 2000; Harold and Murch, 2005). Research on shared parenting arrangements after separation also found that although some children benefited, others struggled, particularly as they got older and wanted to alter these arrangements but fathers were inflexible to change (Neale et al, 2003; Smart, 2004).

The most recent research review commissioned in 2009 by the Department for Children, Schools and Families concluded that

> children do not benefit from contact with the non-residential parent when they do not have a good relationship with that parent, where the contact is against their wishes, or where there is abuse or poor parenting (Mooney et al, 2009, pp 3-4).

Although this seems obvious, it has taken 20 years to reach this conclusion, which is still not accepted in UK government policy and is only just beginning to affect some practice in the family courts. This is partly because of the impact and influence of fathers' rights movements, which is discussed further below.

Fatherhood movements and fathers' rights

No discussion of the influences on current policy approaches to fatherhood and domestic violence would be adequate without reference to the impact of fathers' rights movements. Fathers' movements are specifically about 'masculinity politics,' (Gavanas, 2002) and have been characterised by the social masculinity theorist, Connell, as 'those mobilisations and struggles where the meaning of masculine gender is at issue, and with it men's position in gender relations. In such politics masculinity is made a principal theme, not a taken for granted as a background' (Connell, 1995, p 205).

Historically, the emergence of politically motivated fatherhood movements in countries such as the US, Australia, Canada and the UK originated in some fathers' perceptions of their loss of paternal control and decision-making rights over women and children when mothers were legally accorded equal parental rights during the 1970s. This initially coincided with New Right concerns about the dissolution of the traditional family, which linked father absence to a variety of social ills (Graycar, 1989; Smart and Sevenhuijsen, 1989; Bertoia and Drakitch,

1995). Yet these movements have drawn on a number of other discourses, including using the rhetoric of oppression and inequality to define fathers as victims of the state and of women in family law, as well as child welfare discourses on father involvement, where fathers' movements emphasise the different, unique and superior contribution fathers make in their care of the children, often using socio-biological arguments to support their case.[1] According to Rosen and et al (2009), fathers rights and responsibility movements have mobilised around feminist challenges to male privilege and dominance, viewing their activism with other men as forms of resistance where they seek to 're-naturalise and re-centre hegemonic masculinity', although, as Gavanas (2002) has noted, elements have also been about more marginalised minority men seeking the same masculine advantages as the white, male middle class in the US.

Fathers' rights and domestic violence

While the aims of fathers' movements vary, they retain commonalities, particularly in their opposition to mothers' equality and autonomy, in their assertion of fathers' 'inviolable rights' to their children and in their denial and discrediting of women's discourses of domestic violence and child abuse. The latter is not a side issue, but has been, and remains, central to the aims of fathers' rights organisations, since it is in this area that assumptions of male dominance have been most contested through research and advocacy, as well as by individual mothers in the family courts, although often on behalf of children rather than in terms of mothers' rights per se (Smart and Neale, 1999; Reece, 2006). Thus, as Jaffe and colleagues (2003) have noted, fathers rights groups (FRGs) have used particular rhetorical devices to discredit women's advocacy, through claiming that the extent of fathers' domestic violence is exaggerated; making counter allegations of women's violence; and minimising and trivialising the impact of fathers' domestic violence on children and claims that mother's allegations of violence and other forms of child abuse are false. Related to this are the broader rhetorical strategies used by FRGs as summarised by Collier (2005, p 5), including, perhaps most significantly:

- 'a conflation of the interests of fathers and children in such a way that they become in effect one and the same thing';
- appeals to treat fathers 'equally' through formal legal rights;
- 'claims to victim status' through the use of selective statistics;
- emotional appeals to the suffering of individual fathers; and

- concerns to defend the heterosexual family from the social ills of father absence and the problem of lone mothers.

Collier notes that the latter has involved specific misogyny towards mothers, who have been variously represented as 'alimony drones,' 'mendacious and vindictive' and selfish and irresponsible figures. Mothers in particular are viewed as the 'cause and consequence of social/family breakdown' in contrast to fathers, who are represented as 'respectable and socially safe' and who want to share family responsibilities. Another significant commonality is the consistent and powerful way in which FRGs have mobilised, from lobbying and obtaining positions on key committees and organisations to internet networking, direct action and threats and use of actual violence to influence and change policy (Bertoia and Drakitch, 1995; Collier, 2005; Rosen et al, 2009). Further, because they have been able to use this social power as men, they have had far more influence than women's advocacy on social policy changes, as illustrated in the brief history of UK FRGs below.

The UK Families need Fathers (FNF) pressure group was set up in 1974 as a direct result of married women being given equal parenting rights in law. There was an emerging resentment against mothers usually keeping custody of children on separation and divorce, while in practice fathers rarely contested such decisions (Eekelaar and Clive, 1977). FNF argued that fathers were being discriminated against in these circumstances and from the beginning wanted joint custody over children on separation as well as automatic rights of access to children, including for unmarried fathers, regardless of some fathers' violence.

At the first Parliamentary Select Committee on Violence in Marriage (1974-75), FNF used the threat of violence, even murder, if fathers were excluded from having child contact, the implication being that this would be justified in such circumstances (Harne and Radford, 1994). However, by the early 1990s FNF was proclaiming the 'greater prevalence of female-instigated violence' and, drawing on discourses of the significance of fathers' emotional involvement with children, arguing that 'where there is a loving and spontaneous father/child relationship in the family, the violent-wife, frequently becomes jealous of the relationship in a way that further fuels her violence' (Bruce Kent, FNF at Home Affairs Committee, 1993, p 54).

FNF's emphasis on fathers' emotional relationships with children at this time appeared to reflect a shift characterised by Beck (1992) and illustrated earlier in Lupton and Barclay's (1997) research where some men, motivated by lack of satisfaction in the workplace and uncertainty about the permanence of heterosexual relationships, regarded an emotional 'investment' in children as giving them a sense of security. However, it did not mean a shift away from FNF's aim of masculine control and dominance over families; rather, the emphasis on fathers' perceived emotional connectivity with their children, however genuine, was another weapon used to invert and discredit feminist research about fathers' domestic violence and maintain the illusion that fathers were the 'real' victims in family law processes. Thus, by the end of the 1990s, FNF was arguing that family law policies were making separated fathers 'grief-stricken' at the loss of their children (Parton, 1998, p 775), although in reality they were rarely denied contact by the family courts (Hester and Radford, 1996; Smart and Neale, 1997). In this regard, Smart and Neale, citing their research on post-divorce parenting, found that all the fathers they interviewed viewed their legal contact rights to children as inviolable, quoting one father who said, 'Well you get serial killers and rapists still have contact with the kiddies – doesn't mean to say they are a bad father' (Smart and Neale, 1997, p 335).

During the same period, the FNF was flexing its patriarchal muscles in organising opposition to the 1991 Child Support Act together with other fathers' campaigning groups such as Dads after Divorce. They claimed that the child support payments they were expected to pay were unfair to those who had second families and that there should be no payment without increased child contact. Their power as a fathers' movement succeeded in bringing about significant changes to the Act and in aligning child support payments with their amount of contact post-separation. As Lewis (2002) has noted, the resistance of men's groups such as FNF to the Child Support Act was about control. Fathers were unwilling to fulfil their provider responsibilities without their traditional rewards of having some control over mothers and children and the Act had removed these traditional rewards. Nevertheless, FNF, through its discourses of discrimination, managed to reposition itself as 'victim' and thus rendered invisible this controlling aspect.

FNF has had considerable impact on legislation and policy on parenting post-separation, achieving joint parental responsibility for separated married fathers in the 1989 Children Act and the legal principle of ongoing contact with the non-residential parent in almost all circumstances, developed through judge-made case law (see below). By the beginning of the 21st century, it had a place on the influential Children Act sub-committee, which informed further policy and legislation subsequent to the 1989 Children Act including legislation to enforce contact on reluctant children (2006 Children and Adoption Act), and increased its influence by gaining membership on local family justice councils (FNF, 2009a). It has continued to demand legal change to make 50 per cent shared parenting the norm for children on separation and divorce (FNF, 2009b), choosing to disregard the research that this is not something children necessarily want since it means living between two households and involves major disruption to their lives (Neale et al, 2003; Smart, 2004). While it has not yet succeeded in this aim, it has managed to increase the number of shared residence orders made by the family courts (Smart, 2004).

Children's voices and fathers' rights

One aspect of the 1989 Children Act has been a constant problem for FNF campaigners, as, for the first time, it granted children the right to voice their wishes and feelings about what happens to them post-separation if the case comes before a court (1989 Children Act, s1.3a). To counter this, FNF has consistently campaigned for legal recognition of 'parental alienation syndrome',[2] arguing that where children express reluctance to see their fathers in such circumstances they have been encouraged by selfish, hostile mothers to express such views and that this constitutes emotional abuse of the child (FNF, 2008). FNF also promotes shared parenting by agreement through in-court mediation with family court advisers, thus bypassing the necessity of seeking children's views (FNF, 2009b). It states that 'shared parental responsibility' includes 'most significantly, the right to control or direct the child's upbringing' (FNF, 2009b, p 4), suggesting that paternal control, rather than the needs of children, remains a central concern. Further, although it has abandoned the discourse that domestic violence is mainly committed by mothers and recognises it as an issue of 'personal safety' for children, it continues to argue that many mothers make false allegations, claiming that 'it is an easy way of depriving the other parent of contact and the opportunity to parent the child' (FNF, 2009b, p 4).

While FNF is now accepted as the respectable face of fathers' rights groups in the UK and has received funding from the Human Rights Commission, the more militant Fathers4Justice group founded in 2002 has also had a considerable impact (Collier, 2005). Members of Fathers4Justice have physically attacked the offices of Child and Family Court Advisory and Support Service (Cafcass), and other high-profile incidents including camping outside the homes of judges and on the roof of former Minister for Women and Equality Harriet Harman's house in 2008, as well as throwing a condom of flour at the then Prime Minister Tony Blair in 2004. Collier has argued that since Fathers4Justice has been active, it has influenced some senior judges who have publicised their own beliefs 'that the family justice system has frequently failed fathers' (Collier, 2005, p 511). Undoubtedly, the group has contributed to a shift in government policy, namely that in most cases contact arrangements should be agreed by parents through in-court mediation rather than being disputed in court hearings (DfES, 2004, 2005). In 2006, the government introduced legislation to penalise resident parents (usually mothers) for failing to comply with contact orders through the Children and Adoption Act. At the same time, the Conservative Party leader (now Prime Minister) David Cameron promised a 'strong presumption' in favour of fathers 'equal rights' if the Conservatives won the next election and stated that the debate had shifted recently 'as a result of protests by fathers' (Collier, 2005, p 511).

However, in 2004 when Fathers4Justice was most active, an undercover media investigation (*The Mirror*, 2004) found that all of the group's main instigators, including its leader and deputy leader, had convictions for domestic violence and that meetings were characterised by exposing the children present to 'lurid sex stories' and circulating pornographic images of women supporters. This led to the resignation of some senior members.

One of the main impacts of fathers rights' movements both in the UK and internationally is that through their rhetorical devices they have contributed to the dominant discourse that fathers are always good for children (Kaye and Tolmie, 1999; Collier, 2005; Rosen et al 2009), making it virtually impossible to question a father's capacity to parent until very recently (Smart and Neale, 1997; Kaganas and Day Sclater, 2004). Furthermore, their discourses have served to obscure the harm violent fathers can inflict on children during parenting.

New Labour and the failure to recognise fathers as risks

As Scourfield and Drakeford (2002) have argued, New Labour drew heavily on the ideology that father involvement was invariably beneficial to children, as well as embracing discourses that fathers have been disadvantaged and excluded in family and child welfare policies and services. It noted that early ministerial statements emphasised the 'crucial importance of fathers to children's well-being and boys especially', with ministers referring to 'unspecified research' on father absence to support their arguments and 'the equivocal' and often 'spurious' nature of this research (Scourfield and Drakeford, 2002, p 624). New Labour followed this approach soon after it came to power in 1997 (Home Office, 1998), with funding being made available for father-promotion projects such as the Fatherhood Institute, and the introduction of legislation that would remove the perceived 'institutional barriers' to fathers' exclusion and engagement. Further, although Scourfield and Drakeford (2002, p 625) indicated that New Labour was claiming to be tough on criminal men, 'wife-beaters and sex offenders [were] constructed as non-fathers'.

As in New Right discourses, New Labour regarded fathers' engagement in families as an all-embracing solution to the problem of the 'crisis of masculinity', where men are viewed as producing destructive forms of masculine behaviour because they are uncertain and insecure about their roles. However, they also saw fathers as 'carers of children' and argued that mothers and the state were preventing this care. Fathers thus became constructed as victims in what has come to be known as the 'poor men syndrome', since such arguments denied that fathers have considerable social power as men. Scourfield and Drakeford also noted that New Labour focused on sustaining dominant masculinity in the projects they supported and failed to recognise that most girls and women do not have *actual* equality, either in familial social relations or in the wider public sphere.

It is clear that in taking this approach, New Labour largely followed Anthony Gidden's 'third way' politics (1998) and the recommendations of Burgess and Ruxton (1996), then at the Institute for Public Policy Research, who proposed a complete overhaul of social and child welfare policies to address their purported lack of rights. These included increasing 'the rights' of unmarried fathers, as well as encouraging young and teenage fathers, criminal fathers and those in prison, to engage with their children. Contrasting their policies to those of the New Right, Burgess and Ruxton argued that biological fathers had been deskilled through social policy, which only viewed them as economic providers, disciplinarians and authority figures. They claimed that fathers could be just as good carers of children as mothers, stating that this was an 'equal opportunities' issue for both men and women that could free up women to work. However, in contradiction to this 'equal opportunities' rhetoric, they contended that fathers had been negatively stereotyped as 'abusive' and argued that such representations actually applied to 'very few fathers'. Further, they argued that mothers' rights to autonomy and freedom from violence and abuse should be overridden to accommodate children's 'best interests' to see such fathers, failing to recognise the harm this could have on children themselves.

In a later publication by one of the authors, it was suggested that if violent and some sexually abusive fathers were to 'spend increased time with children this might lead to *reduced* violence and abuse in some cases', since 'some fathers might have less need to demonstrate dominance' or, in the case of sexual abuse, find 'other ways of achieving intimacy' (Burgess, 1997, pp 213-14). However, such arguments demonstrate a failure to understand the attitudes and motivations of violent and abusive fathers and followed in practice would put children at much greater risk of harm, indicating an overwhelming focus on fathers' 'needs' rather than on children's safety and welfare.

Government policy, domestic violence and children's safety

Scourfield and Drakeford (2002) suggested that, rather than constructing fatherhood in an entirely positive way, New Labour had taken a tougher approach to men as perpetrators in its criminal justice policies. They argued that this was partially illustrated in government strategies and policies for dealing with domestic violence where protection for victims was viewed primarily as an issue that should be addressed by taking perpetrators through the criminal justice system. However, as fathers have been constructed as 'non-offenders', this has created uncomfortable contradictions in policy and practice by rendering invisible the fact that some fathers are also perpetrators of domestic violence and child abuse. As Featherstone (2000, 2003) notes, the simple view that all fathers contribute to children's wellbeing has bypassed any understanding of the complexity of men's lives and of the dangers that some fathers can pose to children and mothers. It has also created significant difficulties and tensions for practitioners, who are required to have a positive attitude towards perpetrator men as fathers while taking responsibility for protecting victims and preventing further harm from the negative impacts of domestic violence.

Although there is growing recognition in child protection and safeguarding policies that children need to be protected from domestically violent *men* and an increased understanding of the association of domestic violence with other forms of child abuse by the same perpetrators, such offenders are rarely referred to as violent fathers or father figures in policy statements (DH, 1999; DfES, 2007b). This understanding was also reinforced by legislation in the form of the 2002 Adoption and Children Act, which, although not implemented until 2005, amended the definition of harm in the 1989 Children Act to include 'impairment suffered from seeing or hearing the ill treatment of another' (s 120) and required local authorities to investigate whether there has been significant harm and/or to provide services to such children and their families 'in need' (1989 Children Act, ss 47 and 17). Nevertheless, the conflict between supporting fathers and safeguarding children policies has led to split approaches and often irresolvable dilemmas, where children are frequently the main losers in the 'rights and needs stakes' to be protected from harm, as illustrated below.

Violent fathers and criminal justice policies: putting children at risk

The split approach described above is reflected in paradoxical sentencing policies on domestic violence, as well as in prison policies and policing practice. For example, in sentencing policy, exposing children to domestic violence 'directly or indirectly' and 'using child contact to commit an offence' are recognised as aggravating factors that can secure a more severe sentence. At the same time, violent fathers can use the disruption of their relationship with children as a mitigating factor to avoid more serious custodial punishment (Sentencing Council, 2006, pp 5-6). In practice, being a father appears to be a more significant discourse than being a domestically violent offender, something that has been highlighted in research in this area. For example, Hester and colleagues (2003) noted that fathers were usually given lower sentences by magistrates when they claimed their relationships with children would be affected and that these courts failed to understand the risks such sentencing could pose to children. A further problem is that in the minority of cases where they do receive prison sentences, violent men immediately become constructed as 'marginalised' and 'vulnerable' individuals who *need* continuing relationships with their children for their own rehabilitation in terms of their 'emotional growth and wellbeing', regardless of issues of safety and risk to children and their non-abusing mothers (Walker, 2009).

Policing practice and compromising women and children's safety

Research on policing practice indicates that when called to incidents of post-separation violence relating to disputes over child contact, some police advise both parents that contact is in the best interests of the child (Hester, 2009). This is despite the fact that police risk assessments indicate that, in cases of post-separation violence in relation to child contact disputes, the risk of serious injury and possible lethal violence towards children or their mothers or both is very high (ACPO/Home Office 2006). Such practices are even more paradoxical when it is considered that the police force is a key child protection agency and officers are required to make assessments when attending incidents of domestic violence where children are present and refer them to children's social care when they have concerns about their safety (DfES, 2006).

Overall, both the ideology of all fathers as being essential to children's wellbeing and discourses of 'fathers needs' have overridden children's and mothers' rights to protection in the criminal justice system and have compromised their safety as a result. These discourses and practices also convey the message to perpetrator fathers that their violence is not regarded as a serious crime, since they continue to be *rewarded* with contact with their children, despite their criminal behaviour. This is further illustrated by the research findings from an evaluation of multi-agency risk assessment conferences in South Wales, designed to increase the safety of women and children identified as very high-risk victims through coordinated actions between agencies to reduce repeat victimisation (Robinson and Tregidga, 2005). This evaluation found that at the end of a 12-month period, 42 out of 102 women were no longer experiencing further assault, but child contact with the violent father was one of the main reasons given for continuing violence and harassment of mothers and children.

Children's welfare and safety: every father matters, but not children or mothers

Similar contradictions and tensions are evident in child welfare and protection policies more broadly and have increased over the past 10 years as father engagement discourses have developed further. Collier and Sheldon (2008) have noted that the idea of the involved father has formed a central plank of the government child welfare policy framework. Promoting father engagement was, for example, a major part of the Green Paper *Every Child Matters* (DfES, 2003), which aimed to develop a more integrated approach to children's safety and welfare through preventing childhood difficulties such as low educational achievement, anti-social behaviour and teenage parenthood and resulted in further legislation and policy development. This included the 2006 Childcare Act, which required local authorities to provide parents with information on children's education and welfare services, regardless of whether parents presented any risk to children. Another piece of legislation, the 2006 Equality Act, required public authorities to comply with a gender duty to actively promote gender equality between men and women. This Act has been used as a means to promote the interests of men in general and fathers in particular and has made it more difficult to provide women-only services, such as domestic violence support, partly because of competition for funding from services aimed specifically at men and fathers (Harne and Radford, 2008).

At the same time key services relating to mothers' and children's welfare, including maternity and family support services such as Sure Start Children's Centres,[3] were required to proactively involve all fathers. This included fathers not living with mothers, despite the fact that many mothers may have separated from these men because of their violence and abuse (DfES, 2004; Walby and Allen, 2004; DfES, 2007b). As Featherstone and Peckover (2007) note in this regard, government policy has failed to take into consideration the fact that father hostility and violence, rather than lack of father involvement, are key correlates for poor outcomes for children:

> It is problematic to suggest that father involvement per se is good for children as father involvement itself is correlated with mother involvement and encouraging father involvement in the context of, at worst, violent relationships could be deeply counterproductive for women and children. (Featherstone and Peckover 2007, p 190)

With the launch of a further policy paper *Every Parent Matters* (DfES, 2007a), the government appeared to support overtly discriminatory policies and practices in favour of boys and fathers. This is illustrated through press statements such as 'we will put a boys' reading shelf in every secondary school containing positive, modern relevant role models for boys' and '[we are] engaging fathers by running sessions where dads and their children work together on an allotment, visit sports facilities or take part in music or photography projects' (DfES 2007a, 2007b). It could be argued that there is a similar need for mothers to undertake such projects with their children and that promoting positive role models for girls is also necessary. Yet only fathers' involvement is represented as leading to 'positive educational achievement', (DfES, 2007b, p 10), although, as seen above, this is not supported by any substantive research once economic factors are taken into account (Flouri, 2005). As with earlier policies, *Every Parent Matters* emphasised that professionals were expected to engage fathers as much as possible, but no mention was made of any possible risks from domestic violence and/or child abuse, or of how these risks could produce much worse outcomes for children in relation to poor health, low educational achievement, mental health problems and teenage pregnancy. Rather, specific safeguarding policies have been developed separately from other 'preventative' policies to promote children's welfare and, as with criminal justice policies, they continue to inhibit the protection of children and young people in practice.

Violent fathers and maternity services

Professionals in maternity and health visitor services for adult women are expected to create routine opportunities for expectant mothers to disclose domestic violence, while simultaneously encouraging fathers to be involved as much as possible including at antenatal appointments (DH, 2004;Home Office, 2010). This has created specific pressures and difficulties in protecting expectant mothers from the risks violent fathers can pose to them and the unborn child and to newborn children post-birth (Harne and Radford, 2008).

Further, although health policies aimed at women over 18 have at least recognised that domestic violence from fathers is an issue that needs to be addressed, the same cannot be said for younger teenage mothers who have been subjected to partner abuse. Some awareness of how violence from young violent fathers can affect and has affected teenage mothers and their children was raised in an evaluation of a New Labour scheme to improve the health and welfare of this group, known as Sure Start Plus. One of the aims of this scheme was to reduce domestic violence for teenage mothers and their children. This study reported that 14 per cent of teenage mothers had disclosed that they had experienced domestic violence during pregnancy from a young, violent father/boyfriend (Wiggins and Rosato, 2005). Nevertheless, this figure is likely to be an underestimate of these mothers' experiences of domestic violence, given the fact that they may not have been asked about it by professionals (Include, 2006; Warwick, 2006). Moreover, Australian research in this area has found that 30 per cent of teenage mothers experience domestic violence (Quinlivan and Evans, 2001).

Small-scale UK studies with teenage mothers such as that undertaken in Leeds (Include, 2006) have found that participants were not usually consulted by health professionals, and, where they did disclose experience of domestic violence, it was often perceived as 'mutual violence'. As one young mother said:

> 'It were a boisterous relationship, that's how they saw it. I were as bad as him. How could they [think that]? I didn't pour pints of beer over his head. I didn't urinate on him. I didn't attack him with cigarettes.' (Include, 2006, p 3)

Despite this, in its concern to involve putative young fathers the government national service framework on teenage pregnancy and motherhood (DCSF and DH, 2009), to which the Fatherhood Institute contributed, made no mention of professionals asking teenage mothers about domestic violence. Neither did it create routine opportunities for disclosure and support to gain protection. Such an approach continues to put some teenage mothers and their children at risk. At the very least, young mothers under the age of 18 and their children should be offered the same opportunities for disclosure and protection as adult mothers.

Violent fathers and child protection in children's social care

Although safeguarding responsibilities are placed on a number of public agencies, children's social care has lead responsibility for investigating whether children exposed to domestic violence are suffering or likely to suffer significant harm or are in need of services and support, and for coordinating action between agencies (DCSF, 2009). Its response to referrals from other services is therefore crucial. Yet research and serious case reviews have indicated that social workers' responses continue to be highly variable, with a lack of focus on violent fathers' responsibility for harm often being a critical factor in the further maltreatment of children.

This can partly be explained by traditional social work approaches where child maltreatment is viewed through the lens of the 'dysfunctional family', in which mothers, who are regarded as the main carers of children, are the main focus (Hester et al, 2007). Thus social work interventions become centred on abused mothers' capacity to parent and protect the children and violent fathers' responsibility remains unaddressed (Radford and Hester, 2006). In discussing the evidence from research in this area, Farmer (2006) has indicated that fathers' violence against mothers has rarely been regarded as 'significantly affecting the risk to children' in social work case management. Even where violent fathers were also physically abusing children, the focus tended to shift on to the mother's parenting and capacity to protect rather than on the father's behaviour. Farmer outlines several reasons for this. These remain relevant to contemporary social work practice and include social workers' own lack of powers to remove violent fathers from the home, particularly where there has been no police involvement, resulting in pressure being placed on mothers to separate from and exclude fathers.[4] As Hester and colleagues (2007) have noted, placing pressure on abused mothers, including threatening to remove children, can be counter-productive, since this fails to address mothers' own fears of their violent partners and can prevent them from disclosing further abuse. In these circumstances, the lack of recognition given to abused mothers' own needs for protection from the violence means that the children are also unlikely to be protected from harm.

Another reason for the lack of focus on violent fathers is some practitioners' own reasonable fears of engaging with them, a finding that has been noted in other research and means that the focus turns on mothers' parenting for want of anything better (see, for example, Brandon et al, 2006; Littlechild and Bourke, 2006). Some practitioners also identify with fathers' points of view, particularly in cases where they justify their physical abuse on the grounds that the children need discipline. In this regard, practitioners may view a violent father as 'the cornerstone of the family', leading to his dominance in the domestic domain becoming 'more entrenched' while the impact of his violence on the children and the mother are ignored (Humphreys, 2000).

Other research has shown that violent fathers can make counter-allegations of abuse or neglect against mothers, and, in a policy context where father involvement is overvalued, practitioners may be more likely to collude with fathers' views (Hester and Scott, 2000). Furthermore, Farmer and Owen's research (1995) showed that fathers often deny that they have been violent, and where practitioners do not identify a primary perpetrator or make a distinction between abusive and non-abusive parents, they usually assume that the situation is one of mutual harm. In these cases, the focus may shift on to other problems in 'the family', such as the mother's mental health or depression[5] or a father's drink or mental health problems (Farmer, 2006). Humphreys (2006) has also emphasised that moves towards regarding domestic violence as a gender-neutral issue have affected the way social workers and other professionals perceive its occurrence in families, and, as in the example given above in relation to young teenage mothers, may assume that the violence is mutual and that mothers are equally to blame.

The inability to identify fathers' violence and direct abuse as the main source of risk to children has therefore been one of the most frequent findings of serious case reviews since the 1980s. This stems partly from a lack of understanding of the gendered power dynamics in families, where domestic violence and child abuse is frequently escalated by fathers or other father figures in an attempt to maintain their dominance (O'Hara, 1994). For example, Brandon and colleagues found that in two thirds of 161 cases studied where children had either died or been seriously injured the victims had been living with domestic violence 'most often linked directly to the child's father, or mother's partner' (Brandon et al, 2006, p 76). There was also considerable overlap of paternal domestic violence, substance misuse and mental health problems in a third of the cases reviewed. Yet in most instances, the focus remained on mothers' profiles and capacity to parent and it was apparent that fathers' violent behaviour towards mothers and their own abusive parenting practices were rarely assessed in terms of the harm children had already experienced or were likely to experience in the future, suggesting a continuing institutional failure to identify violent fathers as a key source of possibly lethal risk to children.

Subsequently, some local children's safeguarding boards have developed their own domestic violence risk identification and assessment models that include assessment of violent fathers as parents (discussed further in Chapter Three). Nevertheless, the institutional neglect of violent fathers or father figures as major contributors to significant harm to children continues to be highlighted in a number of recent serious case reviews, indicating that such risk assessments are not taking place as a matter of course by children's social care agencies in some local authorities (see Box 2.1).

Box 2.1: The Edlington case

The Edlington case concerned two pre-teen boys, who tortured two other stranger boys of the same age. They were eventually convicted of grievous bodily harm with intent (*The Guardian*, 2010). A notable factor in this case was that there had been considerable involvement from different agencies over several years with the offending boys' mother. However, the serious case review found that it was the failure of these agencies to address the father's violence over a 10-year period and its negative impact on the two boys' development that led to the boys' final violent attacks. It stated that 'throughout the [professional] involvement with the family, the focus was primarily on the boys' mother ... this had the effect of ignoring the perpetrator of emotional and physical abuse [the father] as well as giving insufficient attention to what the children needed in terms of being parented properly' (Doncaster Safeguarding Children Board, 2010, p 6).

One of the key findings of the review in the Edlington case concerned 'the effectiveness of the local domestic violence strategy in identifying and safeguarding children at risk from domestic abuse' (Doncaster Safeguarding Children Board, 2010, p 7). The review argued that that it was the two boys 'sustained exposure to violence and neglect' that led to their own escalating violence towards other children. It also emphasised '*the reluctance* of children's social care services to become involved' (p 5), suggesting a continuing lack of understanding by some social workers of the corrosive impact a father's violence has on children over time.

Other research has indicated that such professional practices continue to occur. For example, in her research on local authority referrals in 40 case files, Baynes (2009) found that while domestic violence from fathers or father figures was one of the most common reasons for triggering a child protection meeting, some practitioners continued to blame mothers through statements such as 'mother attracts abusive men due to her low self-esteem' and 'the mother's emotional needs caused such intensity that disputes started' (pp 2-3). Further, although two thirds of fathers or father figures were known to have *histories* of violence, some continued to be viewed as 'good fathers,' as illustrated in the following statements:

- 'despite father's violence, suicide attempts and intimidation he is still a good father';
- 'father is uncaring and horrible but ... he will be alright with the baby and wants to protect him' (Baynes, 2009, pp 2-3).

The case files also indicated that several practitioners had 'little concept' of fathers' 'failure to protect'; neither were their parenting capacities assessed nor police checks undertaken (Baynes, 2009). Despite their histories of domestic violence being recognised as a cause of harm, violent fathers continued to escape blame and some were even regarded as appropriate parents.

Evidence that violent fathers can still be regarded 'good' or 'good enough' parents continues to raise serious questions about some social work practice and training. At the very least, it highlights a lack of understanding of the abusive impact on children of living with fathers' ongoing domestic violence towards mothers and illustrates a lack of recognition in some social work practice of the connections between fathers' violence towards mothers and their behaviour as parents and carers of children. Nevertheless, given that some government child welfare and safeguarding policies also make the same disconnections between violent men as perpetrators and violent men as fathers, it is perhaps not surprising that some social workers interpret these 'mixed messages' as meaning that they should regard violent fathers in a positive light.

Other contradictory factors in social work policies and approaches are also relevant. On the one hand, social workers are expected to focus on the child's needs to be protected from harm, but on the other hand they are expected to work in 'partnership with parents' and take a 'strength-based approach' to working with 'the family' (DCSF, 2009). This can therefore lead to a focus on parents' rather than children's needs (Calder,

2008). As early as 1983, Dingwall and colleagues identified a 'rule of optimism' to explain social workers 'overly positive interpretation' of parents' capacity to change their abusive or neglectful behaviour, based on assumptions of parents 'natural love' for their children (Calder, 2008, p 76). Munroe (1999) also identified such biases in her research with social work professionals and argued that systematic risk identification and assessment could help overcome them.

Other factors place further constraints on effective social work practice even where a violent father or father figure has been identified as a serious source of harm, including social workers' own lack of powers to exclude fathers from the family home. As a result, they become dependent on the effectiveness of multi-agency working to protect the children and their mother. In cases where mothers and children remain with violent and abusive fathers and possible significant harm is suspected, social workers are left with the choice of removing the children or supervising 'the family'. Recent research indicates that since a spate of serious case reviews, including that of Baby Peter,[6] where violent and sadistic fathers or father figures have been identified as a major source of harm to children, there has been a massive increase in the number of children taken into care compared with the same months in the previous year (Hall and Guy, 2009). At the same time, where mothers and children separate from violent fathers, there continues to be an assumption that these fathers can be trusted with child contact and this is examined in more detail below.

Domestic violence and safeguarding children in private law policies on separation and divorce

As discussed above, the 1989 Children Act forms the basis of private law when parents dispute arrangements for children on divorce or separation, or when they have never lived together, and it embraces the principle that the child's welfare is of paramount consideration when cases come before the courts. It also introduced a seven-point welfare checklist that family courts must take into account when considering making court orders. These include 'the wishes and feelings of the child', 'the capabilities of parents' to meet the child's needs and any harm the child has 'suffered or is at risk of suffering' (s 1.3). However, the Act also enshrines the non-interventionist principle that the court should not interfere with parents' responsibilities by making court orders unless 'it considers that doing so would be better for the child' (s 1.5). This clause therefore assumes that in private law processes, most separated or divorced parents will agree arrangements for contact and residence of the children without the court's interference (Bainham, 1990).

Thus, since the implementation of the Act in 1991, there has been considerable pressure on mothers experiencing domestic violence from children's fathers to agree contact arrangements by solicitors, mediators and court welfare officers without any assessment of child welfare concerns or the need to seek children's views. This was supported by judicial practices in the family courts that constructed abused mothers who disputed child contact through the courts on the grounds of their own and their children's safety as being unreasonably 'implacably hostile' to their children's welfare. As Smart and Neale (1997) noted, mothers who opposed contact in relation to safety concerns for the children (including further domestic violence, direct abuse and fears of child neglect due to fathers' mental health and alcoholism) were regarded as opposing children's 'true welfare' for 'irrational and spiteful reasons'. It was therefore virtually impossible to question such fathers' parenting capacity under the welfare checklist and the courts became increasingly punitive towards mothers who opposed contact orders (Smart and Neale, 1997).

In a number of defining judgements, judge-made case law has created a presumption of contact with the non-residential parent in nearly all circumstances and dismissed the harm to children from violent and abusive fathers on the grounds that they would experience 'greater harm' if they did not have an 'enduring relationship' with both natural parents (*M* (Contact: Welfare Test) [1995] 1 FLR 274). A defining judgement in the mid-1990s known as *Re O*, concerning a case of extreme violence towards the mother, stated that contact is 'almost always in the best interest of children' and argued that although the two-year-old concerned was distressed by having obligatory contact with the violent father, 'the court should take the long term view of the child's development and not accord too much weight to what appears to be short term and transitory problems' (*Re O* (Contact: Imposition of Conditions) [1995] 2 FLR 124). As a result of these judgements, abused mothers were threatened with imprisonment if they did not comply with contact orders. This threat was carried out in at least two cases where the fathers had previously been imprisoned for domestic violence and in one of these cases the father also had convictions for drug dealing and fire arms offences (*Z v Z* [1996] Family Law, 62; *A v N* (Commital: Refusal of Contact [1997] 1 FLR 533). In another judgement (*Re H and R* (Child Sexual Abuse) [1995]), the House of Lords ruled that a higher standard of proof beyond the standard of the balance of probabilities used in civil law was needed where mothers' opposition to contact involved allegations of sexual or physical abuse.

The impact of such judgements meant not only that reluctant and abused children were forced to have ongoing contact with their violent and abusive fathers, but also that when mothers raised concerns about fathers' direct physical or sexual abuse, they were more likely to be disbelieved and regarded as making false allegations. Shockingly, as discussed in Chapter One, in some cases, residence of children, was transferred from mothers to sexually abusive fathers where mothers had opposed contact applications in these circumstances (Hester and Radford, 1996; Humphreys, 1997; Radford et al, 1999).

By the end of the century, case law involving four fathers' appeals against 'no contact orders' challenged the presumption that contact is always in the best interests of children in cases where very serious domestic violence has occurred, including one case where the father had killed the mother in front of the child and acknowledged that it could be a 'cogent reason' for the denial of contact (*Re L; Re V; Re M; Re H* (Contact: Domestic) [2000] 2 FLR 334).

An expert psychiatric report was also commissioned to review the research on the impact of domestic violence on children (Sturge and Glaser, 2000). This report stated that 'domestic violence involves a very serious and significant failure in parenting – a failure to protect the child emotionally (and in some cases physically) – which meets any definition of child abuse' and asserted that

> 'we consider that there should be no automatic assumption that contact to a previously or currently violent parent is in the child's interests, if anything the assumption should be in the opposite direction and the case of the non-residential parent one of proving why he can offer something of such benefit not only to the child but to the child's situation' (Sturge and Glaser, 2000, pp 623-4).

The report also emphasised that such fathers should be able to prove that they are able to respond appropriately to a child's needs and pointed out the harmfulness of forcing contact on reluctant children who have ongoing fears and memories of a father's violence against their wishes.

Unsurprisingly, the appeal court refused these recommendations, but subsequently non-statutory guidance was issued to family courts on considering decisions on contact and residence (CASC, 2000) This included the courts only making orders for contact in cases where the safety of the child and resident parent could be secured. The courts were also expected to hold fact-finding hearings where necessary to establish that domestic violence had occurred, and where it was accepted that domestic violence has taken place, the family court adviser (Cafcass officer) was required to make an assessment of harm to the child and other parent and ascertain the children's wishes. Significantly, the guidance also stated that family court advisers should make an assessment of the capacity of the parent seeking contact, his motivations and attitude towards his violence, his understanding of the impact of his behaviour on the other parent and child and his capacity to change and behave appropriately. The courts were also directed to consider whether a violent parent should be required to seek treatment before contact is ordered.

Nevertheless, research indicated that courts generally ignored these guidelines; for example, a study of 300 cases undertaken by Cafcass officers[7] (NAPO, 2002) indicated that over 60 per cent of disputed cases involved allegations of domestic violence against fathers, yet the courts continued to order direct contact with these fathers in over 90 per cent of these cases. Subsequently, the government argued that only 19 per cent of contact applications to family courts involved domestic violence, based on *unpublished* research conducted for the then Lord Chancellor's department. It also supported the presumption of contact and took the position that *safe* contact could be achieved in cases where domestic violence occurred through an increase in the number of supported and supervised contact centres and proposed to provide a further £2.5 million for these centres through the Children's Fund (Home Office, 2003). This was despite extensive research that indicated that neither supported nor supervised contact centres could adequately protect children and their mothers from further abuse from violent fathers and that a number of children felt unprotected and coerced into having such contact (Aris et al, 2002). It also meant that children were usually forced into having open contact with violent fathers after six months of supported or supervised contact visits owing to the funding limitations on such provision.

In consequence, government policy shifted further to emphasising contact by agreement, partly in response to fathers' rights groups and partly to save court and legal aid costs (DfES, 2004, 2005), although, as seen above, the government was able to find large amounts of taxpayers' money to promote contact at supervised centres in domestic violence cases.

Subsequently, the work of Cafcass officers in private law cases focused on agreement seeking through in-court mediation/conciliation and support to implement contact rather than undertaking welfare reports to assess children's welfare and ascertain their wishes. After this shift in policy, research on in-court mediation schemes found that in only 20 per cent of cases were welfare reports undertaken, and 43 per cent of participating mothers felt that issues of domestic violence and child abuse had been ignored in in-court conciliation meetings (Trinder et al, 2006).

The role of solicitors and legal costs

The then Labour government argued that it undertook this policy on the grounds that only 10 per cent of parents had contact and residence arrangements ordered by the court. Yet, if this was the case, it failed to reflect the pressure placed on abused mothers to agree contact by professionals, including solicitors, often against mothers' concerns for children's safety and wellbeing. A further pressure on abused mothers is the astronomical costs of taking a dispute through the family courts. Following the policy on 'agreement seeking' between parents, the government reduced the legal aid budget even further to divert cases away from adversarial proceedings and to promote consensual resolution of disputes over contact and residence (Harold and Murch, 2005; Masson, 2006).

Masson's (2006) survey of more than a thousand family law solicitors found that restrictions on legal aid meant that mothers who had experienced domestic violence and had concerns about their children's safety agreed to contact because they were not eligible for legal aid (which is set at income support level) and that part-time working and tax credits meant that even fewer qualified. But even where mothers were eligible, legal aid could also be refused when a mother wished to dispute the case in the court on the grounds of a father's violence. However, only a third of solicitors discussed domestic violence with women clients. Nevertheless, 40 per cent of solicitors had experience of consent orders (orders made on agreement between parents) that they believed put the children at risk of harm; a third thought too much pressure was placed on parents to agree and only five per cent believed that the court had had enough information about children's wishes.

Denying children's voices

Harold and Murch (2005) argued that the policy on agreement seeking between parents meant that children's voices would not be heard since the court welfare report is usually the only means through which the court hears children's views. They stated that the deliberate policy to reduce court welfare reports through in-court conciliation schemes was 'tantamount to a denial of children's human rights' and in particular a breach of article 12(2) of the 1989 UN Convention on the Rights of the Child, which recognised children's right to be heard in judicial and administrative proceedings concerning them. Further, the authors noted that even where court welfare reports were undertaken, children's views could be 'obscured from judicial consideration' (Harold and Murch, 2005, p 12).

The beginnings of change

Some changes to these policies began to occur, however, as a consequence of the implementation of s 120 of the 2002 Adoption and Children Act, which, as seen above, required all child welfare agencies to consider the impairment to children 'to seeing or hearing the ill-treatment of another'. Of key significance was a government inspection report (HMICA, 2005) looking at private law family court and, in particular, Cafcass officers' practices. It found that:

> The perception of the presumption of contact in domestic violence cases is experienced by women as dangerous to themselves and their children. In the absence of systematic risk assessment, the Cafcass focus on agreement seeking [between parents] is out of balance because it does not pay proportionate attention to safety issues in domestic violence cases. (HMICA, 2005, p 19)

The report found a catalogue of unsafe practices used by Cafcass officers, including a failure to check police and health and social services' records to find out if there were risks to children and their mothers. Abused mothers were made to enter into unsafe joint meetings with perpetrators and set up contact visits in their own homes or in shopping centres so that officers could observe contact. Further, children were observed as being clearly distressed when asked about violent fathers or observed in contact visits and these observations were not included in welfare reports. Interviews with children were also found to be conducted insensitively and not enough time was taken to seek children's views.

At the same time, new court forms were introduced asking separating parents to disclose issues of harm. Research in this area has indicated that the forms had some limited impact in sensitising welfare and legal professionals to issues of domestic violence and safety and in improving court decision making. There were fewer orders for contact with an abusive parent where there was evidence of a high level of violence, although there were also a significant number of orders for interim and unsupervised contact (Aris and Harrison, 2007).

Child homicide and family justice council recommendations

Further significant developments included a report by Lord Justice Wall in response to Women's Aid research on the killings of 29 children during contact visits that looked at the role of the courts in making consent orders[8] in these circumstances. He stated:

> It is, in my view, high time that the Family Justice system abandoned any reliance on the proposition that a man can have a history of violence to the mother of his children, but, nonetheless, be a good father. (Wall, 2006, p 66)

The report recommended that the Family Justice Council (FJC) should prepare a report to the President of the Family Division on the approach the courts should take to consent orders where domestic violence had occurred and to investigate whether non-abusing parents were being pressurised into agreeing contact arrangements by others (including lawyers) that they did not believe to be safe. This led to the FJC (2006) recommending that a direction (as opposed to guidance) be issued to the family courts, requiring them to consider a number of risk factors in relation to violent fathers and taking account of the welfare checklist before any orders for contact or residence are made. This reinforced new provisions in s 7 of the 2006 Children and Adoption Act, which, although mainly concerned with enforcing contact, also indicated that risk assessments must be made where there is suspected harm to the child.

As a consequence of these developments, Cafcass (2007) produced a safeguarding framework that included a three-stage process for identifying and responding to the presence of risk factors related to domestic violence. This process involved an initial screening of all contact and residence applications or forms responding to the application, with the police and children's social care agencies in cases where parents had indicated harm. Second, it introduced a structured risk identification form to be used at first directions hearings to separate from the in-court conciliation/dispute resolution process those cases where domestic violence or other aspects of harm to children had been indicated by parents and/or through the initial screening process. Third, it required Cafcass officers to undertake more in-depth risk assessment in child welfare reports as well as making full use of the welfare checklist in assessing children's welfare. However, since these processes were not being implemented in all relevant cases, further changes were made in 2008, when the President of the Family Division issued a practice direction to family courts requiring them to undertake risk assessments and follow the guidelines issued in 2001. Cafcass officers were required to screen all applications for contact and residence and undertake risk identification at, or soon after, the first directions hearing. Preliminary pilot research (Harne, 2009) suggests that these changes have made some difference to improving the safeguarding of children in private law proceedings and the use of risk identification assessment is discussed in more detail in Chapter Three. However, further policy changes proposed by government may reverse these safeguarding measures, as pro-father policies continue to be promoted at the expense of children's safety.

This chapter has outlined the continuities, changes and contradictions in the construction of fatherhood policies historically and their impact on children's welfare in the UK. Although there have been considerable changes over the years it seems that in many cases children's safety and wellbeing is as poorly regarded as it was in the 19th century, and that fatherhood policies that support dominant, controlling and abusive masculinities in familial social relations continue to take priority in the 21st century.

Notes

[1] For example, elements of father responsibility movements in the US utilise naturalised discourses to argue that fathers can do what mothers do and do it better, but mothers cannot do what fathers do because they lack the Y chromosome (Gavanas, 2002).

[2] Parental alienation is a concept invented by Richard Gardener and adopted from US fathers' rights groups. Nevertheless, neither US nor UK professional psychological associations recognise it as a psychological syndrome.

[3] Sure Start Children's Centres replaced a previous Sure Start Scheme, which offered a range of support to families defined as experiencing deprivation in England and Wales.

[4] An amendment to the 1989 Children Act (s 38A(2)) allowed a local authority to seek an exclusion order against a violent parent in limited circumstances, although it has never been implemented.

[5] It should be noted that mothers' depression or other mental health difficulties are often a direct consequence of experiencing domestic violence.

[6] Baby Peter died as a result of ongoing physical abuse in August 2007, at the age of 17 months. There was a huge press furore about the case because he had been known to children's social care services and other key agencies such as the police and health services. He had been subject to a child protection plan since December 2006, when physical child abuse had been first identified, but he had not been taken into care at this point. The mother, her abusive boyfriend, acting as a de facto step-father, and his brother, living in the house as a lodger, were subsequently convicted of allowing the death of a child. National concern, however, focused on the failure of the key agencies to act to take the child into care and the failure of social workers to identify continuing abuse, and led to government intervention: the sacking of the Haringey Director of Children's Services and changes in social work practice in taking more children into care who were identified as at serious risk, rather than leaving them in the family (known as the 'Baby Peter effect').

[7] Also known as officers of the Child and Family Court Advisory Service (Cafcass), which replaced the previous family court welfare service in 2001.

[8] A consent order is an order made by the court ratifying agreement between the parents on contact and residence arrangements for children.

THREE

Violent fathering: perspectives, research and practice

Introduction

This chapter begins by critically examining different theoretical approaches that aim to explain fathers' violence towards women. These are significant, since they inform different policy and professional approaches towards addressing this violence as a significant social problem and developing appropriate strategies for change. Second, the chapter looks at the research undertaken with violent perpetrators that informs some of these perspectives. It also examines the limited amount of research that specifically addresses violent fathers as carers of children, including studies where violent fathers have killed their children. These studies contrast with other research on violent fathers that has often been undertaken from a rehabilitative perspective. Third, the chapter discusses some current practice strategies in addressing violent fathering and children's safety. These include the use of risk identification and assessment, perpetrator programmes and parenting programmes for violent fathers.

Fathers as perpetrators of domestic violence

The extent of men's violence towards women in intimate and familial social relationships has led to a plethora of theories and perspectives aimed at explaining why it happens. In general, these explanations fall into three categories, based on biological, psychological and sociological perspectives. What follows is a discussion of the credibility of these different perspectives, drawing on research on violent men.

Biological, psychological and socialisation perspectives

As Stanko (1994) has highlighted, biological explanations may be used both to normalise men's violence and/or suggest it is an aberration. For example, she indicates that discourses suggesting that men are 'naturally' more aggressive than women remain popular in westernised cultures and have been given more impetus through neo-Darwinism, which has informed evolutionary psychology and socio-biological perspectives. At the same time, men's 'excessive' violence may be explained through faulty genes and/or an excess of male hormones such as testosterone and its impacts on the brain through perspectives from developmental neuro-science (Jaffe et al, 2003).

Evolutionary psychology in particular has been taken up by some US researchers who claim that men's violence towards women and children, including killing, has a specific evolutionary function in promoting 'fitness' for natural selection and reproduction (Wilson and Daly, 1998). Wilson and Daly have observed that violent men are often self-interested and controlling, and argue that one apparent motivation for men's violence is 'sexual propriety', which is viewed as an 'adaptive mental mind-set' to 'deal with the problem of paternity uncertainty' and of 'male to male reproductive competition' (Wilson and Daly, 1998, p 213). Thus, although lethal violence towards partners such as killing can to some extent be seen as maladaptive to evolutionary purposes, the researchers claim that it can still be explained through the psychological mechanism of 'sexual propriety', since such behaviour prevents other men from having access to 'their women'. They also claim that such evolutionary 'adaptation' explains why more stepfathers kill their partner's children, since they view them as a threat to their own reproductive capacity. However, these arguments cannot explain why large numbers of biological fathers kill their own *genetic* children nor the extent of biological fathers' violence towards women in pregnancy. The credibility of such a perspective is also challenged through comparative international research, which indicates the high variability in men's rates of homicide between different countries, with the US, Russia, Estonia and Latvia having much higher rates than other countries in Western Europe and other parts of Eastern Europe, and others such as Denmark, Germany, Italy and Norway having very low rates (Barclay and Tarvares, 2003). These differences indicate that the level of men's violence is located within specific gendered socio-political contexts of masculinity and discredit the 'inevitability' of men's violence towards women and children in evolutionary biological perspectives (Hearn and Pringle, 2006). Nevertheless, these types of explanation retain considerable ideological power, since they feed into exculpatory discourses that continue to excuse men's violence in familial contexts as 'normal' and 'natural' and therefore something they cannot help.

Other psychological explanations tend to focus on individual pathology and underlying emotional problems as causal factors. For example, Saunders (1995) argues that although violent men are not very different from 'other men' and only a small number have 'severe mental health disorders', 'broad definitions of psychopathology can be applicable to most abusers' (p 72). These psychological discourses have suggested that violent men have a number of underlying emotional problems, including 'poor impulse control, low frustration tolerance, fear of intimacy, fear of abandonment, dependency, underlying depression and impaired ego functioning' arising from developmental problems in childhood that require psycho-dynamic interventions to lessen their feelings of insecurity and improve their self-esteem. Yet such interventions are notably unsuccessful in changing perpetrators' behaviour because they fail to address the intentionality of the violence and the perceived benefits they gain from it (Adams, 1988, pp 178-80). In addition, their failure to challenge the underlying attitudes and expectations that violent men hold towards women can lead them to support constructions of dominant masculinity that justify the violence (Bancroft and Silverman, 2002). Finally, these types of explanation lack credibility as causal factors, since large numbers of men identified as having the same psychological or emotional problems do not resort to domestic violence (see, for example, Tolman and Bennett, 1990; Gondolf, 1999).

Family therapy and family systems theories

Although less common than in the past, family systems theories where non-abusing mothers and children are seen as contributing to men's violence and abuse of children (Dale et al, 1986; Bentovim, 1987) retain a lingering but powerful hold in some professional practice. These theories argue that any form of 'family violence' is caused by the *interactions* between family members, rather than the perpetrator alone being responsible for his actions. Thus women can be seen as being equally responsible for men's violence through 'provocative' aspects of their behavior such as refusing sex or 'nagging'. Such theories are reflected in family therapy and couple-counselling approaches, which, as Adams (1988) notes, view domestic violence as a problem of poor communication and one of equal coercion by both partners rather than of one partner trying to control and dominate the other. Thus, although couple counselling aims to improve communication and negotiation skills between partners, it implicitly supports the man's violence by seeing it as an 'unfortunate' outcome of the interaction process (Adams, 1988, p 185).

Psycho-social explanations move beyond those based on individual pathology in recognising that social learning may be a cause of men's violent behaviour. Commonly, psycho-social theories of learning and socialisation draw on role theory to normalise men's violence through arguing that gendered identities are learnt through social scripts. Eadley and Wetherell (1996) indicate that role theory developed out of the formulation of masculine and feminine personality types or traits in the 1930s that constructed gendered identities as opposites. The masculine role was thus associated with qualities such as 'aggression', 'roughness' and 'self-reliance' and the feminine role with 'timidity' 'tenderness' and 'dependence' (Eadley and Wetherell, 1996, pp 101-2). Using the metaphor of actors taking on a role in the theatre, role theorists argue that sex positioning as a boy or a girl socially prescribes a set of pre-scripted gender roles based on socially defined norms and expectations. However, as the Australian critical masculinity theorist Connell (1987) has highlighted, although role theory moves beyond the purely biological as a form of explanation, it cannot explain how such gender roles are reproduced, nor why it is the masculine role that is defined as dominant and aggressive, unless it falls back on biological frameworks of gender difference.

Inappropriate role models in families of origin, where boys both witness domestic violence towards their mothers and may be physically abused themselves by violent fathers, are common explanations drawn from role theory, which supports inter-generational transmission of violence theories (Straus et al, 1980; Saunders, 1995). Nevertheless, the research evidence indicates that such explanations are far too mechanistic, since although about a quarter of boys who become adult perpetrators have had such experiences, most adult male perpetrators have not (Stark and Flitcraft, 1996; Cavanagh et al, 2005). Thus, as Connell (1987) notes, role theory assumes that there is some mechanical transmission of specific role models to children, rather than viewing them as conscious social actors who interpret and act on their experiences in different ways and make choices that are informed or constrained by their own social power. One of the problems of role and socialisation theories therefore is that they position violent men as 'equal victims' of the 'sex role system' (Adams, 1988).

Socialisation theories of gender may also be combined with social strain theories to argue that men use violence against their partners as frustration responses to blocked goals when they are unable to meet social expectations of themselves as men (Gelles, 1983; Smith, 1989). Such explanations may be applied to working-class or unemployed men in particular, where it has been suggested that lack of power in the workplace or an inability to fulfil their expected role as breadwinners may lead them to take out their frustrations on women in the home.

However, these arguments do not tend to fit the empirical evidence, which suggests that domestic violence can be carried out equally by men who have more social power, nor do they explain why large numbers of unemployed men do not use violence against their partners. Interventions for change based on social learning perspectives use cognitive behavioural strategies such as anger management approaches that aim to enable perpetrators to recognise situations that may 'trigger' their anger and skills, and to deal with these responses through strategies such as 'time-outs'. However, because they do not address the power and control tactics that are common among perpetrators of domestic violence, anger-management approaches alone have very limited success in reducing such violence (Babcock and La Taillade, 2000).

Sociological theories of gendered power relations

In contrast to these perspectives, feminist, pro-feminist and some critical masculinity analyses view men's domestic violence as being integrally connected to men's *social* power as men, in male-dominating societies and cultures (Dobash and Dobash, 1992, 1998; Hanmer, 1998). As seen in Chapter Two, men's power and control over women and children has traditionally been legitimised and institutionalised in law and social practices in most societies. In late-modern westernised societies, women may have 'formal' legal equality, but the social relations of power continue to be gendered with women having less political and economic power. This can partly be explained by men's individual and collective resistance to women's struggles for equality and autonomy, and may vary in different national and local socio-political contexts (Radford et al, 2000). These varying social contexts allow men's dominance to continue to be practiced by some men in intimate and familial relationships through the use or threats of violence and tactics of control. Such a perspective also highlights the benefits that some men get from being violent and how violence is used to control women's behaviour and maintain assumptions of men's superior social status and privilege (Pence, 1987; Hanmer, 1998).

Hegemonic masculinities

Further, although most westernised liberal states now have policies that criminalise aspects of domestic violence, woman-blaming socio-political and cultural discourses mean that in practice, such abuse continues to be tolerated to a considerable degree. Critical masculinity social theorists have drawn on feminist perspectives on the connections between men's violence and hierarchical gendered power relations by looking at the relationships between power and the construction of masculine identities as socially based practice (Hearn, 1998a; Pirngle, 1998). In particular, the work of Connell (1987, 2002; Connell and Messerschmidt 2005) has been crucial in developing understandings that masculine identities are constructed through social power struggles between men and men and men and women, rather than being the outcome of biological 'sex differences' or 'sex roles' learnt in childhood. Connell theorises the connection between individual and collective social practices and social structures through drawing on Giddens' structuration theory (Giddens, 1984) to account for the way practices become institutionalised and the way social practices are constrained by institutionalisation (Connell, 1987).

For Connell, institutionalisation creates continuities and routines of social practices over time and space, and produces hegemonic (dominant) forms of masculinity that may include male violence and become *embedded* in local and regional contexts and socio-political formations (Connell, 1987). Thus, although the construction of hegemonic masculinities may not 'correspond' closely with the lives of actual men, 'they express widespread ideals, fantasies and desires' (Connell and Messerchmidt, 2005, p 838). They also 'serve as models of relations with women and solutions to problems of gender relations' and 'to this extent contribute to the society-wide gender order as a whole' (Connell and Messerchmidt, 2005, p 838). However, hegemonic masculinities are variable, contingent, contested and open to change, as they interact with other social movements such as struggles for women's equality, globalisation processes as well as phenomena such as war. The concept of hegemonic masculinities is thus particularly relevant to explaining variations in men's violence towards women and children in specific national and local contexts and why their violence towards women and children may increase as a result of the worldwide distribution of pornography through the internet or at times of war or social stress when some men's constructions of their identities as men become threatened. It can, for example, assist in explaining the current extent of physical and sexual violence by some teenage young men towards young teenage women and the impact of peer group pressure in gang-related cultures in the UK. It also serves to explain the impact of the global media on young men's sexually violent behaviour through its promotion of pornography and misogynistic computer games.

Many women do, of course, resist male violence either individually or collectively, and contribute to changing constructions of masculinities, but how far they are able to do this individually depends to a large extent on the wider social context in which the violence occurs and their own resources and access to other support (Cavanagh et al, 2001). Children and young people may also attempt to resist male violence from their fathers or others, but, as seen in Chapter One, are relatively more powerless than adults to challenge it.

Research with adult violent perpetrators

The credibility of these perspectives is supported by extensive research and practice literature undertaken with adult domestically violent perpetrators in the US and the UK, where a majority of violent men hold the view that they have superior social status to women, and assume that they have the right to dominate and control women and have them meet their sexual and domestic needs (Pence, 1987; Ptacek, 1988; Hearn, 1998a; Cavanagh et al, 2001). Misogyny and contempt for women are also commonly held attitudes expressed by such men on perpetrator programmes (Wilson, 1996). It should be noted, however, that much of this research has been conducted with white men and although some research has been carried out with African-American men, far less has been undertaken with minority ethnic men, including men from South Asian communities.

Some critical masculinity research in this area supports the view that violent men use domestic violence as a resource to accomplish their sense of themselves as men through demonstrating their power over women (see, for example, Messerschmidt, 1993; Lundgren, 1995; Dobash and Dobash, 1998). Thus, masculinity can be achieved through violence by 'putting women in their place and showing them who is boss' (Dobash and Dobash, 1998, p 165). In research involving 60 violent men, Hearn (1998a) found that while men's violence was often used as a means to an end, such as having power and control over women, 'some simply enjoyed the violence or said they did' (p 36). He also suggests that emotions can be specifically masculinised through the practice of doing violence. The ideology of love can therefore be contained in discourses of sexual violence towards women partners and in the sexual abuse of children.

In addition, the connection between the macro-social level of male dominance and micro-social level of men's violence towards women in interpersonal relationships is illustrated in studies of men's ways of describing and accounting for their domestic violence. Cavanagh and colleagues (2001) argue that all personal interactions are located within their wider social contexts and are shaped by them. Individual definitions of domestic violence are thus informed by inequalities between men and women in the wider social context. This context enables individual men to have more power to impose their own definitions of what has occurred in violent relationships over women's experiences of abuse, through the use of socially acceptable discourses that neutralise, eradicate or shift blame for their violence. The authors therefore argue that policies to challenge domestic violence need to understand and recognise not only women's experiences of domestic violence, but also the common discursive strategies used by male perpetrators to deny, minimise, excuse and justify it, as illustrated below.

Denials and minimisation

Strategies of denial may involve refusals to remember what has happened, or outright denials, based on the definitions such men give to their violence, as illustrated in the following extracts:

> 'There was no violence towards [partner] though she would have you believe there was. I was never violent just bad-tempered.' (Cavanagh et al, 2001, p 701)

Hearn indicates that denial often involves defining 'real violence' as something that men do to other men rather than what they do to their partners:

> 'I wasn't violent, but she used to do my head in....I picked her up and threw her against a wall.... I've never struck a woman and I never will.' (Hearn, 1998a, p 117)

> 'In the army you're trained to kill. You're a trained killer but its not brought into the family, well maybe it is I don't know. I hit her in the face and I bruised her eye and cut her lip so I did use force, but not as much force as I probably could have. I could have done more damage.' (Cavanagh et al, 2001, p 705)

Minimisation involves trivialising violent events and thus diluting the definition of what counts as violence, through stating that it only happens infrequently or stressing that it is not severe, as in the following examples:

> 'It doesn't happen every week or every couple of weeks. It's just a very occasional time it's happened.'

'I never hurt her badly physically. I never cut her or beat her senseless.' (Cavanagh et al, 2001, p 705)

Hearn describes minimisation as frequently involving claims of mutual violence, where the word 'just' is used to trivialise what is happening, as in the following extract from a man convicted of multiple assaults on his partner:

'Just a few little arguments, just slaps, where she has digged me and I've digged her back.' (Hearn, 1998a, p 120)

Excuses and justifications

Ptacek's ground-breaking research (1988) found that where perpetrators did acknowledge some violence they commonly drew on excuses that could be found in psycho-therapeutic discourses, allowing them to evade responsibility for it. The most common type of excuse used by perpetrators was that the violence was beyond their control. In psych discourses, this may be referred to as 'poor impulse control', resulting in 'irrational episodes of violence' where the perpetrator cannot be held to be responsible (Ptacek, 1988, p 153). Cavanagh and colleagues (2001) show that the use of alcohol can also be combined with the loss of control discourse to demonstrate this lack of responsibility, as illustrated in the following account:

'I never wanted to hit her in the first place. It wis the drink. Half the time I didnae ken [know] what I was doing ... half the time. (Cavanagh et al, 2001, p 706)

Yet, as the researchers note, while the perpetrators frequently blamed alcohol, they rarely acknowledged that they continued to use violence when they were not drunk, as the women's accounts made clear. Other loss of control explanations used by perpetrators relate to the build-up of internal pressure, frustration, stress or insecurity. However, as Ptacek found, these types of discourses were frequently contradicted in perpetrators' own accounts where they indicated that their violence was deliberate and provoked by their partner's and sometimes children's own behaviour, as is illustrated in the following extracts:

'It's a condition of being out of control.... She's going on and on about how much money we need ... and I'll listen to it for a while, but then you gotta get up and do something, you know ... the way to do it was to go over and try to shut her up physically.' (Ptacek, 1988, p 147)

'I think a lot of it was frustration about not being able to handle the children. You know they would tell me to shut up. "You're not going to tell me to shut up." And then my wife would tell me, you know, "Let me handle this." I said, "I'm the man of the house." Then we'd start arguing. That's basically how they [the violent incidents] used to happen. (Ptacek, 1988, p 149)

Hearn (1998a) defines making excuses as accepting blame but not responsibility for the violence, while justifications involve accepting responsibility but not blame. In justifications, for example, women can be blamed for refusing sex, not dressing appropriately, not being thin enough, not doing the housework correctly, not paying the perpetrator enough attention, not restricting her own autonomy, not being deferential enough or not being faithful. However, as seen above, excuses and justifications frequently merge through the discourse of provocation where, for example, women who assert their autonomy, make decisions and have their own friends can all be seen as provoking or triggering the perpetrator's 'uncontrollable' violence. Underlying these justifications is also a sense that violent men regard their partners as possessions. Jealousy is thus a socially acceptable discourse used to justify violence and relates not only to contacts or suspected contacts with other men, but also to women seeing family or friends, or focusing on the needs of the children rather than on the perpetrator (Mullender et al, 2002; Harne and Radford, 2008).

Excuses and justifications also echo traditional patriarchal criminal justice discourses that have allowed violent men to 'get away with murder' in English law through the legal concepts of diminished responsibility and provocation. 'Nagging' (a specifically gendered concept applied only to women) or leaving an abusive relationship thus continues to be an acceptable defence for men's violent behaviour towards women, as does suspecting that a partner has been unfaithful or is intending to leave. Such a defence may even reduce a charge of murder to manslaughter (Justice for Women, 2006). Moreover, contained in these discourses is the perpetrator's sense of male privilege and ongoing sense of self-righteousness or rightness, in that he assumes he has the right to have his expectations and demands met by his female partner (Ptacek, 1988; Dobash and Dobash, 1998; Hearn, 1998a).

These studies point to the need for professionals to show considerable caution in accepting violent fathers' accounts as 'credible versions' of what has occurred. It should also be noted that such accounts are often contradictory, and that denials and minimisation may later be contradicted by admissions of guilt. Perpetrators then often excuse or justify their actions, and any remorse they show is rarely unqualified (Hearn, 1998a; Cavanagh et al, 2001).

Change interventions based on the analyses discussed above aim to enable violent men to take full responsibility for their violence and accept blame, as well as challenge men's assumptions and patterns of power and coercive control and their male-dominating attitudes towards women. This is discussed in more detail below.

Research on violent men as fathers

Although the research detailed above informs understandings of fathers as perpetrators of domestic violence, it rarely addresses the connection between fathers' perceptions of their violence towards mothers and their own views of their relationships with children and their fathering practices. This is discussed further in Chapter Four in an analysis of the author's own study. The section below discusses the limited research that has been undertaken in this area by others.

Violent fathers as carers of children

As seen in Chapter One, some knowledge about violent fathering has been gained from the child protection literature and by seeking children's views. Other information has come from research with abused mothers looking at the impact of fathers' domestic violence and fathers' abusive behaviour towards very young children themselves. Holden and Ritchie's US research (1991) was an early study which looked specifically at aspects of violent fathers' parenting with abused mothers. It compared the views of 37 mothers of children aged between two and eight living in shelters with those of a community sample of mothers who had not experienced domestic violence. Abused mothers reported that violent fathers were more likely to be angry and irritated by children and more likely to over-punish children than those in the comparison group. A much-reported finding was that violent fathers were viewed as being less involved in childrearing activities than non-abusive fathers. A later UK study with 129 abused mothers (Radford et al, 1999) looked at the mothers' perceptions of harm to their children from violent fathers in the context of child contact and also suggested a low level of involvement of violent fathers in childcare and time spent with their children. Nevertheless, about a fifth of these fathers were reported as having been involved in some childcaring activities, with those who were misusing alcohol or drugs being reported as having the lowest level of involvement.

These studies appeared to connect neglectful and abusive parenting by domestically violent fathers with a lower level of involvement in childcaring activities than non-violent fathers. However, the findings from the UK study were similar to those from studies of fathers' level of involvement in childrearing activities in the general population (see, for example, Warin et al, 1999). A more recent US study based on the national household survey also appeared to refute this connection (Fox and Benson, 2004). This study found that although violent fathers were more likely to be punitive towards their children, they spent the same amounts of time with them as non-violent fathers, suggesting that abusive parenting by violent fathers is not related to the sexual division of labour and a low involvement in childrearing. In contrast, and in line with the research on serious case reviews, other studies have indicated that an increased level of childcare involvement from some violent fathers may lead to increased physical abuse and the ultimate killing of their children. This is discussed in more detail below.

Child killings and the use of violence in constructing fathering identities

Alder and Polk's (1996) research on child homicides committed by Australian men is a rare example of a study that cites the reasons given by perpetrator parents for killing children from their own accounts. The aim of the study was to illuminate the constructions of varying masculinities through child homicide in different settings.

In the familial setting, one type of killing occurred where mainly young, de facto stepfathers 'played a substantial role in the "caring" of the children', as reported by the children's mothers (Alder and Polk, 1996, p 404). In these circumstances, the children killed were very young (aged two or under) and had usually suffered prior physical abuse from the father figure before the killing. As in other studies, the mother had frequently experienced domestic violence from this father figure. Although these kinds of killing were frequently excused as extreme physical discipline, the perpetrators' accounts illustrate the intentionality behind their violence, as is seen in the following accounts:

> 'I went down the park with Sam ... he was good as gold, then he fucking shit, put shit all over the place and I belted him.
>
> [...]

'Austin was sitting on the floor eating a packet of chips and he started crying. I picked him up and whacked him on the bum a few times with an open hand. He was still crying. I picked him up [to] shut him up ... I didn't lose my cool, I was just annoyed ... I was just annoyed because I couldn't hear the video. He was getting on my nerves.' (Alder and Polk, 1996:404–5)

These children were not killed because of the father figures' low level of involvement in childcare; rather, the killings were associated with a high level of father 'care' as described by the stepfathers and in the accounts given by the children's mothers. These demonstrate that the care these fathers gave was very abusive, eventually resulting in death because the children were viewed as provoking and deserving the violence by not obeying or conforming to paternal authority or unreasonable expectations of how they should behave.

The same study identified cases where children were killed mainly by older biological fathers involved in custody disputes. In these cases, the father had frequently displayed or threatened physical violence towards the mother, but had shown no prior physical violence towards the children. Some fathers had committed suicide, but those who survived and were prosecuted frequently cited vindictiveness against mothers for leaving the relationship as a reason for their behaviour, along with the emotionality associated with their loss of power and control over these women and children, whom they had previously regarded as their possessions. One father stated that if he 'couldn't have Maria [his partner] then no one would' and that he would 'use the children' to prevent her from leaving (Alder and Polk, 1996, p 405). In these circumstances, Alder and Polk argue, 'the children become a vehicle in order to cause pain to the mother' and this loss of 'possession' is connected to a masculine sense of identity and 'self-worth'. They also claim that the fathers' accounts illustrate constructions of fathering that are extremely self-interested, where children's lives are taken in order to meet fathers' needs for revenge, or reflect extreme control of very young children who are seen as defying paternal authority and fathers' own needs. In interpreting their findings, Alder and Polk draw on Messerschmidt's (1993) analysis of masculinity being situationally and differentially accomplished through violence, that is, the perceived threats to the men's constructions of their masculinity and the triggers for the child killings differed depending on the situations and circumstances of the fathers involved. Nevertheless, there was also a commonality between cases where fathers used violence instrumentally to assert their dominant masculinity and authority when they believed that they were in danger of losing mothers and children (that is, their masculine 'possessions') or that their authority was being threatened or their wishes defied by very young children.

There were similar findings in a UK study of men who kill their children (Cavanagh et al, 2005, 2007). Looking at a sub-sample of 26 fathers who had fatally assaulted their children, the authors found that both biological fathers (10) and social fathers (16) killed very young children (under the age of four) when they were in their care (Cavanagh et al, 2007). All had a history of physical abuse towards the children, and all but one had been physically violent towards their partner. As in the Alder and Polk (1996) study, these fathers frequently had unreasonable expectations of how very young children should behave. They were killed by extremely violent means because they had defied their fathers' wishes by 'crying', 'wetting the bed' or 'messing around ', as fathers put it in the accounts given in court reports. Some fathers also spoke of their resentment towards the children and were jealous of the attention they got from their mother. In discussing the intentionality of these fathers to harm the children, if not to kill them, the authors suggest that their motivations were clearly 'to silence, discipline and punish the child' and were rationalised by the fathers because they believed that 'their *rights* to attention, silence [from the children] and time with their partners had been infringed by the child' (Cavanagh et al, 2007, p 12).

Again reflecting the findings of Alder and Polk (1996), Cavanagh and colleagues (2005) found that biological fathers also killed children in revenge for a partner leaving or threatening to leave, and in two thirds of such cases partners had previously suffered ongoing physical violence. A more recent UK study of 182 child homicides between 2004 and 2008 (Ferguson, 2009) found that fathers pre-planned 'separation' killings and that over-controlling behaviour towards the mother and children was more likely to be a key feature of the killing than physical violence This research suggests that it is loss of control over the whole family and not only the motivation for revenge that is a key feature of this type of killing, and that it is the extent of control over mothers and children rather than the frequency of physical violence that indicates that such fathers are at high risk of killing children.

Fathering as a rehabilitative context for violent men

The 'good' violent father

In contrast, some US studies have argued that domestically violent fathers' 'investment' in fathering identities may contribute to their rehabilitation and change. For example, a small-scale qualitative US study of eight violent fathers attending a perpetrator programme (Fox et al, 2001) noted that these men had made considerable investment in their identities as fathers and were remorseful about the damage they had caused to their children and wanted to make amends.

A more detailed Israeli qualitative study (Perel and Peled, 2008), undertaken in 1999 and involving semi-structured interviewing with 14 violent biological fathers attending perpetrator programmes, took a similar approach. The research investigated the men's fathering activities and experiences, perceptions of their fathering relationships with their children and ex-partners and fathers' views of the connections between their fathering and violence. Most of the fathers were described as married, with only three being divorced or separated from partners and children, and the study was framed by a traditional religious context.

The research found that all the perpetrator parents perceived themselves as good fathers, with many saying that they 'lived for' their children. Children were regarded as prize possessions and accomplishments, represented through biological and religious discourses. For example, one father described children as 'the blood of your blood; the soul of your soul' (Perel and Peled, 2008, p 465), and fathers regarded very young children as a source of 'great' happiness and joy. They also constructed images of themselves as 'good fathers' through traditional patriarchal discourses where they were the main providers, educators and protectors of children. However, as with other traditional discourses on fathering, the role of educator was perceived as being one of controlling children's behaviour. At the same time, these fathers argued that it was important to have 'warm and frequent contact' with their children. This 'ideal representation' of fathering was contrasted with their childhood experiences of their own fathers, who were perceived as distant and often aggressive and hostile.

Denying the impact of violence and authoritarian fathering

These men's constructions of themselves as good fathers led most to deny that their violence towards mothers had had any impact on their children. Further, while some fathers acknowledged that they had exposed their children to domestic violence, they failed to view such exposure as harmful. Some fathers said they did not understand why their children withdrew when they witnessed violence, while others described using 'dydatic' or 'forceful measures' to explain the violence to the children and minimise its effects, describing it merely as 'quarrels'. Many adopted a 'narrow' authoritarian fathering style, using extreme power and control tactics over their partners and the children themselves. They described spending their time issuing orders to children, shouting at them or shaking and physically punishing them to get them to accede to their demands.

The 'poor me' syndrome: violent fathers as tragic victims

In Perel and Peled's (2008) study, fathers also tended to view themselves as tragic victims, unable to comprehend what they were doing wrong and failing to recognise why children did not want close relationships with them, despite criticising their own fathers for being distant, hostile and aggressive. They blamed the mothers, describing them as the dominant parents preventing them from getting close to their children, rather than acknowledging that it was their own violent and abusive behaviour that prevented the children from showing them any affection.

In interpreting these findings, Perel and Peled focus less on the harm to children and their mothers caused by the fathers' violence and controlling behaviour and more on how fathering identities are 'constricted' by 'conflict' and 'breakdowns in communication' with mothers, reflecting the family systems approach discussed earlier in the chapter. They argue for an analysis that addresses the 'yearning' of violent fathers for a closer relationship with their children and recognises this when child contact is being considered post-separation. They also suggest that violent fathers should be regarded simultaneously as 'harmful' and 'vulnerable' in change interventions.

Part of the problem with such an analysis is that it feeds into the split perspective discussed in Chapter Two, where men's violence is viewed as separate from their fathering and mothers are blamed for failing to allow violent parents to be 'involved' fathers. It also supports fathers' denial and minimisation of the impact of violence on children and of directly abusive parenting practices. This allows fathers to play on the 'poor me syndrome' and use their own 'needs' as an excuse for their abusive behaviour.

A more critical approach was undertaken in a US focus group study with African-American fathers on their perspectives on parenting when victims had separated from them because of their violence (Bent-

Goodley and Williams, 2007). As in Perel and Peled's (2008) study, these men demonstrated traditional patriarchal attitudes towards their fathering. They believed that they had superior status to mothers as well as children, and they viewed their prime role as that of 'disciplinarian', making statements such as 'men should be in charge ... and I should be the man of the house and the disciplinarian' and 'we need to be there to discipline the children ... like children, she [the mother] needs to be disciplined too' (Bent-Goodley and Williams, 2007, p 32). Moreover, while there was some acknowledgement that children's exposure to violence may be harmful and may affect children's feelings towards them, they still believed that they had rights of contact and had something to offer their children.

Other US research has focused on whether there are differences between biological and social fathers in relation to their awareness and concerns about the impact of their violence on children (Rothman et al, 2007). Such research hypothesises that biological fathers have more investment in their own children from evolutionary psychological perspectives and are therefore more likely to be concerned about their children and be prepared to take action to change their behaviour. However, the findings of the study showed that although biological fathers were slightly more concerned than social fathers about the impact of their violence on children, there was no difference between the two groups of fathers in terms of the actions they would take to stop their violence if they saw it was harming the children, with less than half being prepared to undertake counselling or leave their partners.

While these studies on violent fathering are limited and reflect their different contexts, they provide some insight into the way violent fathers view children in their care as objects and possessions rather than people in their own right, and how their own self-interested concerns override those of their children.

Practice perspectives

Practice-based perspectives have developed around the identification and assessment of the risks posed by violent fathers, and around 'treatment interventions' to render them safe as parents. In many ways, this dual focus reflects the contradictory welfare discourses discussed in Chapter Two, where on the one hand all children are viewed as essentially needing fathers and fatherhood is seen as a significant resource to promote their wellbeing, while on the other, there is increasing recognition of the risks posed by violent fathers and the need to identify, prevent or manage these risks.

Violent fathers as extreme risks

While the risk assessment of offenders in general has a longer history, structured assessments of risk (the likelihood of future harm to victims) in the context of domestic violence have mainly developed to identify the most dangerous perpetrators and target resources to prevent harm to those victims at highest risk of further severe violence or lethal harm. This kind of risk assessment can thus be viewed both as a response to victim needs and a means to limit access to interventions and resources. The use of risk assessments to prioritise only the highest risk cases because of limited resources is illustrated in research undertaken in the UK on multi-agency risk assessment conferences (Robinson, 2004; Robinson and Tregidga, 2005), where different local agency members meet together monthly to discuss continuing actions to protect those victims who are most at risk from a perpetrator's domestic violence.

> 'I think the biggest threat to women's safety is the numbers – we can only look at those who are very high risk as perceived by a risk assessment which is a crude tool.... I think that is the biggest weakness but there is no solution – there are thousands to deal with.' (Women's Safety Unit member, cited in Robinson, 2004, p 19)

In this approach, the main focus is on perpetrators' violence towards women, while children are usually viewed as 'secondary' victims who have witnessed severe violence or experienced the loss of their mothers. However, as seen earlier, violence towards mothers is a key risk factor for severe or lethal harm to children and such assessments are therefore highly relevant to children's safety (Humphreys, 2007).

Risk assessment models

In the domestic violence field, most evidence-based models of identifying and predicting future risks emerged initially in the US, largely as a response to the inadequacy of professional or clinical judgements alone in predicting and preventing further serious or lethal harm to women (Hart, 1988; Campbell, 1995). Clinical or professional judgement on its own has been found to very unreliable in assessing risk, since it is impressionistic and is limited by practitioners' own personal preferences, as well as their professional training and experience (Kropp, 2004). In contrast, predictive or actuarial models use research on known offenders to estimate the probability of the likelihood of future harm within a specific timescale. Structured risk assessment or structured professional judgement combines actuarial assessment where known risk factors from research are used in conjunction with professional judgement. It has considerable advantages over professional judgement alone, since it provides professionals with a checklist of known risk factors, at the same time as allowing some discretion in interpreting combinations of risk factors and judging levels of risk as well as taking account of contextual factors and other information.

Nevertheless, although structured risk assessments have more reliability and validity than professional judgement alone, they are not very accurate in predicting future risks, particularly in relation to lethal harm. They should not therefore be regarded as providing any guarantee of certainty in this field (Kropp, 2004). Further, as Kropp has noted, 'there is no such thing as no risk' in relation to domestic violence, and risk assessments should not be used to marginalise and minimise the concerns of survivors whose partners have been identified as lower risk, since all domestically violent perpetrators can be regarded as 'dangerous to some degree' (Kropp, 2004, p 677). Instead, it is argued that risk assessment can inform the nature and degree of danger. In addition, because domestic violence itself is dynamic, risk assessment should not be seen as an end in itself but as an ongoing process, since a perpetrator's violence can change and escalate very quickly.

The problem of structured risk assessments providing no guarantee of certainty is illustrated by the complex and diverse constellation of risk factors identified from the research that aim to differentiate between lethal and non-lethal violence and to identify those core or primary factors that can highlight the most dangerous offenders. For the UK, this is illustrated in Box 3.1, which summarises research aimed at identifying key factors leading to the killing of women in intimate relationships (ACPO/Home Office, 2006).

Box 3.1: Risk factors in the killing of women in intimate relationships

- Separation or child contact dispute.
- Pregnancy or recent child birth.
- Suspect's escalation of the violence including worsening and frequency, previous convictions, injury and previous injury, use of a weapon, access to firearms, harm or threatened harm to pets or other animals and attempts to choke, smother or strangle the victim.
- Suspect's use of sexual violence.
- Suspect's child abuse or threats to children.
- Victims' isolation or barriers to help seeking. This includes isolation from being prevented from seeing family or friends, or living in an isolated rural community. Barriers due to language difficulties or disability, ill-health or substance misuse, forced marriage and families being involved in the abuse.
- Suspect's attempts or threats at suicide or homicide.
- Suspect's controlling behaviour, jealousy, stalking and harassment.
- Fear of the suspect (victim's perception of harm).
- Suspect's substance misuse and mental health of suspect.

Source: ACPO/Home Office, 2006, pp 47-8

More recent research adds to the complexity. For example, Dobash and colleagues (2007) argue that although there is a common assumption that an escalation of physical and sexual violence and the use of weapons signifies the possibility of lethal violence towards women, there is 'no simple progression' from non-lethal violence to killing women in the same relationship. Their study, which compared 122 men convicted of non-lethal violence with a 106 men convicted of murdering their partners, found that men who kill their partners are 'more likely to have had conventional childhood backgrounds, education, employment and criminal careers' than perpetrators who had not killed, and were more likely 'to be possessive and jealous; separated at the time of the event' (Dobash et al, 2007, p 1). They were also more likely to have used physical violence towards a previous partner, although 41 per cent had not used physical violence against the woman they killed.

Another recent UK study looked at five cases involving minimal physical violence in the current relationship and found that core risk factors included separation or the threat of separation combined with the perpetrators' coercive control and jealous surveillance, high relationship conflict, perpetrators' depression and threats of suicide, and physical violence in prior relationships (Regan et al, 2007). This research emphasises the significance of coercive control in identifying high-risk abusers even where there has been no or little prior use of physical or sexual assault against the current victim, It also emphasised the importance of professionals finding out about perpetrators' violent behaviour in previous relationships.

Other issues affecting risk assessments

The way practitioners interpret and make judgements about levels of risk still depends on their own understandings and current knowledge of the significance of different risk factors as well as the context and purposes of the assessments required. Professionals are frequently asked to assess high, medium and low levels of risk both in the short term (over the next few weeks) and in the long term, and the former may be easier than the latter (Harne, 2009). Other factors may also inform practitioner assessments of imminent risks, such as pressures of work and the limited time and resources practitioners have to investigate them (Parsloe, 1999).

Other research has shown that victims' own estimations of future risk are often more accurate than structured assessments, such as the SARA (Spousal Assault Risk Assessment guide), undertaken by professionals (Gondolf, 1999; Weisz et al, 2000). Weisz and colleagues (2000) indicate that although some victims underestimate risks, they rarely overestimate them. Structured risk assessments used by professionals should therefore always be informed by victims' own fears for their own safety and how they perceive future risks. Where professional assessments indicate that survivors have underestimated the risks of harm to themselves and their children, they should always be given information about the possible level and significance of identified risks and help with safety planning. The US Danger Assessment Scale (Campbell, 1995) has been specifically developed for use with survivors to inform safety-planning strategies and has been found to increase the accuracy of predicting further violence (Weisz et al, 2000).

In the UK, structured risk assessment has been shown to improve professional decision making and actions taken in multi-agency conferences to protect victims of domestic violence identified as very high risk and prevent repeat victimisation (Robinson, 2004). However, it may neglect other aspects of harm that are specifically relevant to children's safety.

Children's safety and extreme risks in the context of domestic violence

Family separation

As discussed earlier in this chapter, the current literature suggests that very high-risk factors for children need to reflect the different situational contexts in which violent biological fathers and social fathers are motivated to perpetrate child killings. For example, the child homicide studies discussed above demonstrate that in some contexts the risks of lethal harm to children are similar to those for mothers (see Box 3.1 above). This is particularly so in cases of separation and child contact, where child killings can be identified as acts of revenge or extreme examples of fathers asserting power and control (Alder and Polk, 1996; Saunders, 2004; Cavanagh et al, 2005; Ferguson, 2009). Ferguson's (2009) study included 37 children killed by biological fathers post-separation between 2004 and 2008 and revealed that 20 victims were killed during contact visits, although only in four cases had the contact been ordered by the courts. This research points to the need for professionals, including solicitors, whom parents may consult for legal advice post-separation to undertake risk assessments before advising non-abusing parents to agree to arrangements for contact or residence. It also indicates that professionals need to explore the extent of coercive control used by fathers in the family (even where there has been little physical violence) as a core risk factor relating to the likelihood of their killing children.

Direct parenting by violent fathers

The research indicates that direct parenting by violent fathers or father figures is another context in which children are at risk of lethal harm, usually when the fathers are looking after the children on their own. Although most of these cases involve de facto stepfathers, at least a third involve biological fathers (Cavanagh et al, 2007). Existing studies suggest that in these cases, fathers tend to be younger (under 25 years old) and are more likely to be undereducated and unemployed and to have had disrupted childhoods. By contrast, older fathers with more conventional backgrounds are more likely to kill children on separation (Alder and Polk, 1996; Cavanagh et al, 2007). Half of fathers in the former category may also be misusing alcohol or drugs, and/or have mental health problems. They are also more likely to kill children who are very young (under four years old) and those identified as vulnerable such as disabled children (Brandon et al, 2006). Their motivation for killing appears to be linked to their own sense of entitlement to have their needs met by the children as well as by their partners, suggesting that controlling behaviour is also a key feature of these killings (Cavanagh et al, 2007).

To summarise, existing research identifies some of the key risk factors for possible lethal harm to children in different settings within the context of fathers' domestic violence and can to some extent inform preventative measures. However, it should be recognised that biological fathers and social fathers are not necessarily discrete types, and do not necessarily conform to particular types of behaviour, since biological fathers can become social fathers in second families. Further, the focus on prevention of lethal harm (which is, in fact, relatively rare) may obscure how risk identification and assessment is used to inform children's safety and wellbeing more broadly when considering whether violent fathers should continue to be involved in children's lives.

The risks of violent fathering: self-centredness and coercive control

In a different approach to assessment from that discussed above, US practitioners Bancroft and Silverman (2002) drew on their own experience of working with male perpetrators and evaluating violent fathers for the family courts to argue that risk identification and assessment of potential harm to children needs to be informed by violent fathers' capacity to parent children. They argue that perpetrators' parenting cannot be viewed in isolation from their violence towards women, since it is informed by common attitudinal characteristics of entitlement to have their needs met and by their own self-centredness, as was seen in all the homicide studies cited above. Further, although most violent fathers do not go to the extent of killing their children, they frequently fail to prioritise their emotional and developmental needs. They tend to view young children as being there to meet their own needs and expectations, and children's failure to meet these needs may lead to fathers' lack of tolerance of their behaviour and neglect of their basic care. In addition, men's use of coercive control over partners may extend to rigid authoritarian parenting, involving excessive control of children when fathers' expectations of how children should behave are not met. In addition, in some cases, violent fathers' sense of entitlement and ownership of children can lead to the sexual abuse of daughters.

Drawing on their own study of violent fathers, Bancroft and Silverman (2002) indicate that although such men may demonstrate pride in their children, they tend to perceive them as 'objects' to be governed by others, accounting for a common lack of empathy for children's feelings and needs:

> ... a batterer's level of commitment to his children cannot be assessed on the basis of his statements or his expression of emotions such as the shedding of tears while talking about them or the proud showing of photographs. Such displays can be products of manipulation or of self-centredness rather than a genuine connection to the child. (Bancroft and Silverman, 2002, p 33)

This analysis leads them to identify a number of recurring features that need to be assessed when looking at violent fathers' capacity to parent children and be involved in their care. These go beyond the more well-known factors that are generally recognised as being harmful to children in the context of domestic violence and include a father's history of exposing children to domestic violence; a history of physical or sexual abuse towards children; the risk of further post-separation violence; the level of coercive control the father has demonstrated in the past; the risk of abduction; and risks stemming from alcohol and/or substance misuse or mental health problems. Bancroft and Silverman argue that the violent father also needs to be assessed for the following:

- the extent of his sense of entitlement to have his needs met by children as well as by the mother, and, allied to this, the level of self-centredness or selfishness in his focus on having his own needs met;
- lack of empathy for children's feelings, and an inability to prioritise their needs;
- his treatment of children and partner as his possessions;
- his emotional/ psychological cruelty to children;
- neglect of children's physical, health and emotional needs;
- excessive control of children involving authoritarian and intimidatory parenting;
- the extent to which he undermines the mother in front of the children and uses the children as a weapon against her.

Bancroft and Silverman emphasise that violent fathers often perform well under observation and when being interviewed by professionals. They argue that information gathered on fathers' past behaviour, primarily from non-abusing mothers and the children themselves as well as from professionals such as health visitors and children's workers, are likely to give a more credible picture of potential risks than violent fathers' own accounts or short observations of father–child interactions. In the UK, Sturge and Glaiser's (2000) expert report to the family courts indicates that some of these parenting risk factors, such as lack of empathy for children and an inability to prioritise their needs, are highly significant in assessing violent fathers post-separation. However, there is generally very little information on how to specifically assess the risks of violent parenting.

Assessing violent fathers' capacity to change

The UK practice direction to the family courts (President of the Family Division, 2008, s 27d-e) requires the courts to consider the violent parent's 'capacity to change and behave appropriately' as well as their 'capacity to appreciate the effects of their past violence' on the non-abusing parent and the child. However, Bancroft and Silverman emphasise the difficulty in assessing violent fathers' capacity and commitment to change across the range of factors listed above. Such commitment cannot be ascertained, for example, from violent fathers' own vague statements, such as 'I used to have a bad temper, but that was a long time ago and I have grown up since then' or ' this [perpetrator] programme has opened my eyes and I would never do that again' (Bancroft and Silverman, 2002, p 178). Rather, fathers need to acknowledge the unacceptability of, and take full responsibility for, any violence towards mothers and abusive behaviour towards children and demonstrate that they understand its impact without using excuses or justifications, or denying or minimising aspects of the violence. Psychiatric assessments may be unhelpful in making assessments in these circumstances, as psychiatry's philosophical approach does not recognise the need for perpetrators to accept responsibility for their actions, but attributes their behaviour to underlying psychological or emotional problems from childhood, or to particular life stresses. Further, even though violent fathers may accept responsibility for their violence, this does not mean they are necessarily able to change their abusive behaviour sufficiently to be trusted with the care of children. This is discussed further below in the context of rehabilitative measures.

Using risk assessment to safeguard children in child protection and family law practice

As highlighted in Chapter Two, the need for specific, structured risk assessments to ensure children's safety has been recognised partly as a consequence of recent policy changes in public child protection as well as private family law, which now acknowledges that witnessing domestic violence may cause harm to children.

Risk assessment in child protection

Some child protection agencies have developed specific risk assessment models in relation to domestic violence (Bell, 2007). Others work with organisations that conduct risk assessments on their behalf, such as the London-based Domestic Violence Intervention Project (DVIP) (Radford et al, 2006). Nevertheless, the main focus of these interventions is limited to the more obvious harm to children from being directly physically or sexually abused by violent fathers, the emotional harm experienced through witnessing domestic violence and the mother's capacity to parent and protect the children, although aspects of the perpetrator's parenting are also addressed. One aim of the DVIP approach is to assess the perpetrator's 'capacity for change to stop the violence and to support a healthy relationship able to address the emotional and developmental needs of the child' (Radford et al, 2006). However, the project takes a gender-neutral approach to assessing both non-abusing mothers and violent fathers' 'parenting capacity' and 'ability to empathise with the child', partly as a consequence of the demand for dual assessments by the family courts in public law cases where there are often perceptions of 'mutual violence'. At the same time, the project recognises that through these assessments it needs to establish whether there is a primary physical aggressor and to explore the nature of the violence and gendered power relationships between the parents by working with them separately and recognising that support to improve the safety of mothers and their children can enhance their parenting capacity.

Structured risk assessment models are also beginning to be used in multi-agency child protection contexts such as safeguarding children boards (see, for example, London Safeguarding Children Board, 2008). This model aims to assess and support children's and mothers' needs as well as those of the perpetrator and to identify safeguarding thresholds for intervention by children's social services using a risk assessment matrix developed by a voluntary sector agency (Bell, 2007). This recognises that babies and young children under the age of seven are particularly vulnerable, as are disabled children and those living with mothers who have insecure immigration status and/or are at risk of, or have experienced, honour-based violence or forced marriage. As such, they are considered as being 'in need' or at risk of suffering significant harm as soon as they come to the attention of relevant agencies. The matrix also recognises aspects of violent fathers' behaviour as risk factors, or protective factors if fathers demonstrate willingness to engage with services to change. However, a perpetrator's parenting capacity is only considered as a risk factor at the higher levels of intervention and the focus remains on the mother's capacity to protect. There is often also an unrealistic expectation that perpetrators will be willing to acknowledge their violence and will be motivated to change and engage with interventions such as perpetrator programmes and this discussed in more detail below. It can be seen, therefore, that although these types of risk assessment are an improvement on earlier child protection approaches where violent fathers were not usually held accountable for harm to children, they still fall short in a number of respects.

Risk assessment in private family law practice

Risk assessment was introduced by the Child and Family Court Advisory and Support Service (Cafcass) in 2008 in all private law applications for contact and residence when parents separate. It has formed part of the Cafcass safeguarding process in private law proceedings, which involves family court advisers undertaking screening checks on both parents with the police and children's social care services; using a risk identification checklist to undertake an initial assessment of levels of risk at the first directions hearing; and undertaking a safety assessment if the initial risk assessment process identifies safety concerns (Cafcass, 2007). The risk identification checklist used 16 risk factors, which reflect some of the existing research discussed above and included previous harm to children; domestic violence (including escalation); other violence including possession of offensive weapons; jealous/possessive behaviour by an adult in relation to partner or child; post-separation violence; violence linked to contact; threats/fears of child abduction; parental mental health/learning difficulties; previous suicide attempts; drug or alcohol abuse; specific cultural factors; special needs of children such as disability or behavioural difficulties; and high family stress including a high conflict relationship (Cafcass, 2007). A preliminary pilot study (Harne, 2009) suggests that alongside screening, its use has improved the safeguarding decisions and actions of practitioners, and has resulted in fewer abused mothers being pressurised to agree interim contact for their children with violent fathers and more awareness of the need for further investigation of the risks from domestic violence. However, it also shows that practitioners tended to underestimate the risks of verbal threats such as threats to kill, particularly when made in a post-separation context.

At the safety assessment stage, when children are interviewed and a welfare report with recommendations to the family courts is usually produced based on the welfare checklist in the 1989 Children Act, the pilot study found that there were fewer recommendations for direct contact and some increased recognition of the risks to children from harmful parenting by violent fathers, particularly when this was reported by the children themselves. At the same time, there remained problems for practitioners in assessing risks in cases where there was a lack of corroborative evidence from the police, where the violence was denied by fathers and where the family courts failed to make findings of fact that domestic violence had occurred (Harne, 2009).

To date, the small number of research studies looking at the impact of risk identification and assessment processes on professionals' decision-making practices in safeguarding children and their mothers in the context of domestic violence in the UK suggest that it is making a contribution to improving practice in this area. Nevertheless, risk assessment can only serve as a guide for professionals and it cannot substitute for a comprehensive understanding of the harm that children can experience from domestically violent fathers and for appropriate policy and practice measures to ensure their safety.

Perpetrator programmes and children's safety

Perpetrator programmes for domestically violent men have proliferated over the past 10 years in the UK and have come to be viewed as a key means of rehabilitating domestically violent offenders within criminal justice policy and making violent fathers safe to be involved in children's lives in family law and child protection policies (Home Office, 2003). However, the growth in programmes, particularly in the probation sector, has not to date been accompanied by any substantial evidence in the UK that they are more effective than other criminal justice sanctions or that they work in changing violent fathers in the child welfare context. We return to this subject later in the chapter.

The rise in the number of probation-run programmes and court referrals to such programmes as part of a community rehabilitation order can to some extent be seen as a response to government measures to increase the criminalisation of domestic violence through, for example, the introduction of domestic violence courts and the need to have sentencing options for magistrates over and above the ubiquitous fine or custodial sentences (Cook et al, 2004). Nevertheless, as seen in the previous chapter their use as an alternative to imprisonment for serious domestic violence poses considerable risks to mothers and children's safety.

Programme approaches

In the UK, perpetrator programmes may be run by the probation service, which takes men who have been mandated by the courts to attend a programme through a probation order. They may also be run by the voluntary sector and these schemes tend to accept men referred by the criminal or family courts, or by children's services or other agencies. Some violent men may volunteer to attend the latter usually because a partner had threatened to leave them. In general, both these types of programme adopt a gendered analysis towards changing perpetrators and hold them fully responsible for their violence towards women. They regard men's violence as purposeful and their aim is get perpetrators to recognise that they can make the decision not to be violent. Most use a combination of cognitive behavioural techniques and educational approaches to confront perpetrators' beliefs about the acceptability of their violence and their woman-blaming attitudes, and to address their denials, minimisations and excuses. The well-known Duluth programme exemplifies this approach and uses examples from the power and control wheel (see Introduction, this volume) to challenge strategies of coercion and control and develop men's understanding of the impact of their violence on women and children (Pence, 1987). Perpetrator programmes may also use control logs or control checklists with violent men (rather than the anger logs used on anger management programmes) to encourage them to monitor their own behaviour. Most also address the impact of men's violence on children and some offer specific sessions on parenting. This is discussed in more detail in relation to the empirical research in Chapter Five.

Principles and standards

Significantly, these types of perpetrator programme emphasise that women and children's safety must be the main priority and national standards have been developed between practitioners running programmes to ensure that this principle is upheld (Respect, 2008). Perpetrator participants are thus not accorded confidentiality, since they may pose a risk of further violence and abuse. Basic programme principles include the need to monitor a perpetrator's behaviour while on the programme to assess his level of risk and obtain feedback from his partner or ex-partner on any changes to his behaviour if it is safe to do so, and the need to provide a woman's support service alongside the programme. This service should be proactive in making contact with men's partners and ex-partners and manage the flow of information on the perpetrator and the risks he poses. Women's support services should also inform partners or ex-partners that perpetrators may not change as a result of their programme attendance and give them advice and support about safety planning, including leaving their partners where appropriate. Some support services also offer group support and programmes that help to build women's confidence and increase their own understandings of the impact of their partners' abuse. Programmes should also have a child protection policy, consider 'the safety and needs of children in all aspects of their work' (Respect, 2008), be accountable to their local communities, and work in conjunction with local services and domestic violence fora.

Programme effectiveness

Programme effectiveness is a crucial question, particularly in the context of this discussion when they are viewed as a means of changing violent fathers and making them safe to be involved in children's lives. Yet to date, there have been few published research evaluations in this area in the UK, and knowledge largely relies on US research evaluation studies. However, as the US researcher Gondolf (2004) has noted, different research designs have led to contradictory and ambiguous evidence about their success. One key aspect to have been highlighted is the outcome measures used to evaluate effectiveness. It is now widely accepted that perpetrators' self-reports are unreliable measures of whether programmes have worked because perpetrators learn to 'talk the talk' when attending programmes and manipulate the system (Burton et al, 1998; Gregory and Erez, 2002). Other factors such as a decrease in recidivism measured through reports to the police are also unreliable because of the high level of under-reporting by domestic violence survivors. Since one of the primary aims of programmes is to increase women and children's safety, it is argued that women's self-reports are the most effective measure of change. Nevertheless, as with some risk assessment models, this approach neglects children's specific safety concerns and their fear of violent fathers and most US outcome evaluations of perpetrator programmes to date have not addressed this issue. Yet, despite this, some research evaluators have acknowledged that perpetrators use their attendance on programmes as a means to enhance their position with family courts in relation to contact and custody applications, and to get their revenge on mothers (Rittmeester, 1993; Bennett and Williams, 2001).

Even in assessing improvements to women's safety, however, many US evaluations' main outcome measure is a reduction in the physical assault of women according to their own reports. This omits the range of other intimidatory and coercive tactics that perpetrators use against their partners and that have been shown to increase in some UK and US qualitative programme evaluations even where the physical violence may have diminished (Burton et al, 1998; Gregory and Erez, 2002; Gondolf, 2004).

A further issue is that many evaluations are not able to show whether it is their intervention that has had made a difference, since they have not provided a comparison group of men who have had no intervention or who have had different criminal justice interventions. In the UK, there has only been one published evaluation of this type to date (Dobash et al, 1996), although other studies are now in progress (Respect, 2008). The earlier study (Dobash et al, 1996) looked at the outcomes for women whose partners had been on Duluth-type programmes compared with outcomes for women whose partners had received other criminal justice sanctions (mainly fines). However, although this study indicated that women partners of men on programmes experienced less violence and abusive behaviour one year after the programme ended than those women whose partners were merely fined, the numbers of women reporting were too small to be conclusive.

Messages from evaluations

US reviews and meta-analyses of different research studies are unable to provide conclusive evidence of the effectiveness of such interventions, even when the methodological design is rigorous (Feder and Forde 2000; Gondolf, 2004). Gondolf states that this demonstrates that 'we have no substantial evidence that programs are effective or highly effective' (Gondolf, 2004, p 9). At the same time, he argues that his own four-year multi-site evaluation of four different programmes in different settings and of varying lengths demonstrates that some programmes contribute to a reduction in physical reassault [of women] but this is related to 'the intervention system of which the program is a part,' (Gondolf, 2004, p 2).

Programme drop-out and non-attendance

Drop-out and non-attendance is a perennial problem for perpetrator programmes. US evaluations have identified drop-out and non-attendance rates as high as 55 to 80 per cent in some cases, even where men have been mandated to attend by the criminal courts. Gondolf's multi-site evaluation showed that attendance and completion rates could be vastly improved by applying external pressure. For example, in one programme in Pittsburgh, perpetrators were mandated by court to attend pre-trial sessions for three months, with a penalty of 28 days' immediate imprisonment for non-compliance. They were also required to appear in court regularly to confirm their attendance. These measures produced an initial attendance rate of 95 per cent and a completion rate of 70 per cent of all men mandated (Gondolf, 1998). In the UK, there are ongoing problems of attendance on programmes and the courts failing to take action on breaches of orders through re-sentencing and imprisonment (Cook et al, 2004). However, non-attendance is a much greater problem for voluntary sector programmes where men have been referred by agencies such as children's services or have self-referred because there are no adequate sanctions to enforce attendance and keep them in the programme. This is demonstrated by a recent voluntary sector process evaluation, where, of 166 men referred, 68 chose not to continue even to the first assessment phase, only 18 attended any group sessions and only seven completed the programme (Williams and Hester, 2009). In addition, Goldolf's (1998;2004) research demonstrates that men who volunteer to attend are more likely to drop out when partners decide to leave them. This latter research also shows that drop-out is more frequently related to marginalised men and those from Black and minority ethnic groups, suggesting that specific provision needs to be made for these men, run by programme leaders from the same backgrounds. In the UK, programmes specific to minority ethnicity are scarce, with little provision for South Asian men in particular (Izzidien, 2008).

Length of programmes

In Gondolf's multi-site research, where programmes ranged from three to nine months, the length of the programme appeared to make little difference in terms of programme effect; rather, it was the system keeping men in the programme that had an impact on women's safety, and where men changed their behaviour they tended to do so in the first three months of programme attendance (Gondolf, 2004).

However, at the 15-month evaluation point, there was a significantly lower reassault rate for the nine-month programme, although this was partially attributed to the fact that this project provided services to deal with men's drug and alcohol misuse (Gondolf, 1998). In general, however, the study found no causal relationship between drug and alcohol misuse and the extent of men's domestic violence.

Women's support services

In the UK, one early process evaluation of the DVIP programme (Burton et al, 1998) found that it was the women's support services rather than men's programmes that was the major factor in affecting women's perceptions of safety and helping them leave their violent partners. Another more recent process evaluation (Williamson and Hester, 2009) found that women engaging with support services found such intervention helpful, and far more women engaged with these services, despite their partners' non-attendance on the perpetrator programmes. Gondolf's (2004) research found that women's support services needed to extend beyond the length of men's perpetrator programmes for the men in order to increase their safety.

The US multi-site evaluation found a small effect where perpetrator programmes offered separate services to treat men who misused alcohol or drugs. However, they found no causal relationship between this misuse and the extent of men's domestic violence. This study also found that the programmes were less effective for the chronic most violent perpetrators, suggesting that custodial sentences are more appropriate for this group.

In summary, existing evaluations indicate that although perpetrator programmes may have a small impact in terms of reduced levels of domestic violence towards women, they do not provide a panacea for changing violent men's behaviour, and the evidence base for significant public investment in such programmes in the UK is weak. Moreover, current research has little to say about whether perpetrator programmes change violent men as fathers. Below we look at more specific provision in this area.

Parenting provision

Programmes aimed specifically at addressing the problem of violent fathers' harmful parenting of children have been developed in North America. Most notable among these is the Caring Dads programme, initiated in Canada in 2001. The programme's founders argue that general parenting skills programmes are not suitable for violent and/ or abusive fathers, because their sense of entitlement leads them to 'feel that they deserve unconditional love, respect and compliance from children', resulting in abusive control and a failure to prioritise the feelings and needs of children. It has therefore been recognised that specific programmes are needed to counter such attitudes if these fathers are to benefit from learning parenting skills (Scott, 2004). The content of the Caring Dads programmes also aims to address the failure to value children through challenging a range of abusive parenting practices from emotional cruelty and neglect to ignoring children's development needs, abusing others close to the child and using children as a weapon against mothers, and physical and sexual abuse (Scott, 2006).

As with domestic violence perpetrator programmes, accountability standards have been developed where the safety of children and their mothers is given priority whether or not the intervention changes the fathers' attitudes and behaviour. Programme initiators therefore recommend that outreach and advocacy services and information are provided to mothers whose (ex-)partners are participating in the Caring Dads programme (Scott et al, 2007).

However, as with perpetrator programmes, it seems that drop-out from such parenting projects remains a major problem. An initial pilot evaluation of the first two Caring Dads programmes, for example, showed that only six out of 17 fathers completed the programme. It also found that fathers' self-reports were not adequate indicators of their risk of further abuse (Scott, 2004). This confirms findings that fathers' accounts are unreliable indicators of change and that adequate outcome measures that include obtaining the views of children and their mothers need to be sought in any effective evaluation.

Mathews (1995) has carried out one of the few other existing evaluations of a parenting programme for domestically violent fathers in the North American context. This qualitative study found that many violent fathers resisted changing their physically abusive behaviour towards children and were reluctant to give up the benefits they had gained from having power and control over their families. Mathews also found that fathers generally lacked empathy for children and this prevented them from acknowledging children's needs.

In the UK, Caring Dads programmes are currently being piloted by the London Probation Service and in North and South Wales, although there has as yet been no published evaluation of their effectiveness. Moreover, there are concerns that as stand-alone interventions such programmes do not adequately address fathers' violence towards mothers.

In conclusion, the discourse that violent perpetrators can be good enough fathers is beginning to be challenged in the research and practice literature, with a growing recognition that violent fathers' sense of entitlement to have their own needs met frequently extends to their perceptions and treatment of children through their parenting practices. How far these can be effectively changed through rehabilitative interventions remains an open question and is discussed further in the next two chapters.

FOUR

Abusive fathering

Introduction

This chapter discusses the author's own exploratory, qualitative UK research with 20 domestically violent fathers. Overall the study aimed to look at fathers' own perspectives on their violence, its impact on their relationships with children and their parenting practices. The need for such research was highlighted by the fact that there were no other UK studies that specifically interrogated violent perpetrators' views of themselves as fathers. The policy context also demonstrated a lack of questioning of violent fathers' parenting and the impact it could have on children. One object of this research was therefore to provide an insight into violent fathers' own views of their parenting and the meanings they give to it when still living with families or in the context of post-separation child contact, in order to highlight the need for policymakers and professionals to pay greater attention to these areas when making decisions about children's safety and wellbeing. A second aim was to look at the impact of perpetrator programmes for domestically violent men on the fathers' understandings of their effects of their violence, since all the fathers who agreed to participate in the research were drawn from such programmes. These findings are discussed in Chapter Five. In addition, in a separate sample, the research sought the views of 10 mothers who had experienced violence, on their ex-partners' fathering, when still living with the family and during child contact, post-separation to provide comparative perspectives. The perceptions of mothers provide a powerful contrast to the fathers' accounts in this chapter, particularly in highlighting the impact of fathers' abusive behaviour on children, which was often minimised or omitted in the fathers' narratives.

Methods

The main methodological approach[1] in this study took the form of semi-structured interviews. Violence and control checklists were also used with the participants to enable the violent fathers to disclose on paper patterns of abusive and coercive behaviour they may not have been prepared to talk about in the interviews. Such checklists are commonly used with violent men on perpetrator programmes as a means of monitoring their behaviour towards partners/ex-partners. Research in this area has shown this to be a useful way of gaining a fuller picture of men's violence and control strategies (Dobash et al, 1996). The checklist used in this research also included added factors developed by the researcher that asked fathers about specific emotional and physical abuse towards children.

The first part of this chapter gives information about the fathers' backgrounds and summarises their familial situations, child contact arrangements and histories of violence and abuse towards mothers and children. These details were gained mainly from the control checklists in order to provide some context to the men's accounts. In addition, summary information is given about mothers' experiences of violence. The findings from both the mothers' and fathers' accounts are discussed in the second part of the chapter. In discussing the findings, personal details such as names have been changed and some details omitted in order to retain anonymity for the participants and the partners and children they refer to.

Background and summary information on violent fathers

Who were the fathers?

The 20 fathers who participated in this study were recruited from four perpetrator programmes for domestically violent men in different parts of England. Two of the programmes were probation-led and took perpetrators who had been mandated by the criminal courts to attend the scheme following a conviction for violence. The other two programmes were based in the voluntary sector and took a mixture of perpetrators who volunteered to attend, those who had mandated to do so by the criminal courts, and those who were referred by the family courts or social services. The fathers' occupational backgrounds ranged from professional, managerial and technical to semi-skilled and unskilled. Three of the men were unemployed at the time of interview and three had substance abuse or mental health problems. Their ages ranged from early twenties to late forties. All except one man were white and all were born in the UK.

The views expressed in this research are therefore limited and do not reflect those of minority ethnic or migrant fathers. The fact that all the fathers were attending or had recently attended perpetrator programmes also meant that this context could have some impact on the views expressed and could differ from those of violent fathers who had not attended such programmes.

Fathers' familial circumstances and kinship relationships with children

The fathers' relationships with children were highly diverse and changed over time, reflecting the fragmented nature of families in the early 21st century. An important focus of the research was to look at the perspectives of separated fathers particularly in relation to child contact and all except two participants were separated from children of first families. However, as the research progressed, it became apparent that almost half (nine) were still living with, or had recently separated from, children in second families, with one being separated from children in three families. These children could be their own genetic children, and/or stepchildren. The term 'stepchildren' is used here to encompass all children with whom men perceived themselves as having some kind of 'fathering' relationship, where there was no genetic connection, irrespective of whether the men were married to their partners. In three cases, fathers also had connections with stepchildren from first relationships. In four cases, fathers were still living with second families, comprising both genetic children and stepchildren. To a greater or lesser extent, the men viewed themselves as being 'social fathers' of stepchildren.

This complexity meant that in looking at fathers' violence and its impact on children, there was a need to broaden the research focus and to take account of the men's relationships with stepchildren, and children and mothers in both first and second families. As a result, it was clear that far more children were affected by fathers' violence than was initially apparent. In all, the fathers had some kind of parenting relationship with 55 children of varying ages and sexes. Of particular concern was the number of young children affected at the time of interview, since younger children are more likely to be seriously affected by a parent's violent and abusive behaviour (Hester et al, 2007). Half of the children in the current study were under the age of 10 and 18 of these were under the age of seven.

Fathers' living situations at time of interview

The complexity of fathers' familial circumstances is reflected in their living situations at the time of interview. All the fathers except two were separated from children from first families at the time of interview. These two had recently returned to live with first families after periods of separation of over a year or more. In one of these latter cases, the children were teenagers and one had recently left home at the age of 17. In the other, both children were under five. Four fathers were also living with second partners and children where the ages of children ranged from babies to teenagers. One father had never lived with the mother and baby of a first family. In addition, five fathers were recently separated from second families or, in one case, a third family because of their violence.

Table 4.1: Fathers' living situations at the time of interview

Separated from first families	18
Returned to live with first families	2
Separated from second or third families	5
Living with second families	4
Never lived with first family	1

Contact arrangements

Fathers' contact arrangements varied greatly. They had also changed over time and were continuing to change. Some fathers were unwilling to give specific details about why they had changed. This is discussed more fully below, but some general points can be made about the different types of contact arrangement and the circumstances in which there was little or no contact.

Most fathers said that contact had been agreed with mothers, although they did not explain why the mothers had agreed this, and the fathers' accounts can be viewed as particularly unreliable in this respect. Other research has suggested that abused mothers agree to contact for a variety of reasons (Radford et al, 1999; Masson, 2006) and the mothers themselves shed more light in their own accounts in the current research. However, the amount of contact fathers had with older children (aged between 11 and 16) appeared largely to have been determined by the children themselves.

Just under a third of the sample (six) had sought contact through the courts because mothers were opposing it. These cases tended to involve both genetic and stepchildren in first families. In three of these cases, there had been prior social services involvement because of safety concerns over children who had been physically abused. In one case, the direct contact ordered had been very limited for a number of years (one three-hour visit every six weeks) and was supervised by a social worker because of the extensive nature of the abuse. This was the only case where, according to the father's accounts, contact was being formally supervised at the time of interview. Two cases had led to no contact. In one case, this was because the father withdrew after a preliminary hearing after 'losing his temper in the court', and in the other, because the child in question, who was 15 years old, had refused contact. One court case was undecided at the time of interview.

Contact and children's age

In general, fathers who were separated from older children who were over 11 years of age stated that they had infrequent contact. This was mainly because the children 'chose not to', and, in two cases, teenagers had chosen to have no contact at all. Only in one case did a father have regular weekly staying contact with his two children aged 11 and 13, although at the time of interview this had been thrown open to question because the children had heard of the father's assault on a second partner. While older children often chose to limit or have no contact with violent fathers, there was some concern over fathers' contact with younger children (aged 10 or under). Contact in these cases tended to be more regular and more frequent and usually took place on a weekly basis. This is discussed further in the fathers' accounts.

Contact with children from second and third familial relationships

Whether fathers had contact with children from second and third relationships seemed to vary and depended on a number of different circumstances. One father, who had three genetic children from three different relationships, had weekend staying contact with all these children at the same time every three months, and stated that this had been agreed with their mothers. However, another father whose violence was the cause of his recent separation from a partner with whom he had lived for a number of years felt that there was no point in seeking contact with her genetic children. This was explained in terms of these children already having contact arrangements with their 'natural' fathers, one of whom had also been violent towards the mother concerned. The father mentioned above, who had recently separated from a second family of mother and baby, stated that he would not be seeking contact with this child, because he felt he would be unlikely to get it, due to his further recent violence towards the mother.

Fathers' involvement in childcare when living with families

Although most of the fathers in this study did not have the main responsibility for looking after the children when still with families, their level of involvement was greater than has been indicated in earlier research with mothers (Holden and Ritchie, 1991). Some fathers cared for children regularly when mothers were working either full or part time. Two thirds of these fathers described themselves as regularly looking after young children (under the age of six) for a few hours a day when mothers were working and two fathers said they did more than that where their partners were the main breadwinners. Only three fathers subscribed to the traditional view of childcare being mothers' responsibility, although they had had some involvement at mealtimes or bedtimes. While some of the fathers may have been exaggerating their childcare roles, almost half of the mothers participating in the study said that their partners undertook some regular childcare and in three cases this was where mothers worked. In another case, the father was described as trying to prevent the mother from participating at all in the care of her baby because he wanted complete control over the child.

These changes reflect general economic shifts in the labour market and in government policy, which promotes mothers' participation in paid work and fathers' involvement with children, as well as the shifts in the social significance fathers have accorded to children which have developed in the UK and elsewhere in the late twentieth century, as discussed in chapters two and three. Along with fathers more generally, these division of labour shifts in the home led to conflict and resentment over household chores and childcare with their partners (Lupton and Barclay, 1997). However, for these fathers such conflicts often led to violence and this is discussed further in the fathers' accounts.

Fathers' experiences of childhood abuse and violence

Just under a third of the fathers (six) used their own childhood experiences as one of a number of explanations for their violence towards women and/or their own abusive parenting practices towards children. Five fathers described their own fathers as being violent towards their mothers and towards themselves, and one father, who was brought up by his mother and grandmother, experienced physical abuse from his mother. In this example, however, the father's experience of abuse was complicated by the fact that he also admitted to 'seriously' assaulting his mother at the age of 12. The most common explanations for their violence included 'having uncontrollable tempers' that were further 'provoked' by their partners' and children's actions; women's and/or children's failure to meet fathers' expectations of how they should behave; claims of 'mutual violence'; and, occasionally, a belief that violence constituted 'normal' masculine behaviour. This study does not therefore provide any strong evidence of the 'cycle of violence' theory. Rather, as seen in Chapter Three, fathers tended to draw on strong cultural discourses used by other violent men to excuse and justify their own violence and abuse.

Fathers' histories of violence

As the research progressed, it became increasingly clear that all of the fathers had a history of domestic violence; that is, their violence was not related to single incidents or events but had been ongoing for at least part of their individual relationships with women. Most had perpetrated the violence for several years. However, since they often minimised their histories of violence, it was not always possible to know when the violence had started, although there were indications that in some cases it had intensified when their partners became pregnant, after the children were born or at the point of separation.

Significantly, in the case of almost half (nine) of the fathers interviewed, the violence had been perpetrated in two relationships where children were involved. One father admitted to being violent in three different relationships with women where he also had genetic children with whom he had contact. Thus, as has been indicated in other research, some fathers had moved through 'careers' of domestic violence, where violent practices in familial relationships were habitual and were carried over from one relationship to the next, increasing the numbers of children and mothers affected.

Convictions for domestic violence/child abuse

Ten fathers admitted to having convictions relating to domestic violence and these men could be described as 'working class' in occupational terms. Two fathers had been convicted for physical assaults on their children, with one being identified as a 'schedule 1' offender for having several convictions for cruelty against children, as well as for violence against the mother. Three fathers' convictions included actual bodily harm to mothers and two for threats to kill and harassment of ex-partners under the 1997 Protection from Harassment Act (PFHA). Three had more than one conviction relating to domestic violence, with one having convictions for actual bodily harm and harassment.

Two other fathers stated that they had had multiple convictions for violence, although they were vague about what these actually were. One of these fathers had been convicted in his teens for assaulting his mother and stated he had other convictions for violence against men. Two fathers also had convictions for other offences not related to their violence. However, half the fathers participating in the research (10) had no convictions for perpetrating violence and they described themselves as 'volunteers' on the perpetrator programmes, usually at the instigation of second partners who threatened to leave the relationship unless the men changed. In a few other cases, fathers had 'volunteered' to attend to demonstrate their 'fitness' for contact with their children, either to the family courts or social care agencies. A quarter also admitted to having been physically violent very recently while they were on the programmes, either to current partners or to ex-partners. Such incidents included post-separation violence. Nevertheless, in relation to the extent and forms of violence admitted to by the fathers most explicitly in the checklists, there was, on the whole, little difference between those who had convictions for violence and those who did not (see below).

Civil injunctions

Most of the fathers who admitted to having injunctions against them also had convictions for violence. Four fathers with convictions had injunctions (exclusion orders) to stay away from mothers and children and one father had a restraining order under the PFHA. In two of these cases, fathers stated the injunctions had been as a result of their convictions for physical assaults on children rather than violence towards partners. Only in two cases did men state that there were injunctions against them where they had no convictions.

Fathers' violence and abuse control patterns

As found in other studies with violent men, the fathers tended to minimise their violence and abuse in their interviews. The checklists (see Appendix 1) used in combination with the interviews showed that most fathers had carried out a range of physical violence, sexual violence and coercive control towards mothers. While fathers varied in the type and amount of physical and sexual violence and intimidation to which they admitted, the following example, from Father A, is typical.

Pin her to wall or floor; sit or stand on her; bang her head; rip her clothes; throw her around; punch her with fist; pull her hair; pound walls with fists; throw food or objects around; prevent her from leaving, shout, swear and scream; threaten to harm children; touch her sexually without consent; get angry if don't have sex. (Father, no convictions for violence)

Sexual violence

Only one man talked about sexual violence during his interview and its more frequent occurrence was revealed only through the use of the checklist. Over a third (seven) admitted to some form of sexual abuse of their partners, which ranged from treating their partners as a sex object to getting angry when they refused sex; making fun of partners sexually; using threats to get sex; making partners perform sex acts against their will; sexual touching without consent; physically attacking sexual parts of the body; and forcing partners to have sex. This could be combined to a greater or lesser extent with other forms of behaviour, which indicated that women partners were often regarded as sexual possessions. Telling women what to wear was a common form of sexual control, as well as checking up on them and accusing them of having affairs.

Psychological/emotional abuse and coercive control

This type of abuse involved strategies of isolation, intimidation, coercion and humiliation, designed to limit partners' autonomy and undermine women's sense of self while ensuring men's own needs were met. In general, more fathers acknowledged carrying out these strategies in the checklists rather than in the interviews. Most fathers admitted to using some of these strategies, with a few disclosing more of this type of abuse than physical violence. This is illustrated in the checklist of Father B, who admitted to:

Opening his partner's mail, listening to phone calls, depriving her of food or sleep, preventing contact with friends or family, not letting her go out, making out she was stupid or mad, criticising and calling her names, threatening to harm the children, accusing her of having affairs, not letting her speak, telling her what to wear, forcing her to do housework to his standards.

While most fathers admitted to using a combination of strategies in the checklists, together with multiple forms of physical violence and threats of violence, the most common forms of psychological abuse included humiliation and making fun of partners; criticising and blaming them; making them out to be stupid or mad; not letting them speak or ignoring them. Isolation strategies such as preventing contact with friends and family and preventing partners going out on their own were also common.

Post-separation violence and abuse

There was no checklist aimed specifically at identifying post-separation violence or abuse. However, a third of fathers admitted during their interviews to having used such violence. It was also evidenced by some of the men's convictions of under the 1997 Protection from Harassment Act. For example, two fathers had convictions for telephone harassment, stalking and threatening mothers and children in the family home. Three other fathers said they had used physical violence against mothers post-separation, including two who admitted physical assault during contact visits at the mother's home. In addition, three fathers disclosed using threats of physical violence to coerce either first partners or second partners who had left the relationships to return to the family home and, in two of these cases, the abduction of children was used as part of this coercion. Further, several fathers talked about threatening mothers through the children during contact visits, although they did not usually acknowledge this as abusive behaviour.

Fathers' abuse of children

Fathers' acknowledgement of the abuse of children was obviously constrained by the focus of the research as well as by how far they were prepared to define certain behaviours as harmful to children. As has been seen in Chapter One, emotional/psychological abuse can be seen as a consequence of children's experiences of fathers' ongoing violence, threats and psychological strategies of control towards mothers, which can engender extreme fear and anxiety in children. In this study, very few fathers defined their violence and abuse towards mothers as emotionally abusive of the children even when they were using children in the abuse of the mother, for example, by abducting children or taking advantage of contact time post-separation by getting children to take threatening messages to mothers. Some fathers were prepared to acknowledge direct intimidatory or physical abuse of children in their interviews, while others only disclosed it in the checklists, where specific aspects of child abuse had been developed by the researcher.

Almost half the fathers (nine) admitted that they had used physical violence against children, with most using it more than once. This could involve the use of weapons such as leather straps and hitting children 'hard' across the face and head as well as bruising their bodies. Fifteen fathers also admitted to intimidating and threatening children through banging furniture, breaking or throwing objects and/or through shouting and swearing at them. Other kinds of intimidatory and threatening behaviour towards children to which fathers admitted in the checklists included threatening to hurt mothers, threatening pets, threatening to put children in care, forcing children to eat and breaking their possessions. Some fathers also admitted to regularly humiliating and criticising children, including in front of friends, ignoring them and forcing them to keep secrets from their mothers.

From this, it can be seen that these fathers' violence and control of mothers was chronic and frequently severe and, in some cases, extended into the post-separation context. It also affected a much larger group of children than originally anticipated because it included those in second familial relationships. In addition, most fathers in their control checklists disclosed a range of simultaneous and direct abuse of children, which included physical abuse, intimidation and emotional abuse. As has been seen above, much of this abuse involved very young children – that is, children under the age of six – and the implications of this must be of particular concern. However, the way these men portrayed their abusive behaviour and described its impact gives a very different picture.

Summary information on mothers

The mothers' sample comprised women drawn from two different support groups/networks for separated mothers and children experiencing domestic violence. All of the women were living on their own with their genetic children at the time of the interview, having been separated from their most recent partners for varying lengths of time. Two mothers were separated from two violent partners with whom they had had children. These mothers had been specifically targeted by these violent men when they were vulnerable after leaving the first violent relationship.

In all, 25 children had been living with abused mothers and violent fathers before separation. Ten of these children were under the age of five at the time of separation. Most mothers had initially agreed that their children could have contact with fathers following separation, usually on the advice of a solicitor who had told them that they had to agree. In four cases, contact had initially taken place at a contact centre. Two mothers had initially organised contact informally without taking legal advice, because they believed the children should have a father's influence. However, at the time of the research interviews, the family courts had finally ruled against contact for the children of seven mothers because of ongoing violence or abuse of children.

Mothers' and children's experiences of violence and abuse

Mothers' experiences of violence and abuse had usually begun with coercive control, which was later accompanied by physical and sexual violence when they began to live with their partners, during pregnancy or soon after the children were born. Half described the use of sexual violence as a form of reproductive abuse, with one mother saying that three out of four of her children had been born as a result of rape. Most had stayed in relationships through fear, with some describing being constantly watched and checked up on so that they could not leave. None had felt able to report the violence to the police. Some were also told by fathers that they would never escape, because the family courts would grant them access to the children. As indicated in earlier research, mothers left when the violence escalated, for example because fathers had tried to strangle them or threatened to kill them or their children, and/or because mothers had become increasingly aware of the harm being done to their children through witnessing violence or because the children themselves were being abused (McGee, 2000; Humphreys and Thiara, 2002; Mullender et al, 2002). In contrast to the fathers, some mothers described extensive and deliberate use of sexual, physical and psychological violence in front of very young children, and children being deliberately harmed or threatened with harm in their presence.

Post-separation harassment and violence

All the mothers had experienced serious post-separation harassment after separation, which was designed to create fear in whole families. This included stalking, silent phone calls, entering the home while mothers and children were out and leaving live electric wires exposed, slashing car tyres, having the services in the house cut off, driving up and down outside the home to instil fear and ensure the family knew they were watched, and reporting mothers to social services for allegedly harming children. In one case, the mother was harassed at work in an attempt to make her lose her job. Half of mothers had also experienced serious post-separation violence, often during contact handover, with two mothers being stabbed in front of their children and another being dragged along the ground in a moving car. As a consequence, three mothers obtained convictions of their ex-partners for post-separation violence and the police gave one mother a panic alarm. Five fathers had also made allegations to social services that mothers were abusing the children as a form of revenge for leaving them. One father made allegations on three occasions before social workers finally realised that he was deliberately making false allegations to harm the children and their mother.

Children's experiences of direct abuse

Mothers' accounts gave examples of children being directly abused as well as frequently having to witness violence towards their mothers. Mothers reported physical abuse and intimidation of very young children when fathers were looking after them on their own for a few hours a day, either when mothers were at work (in five cases) or out of the house for a short time. It should be noted, however, that mothers were not always aware at the time that such abuse had occurred and had only found out later from children's accounts. In contrast to the fathers' accounts, three of the mothers disclosed incidences of sexual abuse by biological fathers, with one describing a father grooming three children (aged 7, 9 and 11) by showing them pornographic films while the mother was at work. Mothers also described children being directly intimidated and emotionally abused when they were present in the home and the impact of this is discussed further below. Mothers who had second partners described different forms of abuse being directed at biological and stepchildren. For example, two mothers described second fathers as trying to drive older stepchildren out of the home through physical abuse while exerting extreme control over their own biological infants. One of these fathers would not allow the mother to feed or look after the baby at all, or, as he got older, allow him to play outside the home. Mothers' perceptions of neglect of children's basic health and developmental needs, particularly when fathers had contact with very young children such as babies and toddlers, were also significant aspects of harm to children, which were not mentioned in the fathers' accounts.

Findings from fathers' and mothers' accounts

Fathers' accounts of their violence and its impact on children

As in other research discussed in Chapter Three, fathers tended to partially deny and minimise their violence in their accounts (despite having acknowledged extensive violence in their checklists) and this affected how far they acknowledged its impact on the children themselves. They drew on strategic responses similar to those described by Cavanagh and colleagues (2001), using socially acceptable discourses to excuse the violence and mitigate their own culpability.

Denials and minimisation

Although it was difficult for the fathers in the context in which they were being interviewed to deny outright that they had been violent, some with convictions for violence attempted to do so through claiming that mothers had made 'false allegations' about particular incidents and arguing that they were the 'real victims'. For example, in describing an incident when he was arrested for violence towards his second partner, Collin stated:

> "The charges were for assault, criminal damage, which I got found not guilty for. I actually got found guilty of threats to kill her, which I know wasn't the truth – but when you put on tears for the court...."

Later in his account, however, it became clear that he had threatened to kill his partner with a knife in a struggle over a 'suspicious phone call' that his seven-year-old daughter had witnessed, although he made no comment about this, except to refer to his daughter as a witness to what 'really happened'. It also became apparent that he was awaiting trial on yet another charge of actual bodily harm, which related to yet another violent 'incident' following separation.

Another father, Geoff, in describing his convictions under the PFHA and the restraining order placed on him, represented himself as a victim of his ex-partner's allegations:

> "She said I was kicking the door down – that I was blocking the phone line with my mobile phone – I was accused of harassing her on numerous occasions – and that I was

following her when she went shopping – *now I'm frightened to go out."* [his emphasis]

Another common strategy used by the fathers to deny and minimise their violence was to limit it to a 'few incidents' of physical violence, where only certain forms counted. In Matt's account, for example, only punching was real violence, anything else was something less. When describing his violence, Matt said:

> "I have hit her. I don't punch her – I'm not the violent type. I've pushed her and raised my voice and tried to strangle her on one occasion."

Later in his account, Matt was to talk about other forms of physically violent and intimidatory behaviour, which clearly also affected the children and created an atmosphere of fear in the home but were not included in his definition of 'real' violence:

> "I threw objects and smashed phones and pictures – I've smashed cups – I've smashed the baby's cup – I've even smashed remote controls, would you believe."

Another strategy to both minimise and justify the violence was to claim it was about mutual conflict, thus arguing that women had provoked the violent response and were equally responsible for it (see also Hearn, 1998a). This was often represented in terms of 'a few little arguments', where 'we were annoying each other' or 'she was the one who started to fight' or, as 'a failure in communication' as in family systems discourses. However, such claims of 'mutual conflict' were frequently contradicted by information given in the fathers' checklists or by fathers' own descriptions of children witnessing or being caught up in violence that had seriously injured mothers. Bill, for example, described his violence in the following terms:

> "It was the fact that we couldn't communicate, that we were both upsetting and annoying each other about what we were saying – shouting matches – shouting and abuse we had come close on several occasions."

Yet in his checklist, Bill disclosed that he had engaged in a range of physical and intimidatory behaviour towards his partner, including head-butting her, banging and punching walls, threatening her when she refused sex, and driving recklessly to terrify her.

'Uncontrollable' violence and mothers' provocation

Where fathers did acknowledge some violence, it was most commonly excused through the discourse of it being out of their control. Several fathers thus described themselves as having 'short fuses', 'bad tempers' or 'uncontrollable rages' (see also Hearn, 1998a). However, this loss of control did not occur in any circumstances, but was regarded as being provoked by mothers often simply because they were not doing what fathers wanted. This is illustrated in the following account by Matt:

> "What winds me up about her is that I have actually raised my voice to my other two girlfriends and once they had seen me raise my voice they knew I was in a bad mood and that would make them shut up – it was enough to make them shut up – it was enough to frighten them, but not this one – she pushes and pushes and I will snap and go and hit her."

Fathers' violence and the division of labour in the home

Most fathers in this study said that they did not see any differences between mothers' and fathers' 'roles' in terms of housework and/or childcare. Yet blaming mothers for not doing enough housework or not doing it according to fathers' standards was a common justification for violence. Jeremy, who was one of the middle-class fathers, explained some of his violence in the following terms:

> J: "Well for years I did the cooking and the cleaning, because she'd never been that way inclined, and rather than negotiating I would shout and scream."
>
> Q: "Because she didn't do it?"
>
> J: "Yes – well to be fair, when we were first married she did, probably because I picked fault with what she did, she said she wasn't going to do it anymore."

Such discourses could also merge into fathers' explanations that their partners were exploiting them as 'house husbands,' and were clearly connected to their own constructions of themselves as men. For example, Guy, another middle-class father, said that he was violent because his partner treated him unfairly, since he had to do most of the housework after the birth of their child:

> "She was the main breadwinner, and when we were living together I did all the shopping, cleaning etc ... it [the violence] was ostensibly to do with housework – my partner was very untidy – I resented doing certain things, like having to go round the shops – *I felt I was being treated instrumentally.*" [his emphasis]

Some fathers also justified their violence on the grounds that mothers' not doing enough housework prevented them from being 'good' fathers. Brian, for example, justified his violence towards his child's mother (where he acknowledged that he had broken her nose in one incident and her teeth in another and had a 'controlling problem') on the grounds that she did not do sufficient housework so he could not spend enough time playing with his son. Brian stated that he did not believe in 'set roles' in the home, but explained his 'violent and controlling' behaviour towards his partner in terms of having to do too many chores and basic childcare because his partner went out 'four nights a week' so he was unable to spend 'quality time' with his three-year-old boy. He said:

> "I've always felt that my wife didn't help with the household chores that needed to be done, like dishes and washing – things like that. I did it all – so I didn't have lot of time to play with my son – I would be cooking tea, bathing [X] or getting him ready for bed, so I didn't have a lot of time for the love side of things."

However, it should be noted that in Brian's control checklist, he admitted to imprisoning his partner to prevent her from going out. In addition, he admitted to stalking her, opening her mail, making physical threats, smashing possessions in the home and using sexual violence. He also initially denied that his violence and controlling abuse had any impact on the three-year-old child or that he was even aware of it, but later he admitted that "when I shouted at her, he would come over and hit me, he was trying to protect her."

In contrast to Brian, Dave initially described his violence as being the result of his (ex-)partner refusing him contact with the children, giving the impression that as a 'good' father he had only been 'legitimately' violent in this context and that it had not occurred while he was living with the mother. For example, he said: "I don't want to minimise anything. I've whacked her across the face a few times during our separation – she wouldn't let me see the kids." Further on into the interview, however, it became clear that there had been ongoing violence before separation and that this was justified because his partner did not 'have his tea on the table' when he came home from work and the house was 'untidy,' and his partner was 'keeping him a prisoner in his own home' because she asked him to attend to the children having their tea. In this regard, Dave stated that his partner was making him appear 'weak' and undermining his sense of himself as a 'real man'. However, Dave was one of only three fathers in this research who explicitly subscribed to the traditional view of fathers as the breadwinners, with mother's role being to do the housework and look after the children.

Other fathers justified their violence towards women during pregnancy because at the time *they* had chosen not to be fathers and their partners were perceived as contravening this choice. In addition, women's state of pregnancy could be seen as threatening the emotional support that the men expected from women and this could be viewed as a justifiable reason for violence. This was directly expressed by one father who stated that he was violent when he found out his partner was pregnant because he felt 'insecure,' and he felt that his partner was not giving *him* 'any support'.

These fathers' accounts can be read on a number of different levels. First, the denials, minimisations and contradictions of the fathers' accounts emphasise their unreliability as credible versions of the violence. Second, they reflect the ways in which fathers strategically used gendered socially acceptable discourses as well as popular psychological explanations to transfer the blame on to mothers and re-present themselves as the victims. Third, the men's status and identities as fathers were constructed in some accounts through their violence, where mothers were regarded as challenging their sense of entitlement to time to play with children and their control over the household and/or undermining their sense of themselves as men. For those fathers who were involved in childcare and household tasks in the home, this became a source of conflict, where violence was used to gain control over the division of labour to their own advantage.

Significantly, however, and as indicated in Perel and Peled's research (2008), children's presence and the impact of violence on them were usually absent in the fathers' narratives and children witnessing the violence were regarded as irrelevant to their constructions of themselves as fathers. Often, it was only when fathers were asked directly about children's presence did it become apparent that children were the observers of their violence. Further, where children were referred to, it was when they were used to promote a view of men as 'good' fathers. This was also illustrated in their accounts of their relationships with the children.

Fathers' views of their relationships with children

Several fathers asserted that they were better parents and that children preferred them to their mothers. In these discourses, children could be afforded significance as sources of pride, enjoyment or love, but, at the same time, any consideration of the impact of fathers' violence on them was usually absent. This was demonstrated by Collin talking about how much he cared about the baby son he had had with his second partner and how much the child preferred him to his mother. In casually describing an incident of violence, however, he acknowledged his son's presence but made no mention of the effect the violence could have had on him:

> "I had a lot of time for the baby but no time for her ...
> I enjoyed playing with him ... he wanted to be with me
> rather than his mother ... in the violent incident when I
> got arrested, she was holding him in her arms and he was
> covered in her blood."

Two other fathers used incidents where they had 'abducted' the children from their mothers as examples of how much they cared about them, while at the same time making it clear that they were using the children to control their mothers.

For example, Phil talked about having a 'special relationship' with his young son from his second relationship and how he was 'so proud of him he could cry with joy' and used this as the justification for taking him away from his mother, saying:

> "I didn't want to lose her and I didn't want to lose my
> son – she did leave me one night but I went into old gear
> and went down her mother's and said 'Get home' and she
> wouldn't – so I took the baby off her and said 'You can
> stay here if you want to' and I knew she would eventually
> come home, because a good mother won't leave her baby."

Thus, as Bancroft and Silverman (2002) have noted, violent fathers' expressions of pride and love of their children cannot be viewed as demonstrations of commitment to their wellbeing; rather, children are viewed as objects and possessions used to fulfil fathers' needs. Very few fathers in this study ever acknowledged that their violence towards mothers could have an impact on children, although most eventually admitted that children were either witnessing violence directly or were present in the home when it occurred, and some described hearing children crying and screaming in other parts of the house. A few eventually admitted that it could have had some impact at the time it happened, but often minimised the effect by describing the children as 'startled,' or 'wary' rather than fearful or frightened. However, they rarely recognised any broader or continuing impact, as illustrated in the following mother's account:

> "The children used to be really withdrawn and subdued –
> now two years on [following separation] they are outgoing
> and lively. Sarah, the youngest [then aged five] was very
> withdrawn for a long time – at one point she was smearing
> faeces on the wall. She had this ongoing fear that she was
> going to be hit next … this came out when we went to see
> the psychiatrist. Sarah is just about calm now … but not in
> all circumstances. Whenever someone gets angry, Sarah will
> get terrified because when he raised his voice she knew I
> would get hit – 'Dad' is a fearful word to her now." (Fiona,
> talking about the impact of her partner's violence on her
> five- and seven-year-old daughters)

In this regard, only one father, Guy, described the long-term 'very negative impact' on his six-year-old daughter as a result of her 'witnessing' his 'explosions of rage and temper' towards her mother: "She's shy – she has a lot of problems going to school and changing class – I think it has had the effect of making her insecure."

Moreover, no fathers were prepared to talk about deliberately abusing mothers in front of the children or using children in their abuse of mothers (although five admitted to this in their checklists) and the impact of this kind of abuse was only apparent in the mothers' accounts.

Pat, for example, described how her partner would deliberately rape her in front of her three-year-old son in order to force her to comply with his sexual demands:

"I didn't want to have sex with him and by that time I disliked him intensely and I would pretend to be asleep and he would cause a scene and wake me up and wake up John – because he would get on top of me – 'You are my wife', 'You are my property' – and then he would just do it to me and John would go 'What are you doing? What are you doing to Mummy?' So I just used to let him do it in the end."

Pat further described how her partner tried to draw the child into his psychological abuse of her:

"I left when I was six months' pregnant with Simon [second child] so he hasn't suffered all that, but John did. He saw the hitting and the shouting and mummy's sick in the head and mummy can't do anything right and mummy can't cook and mummy can't do this or that … he'd take him for a ride in the car and then say it. John would come back and say 'You're sick, mummy.'"

Abusive parenting practices when looking after children

As seen above, most men in the fathers' sample claimed to have some direct responsibility for looking after the children and more so when partners worked. But as their accounts continued it became apparent that far from being 'caring' in the conventional sense of prioritising and meeting children's needs, men were often abusive in these circumstances and children could experience further harm through direct intimidation and threats, emotional cruelty and physical abuse.

In the same way that women were often blamed for men's violence, some fathers justified violence towards children by arguing that very young children themselves provoked such behaviour, by annoying them, failing to meet their own expectations of how children should behave and making unreasonable demands on them (see also Alder and Polk, 1996; Cavanagh et al, 2007).

Ted, for example, who had admitted to convictions for cruelty to children, related how his three daughters provoked abuse because they 'annoyed' him by not behaving in the way he expected of them and not conforming to his wishes. This is illustrated in the following extract:

T: "I would get a bit annoyed if they came home late from school and if they wouldn't sit down and concentrate on their homework, because I thought that was important and if I actually sat say with Paula [five-year-old daughter] and she was trying to read to me and sometimes I would get a bit annoyed if I thought she wasn't trying."

Q: "So you would hit her?"

T: "Yes but it was also more shouting."

Q: "So what effect do you think that had on her?"

T: " She would just get really terrified and curl up in a corner – in the end she wouldn't sit on my knee anymore."

In a similar way to how he viewed his partner as deserving his violence because she would not 'shut up', Matt saw his children as deliberately provoking his 'uncontrollable temper' when he was looking after them while his partner was at work. It is also interesting to note that in this discourse, Matt himself becomes the key 'victim' of his own violence:

"Basically what it is – I'm frightened of my temper. The two of them are little sods together and I'm frightened of doing damage to them when I'm on my own with them and they are misbehaving and I can feel my temper and it does frighten me in case I hit them."

Matt was one of few fathers who acknowledged that both his violence towards the children's mother and his own intimidation of the children had had some impact on them at the time it happened, but he believed that it could be cancelled out by expressions of love and by playing with his three- and four-year-old daughters. He said:

"The youngest seems to cry all the time which I think is through the violence and the eldest will just cry when I tell her to do anything, which I think is due to all the shouting and violence and I'll say, 'I'm not telling you off, I'm not saying you can't do it – wait until tomorrow – we'll play a game of when the police were chasing me' – oh, I love them to bits!"

Yet, as seen in McGee's research (2000), such inconsistent parenting can have a particularly negative impact on very young children. Uncertainty about how their fathers are going to behave towards them may increase their levels of fear, as illustrated in the following mother's account:

> "If he felt like it he would cuddle them, but only when he felt like it. At other times he would kick and throw things at them, just because he was in the same room as them ... this made the children absolutely terrified of him because they never knew what he was going to do next." (Tina, talking about her three-year-old son and six-year-old daughter)

Fathers' blaming of very young children as an excuse for their abusive behaviour, because they were detracting from their own needs, was further illustrated by Tom, who had responsibility for looking after his two daughters (aged two and four) in the evenings when his partner was in hospital for two weeks (they were cared for in a nursery during the day). It should be noted that earlier in his account, Tom had expressed the view that he and his partner should care for the children equally. He said:

> "It was too much for me, I was no good at it whatsoever – I would get frustrated with them and very tired – they wanted to talk to Dad and they were constantly badgering me for attention – [there was] awful shouting and verbal abuse, aggressive abuse to get them to do what I wanted them to do – I was constantly boiling – the slightest thing – if they dropped a spoon when they were eating their pudding – that would be enough to slam my fist down on the table and say 'What the hell do you think you are doing?' and that obviously shocked them rigid."

Tom was the only father who recognised that his intimidatory parenting had had some long-term impact on the children, stating:

> "My four-year-old daughter is not talking well compared with other children half her age – she has these catatonic states – it alarms me – I've seen that when I've been aggressive and smacked her, that is one major effect that I have had on her."

Emotional cruelty and extreme control

A few fathers admitted that they were deliberately cruel to children, describing controlling and frightening them through looks, silence and humiliation rather than through the use of physical abuse. Phil, for example, said:

> "Just being in the same room was enough in the end – it was mental abuse. They were terrified of me – all I had to do was look ... I was quite cruel to be honest with you – at mealtimes I used to sit there and make them eat things they really didn't like and they used to cry. I wanted to make them too perfect. I wanted to make them what I was like."

However, mothers' accounts were far more illustrative of the impact on children of the emotional cruelty they could experience. They also showed how some fathers would target particular children for such abuse when they were involved in their care. Susan's partner looked after her three children regularly for two hours a day while she still lived with him, until she returned home from work, but she only became aware of how her youngest child was being abused when she took him to the doctor for bedwetting:

> "It started when Paul was about four. His father would call him thick and stupid and hit him around the head – when he got glasses he called him 'four-eyes' ... when he was about six or seven he was still wetting himself, so I took him to the doctor – it was only by chance that he let something slip and I realised why he was wetting himself – because his father was humiliating him when he was looking after him, before I got home." (Susan, talking about the youngest of three children)

Other mothers described fathers perpetrating a range of cruel, often gratuitous, humiliation and extreme control of very young children when they were looking after them, or when children were merely in their presence. This not only made children extremely fearful but also, in some cases, affected their behavioural, emotional and cognitive development. Margaret, for example, described how her second violent partner constantly made fun of his three-year-old child for not talking properly, thus delaying his speech development even further. In addition, mothers related how fathers deliberately told very young children how they had killed their pets, threatened to lock toddlers in bathrooms as a form of punishment, threatened to drown or strangle them or told them they would kill their mothers.

One mother described her second violent partner's such extreme control of a very young child that she was also prevented from caring for him.

Intimidatory parenting through physical abuse

As seen above, threatening children through intimidation and deliberate cruelty could also extend to physical abuse when fathers were involved in caring for their children. Other fathers, who had less involvement in childcare, described children as provoking physical abuse at mealtimes and bedtimes when their mothers had gone out and they were looking after them. Dave, for example, related how he had been involved in a child protection investigation. His stepson (then aged six) had been placed on the child protection register because he had hit him 'too hard' and bruised him because he was 'just playing and not going to sleep'. Another father, Jim, felt that 'the only way to get children to do what you wanted' was to hit them. He related how he had been convicted for assault on his disabled genetic child, because he had hit him 'too hard' when he refused to go to bed. Neither of these fathers gave any consideration to the impact the abuse might have had on their children and both felt that they were justified in using physical violence because the children were not behaving according to their wishes.

Nevertheless, only two men in this study viewed their specific role as fathers as being to physically discipline their children. One of these was John, a member of the armed forces who described using 'armed forces discipline' on his children, which he later recognised as having had a 'horrendous impact' on them. However, it was only in the mothers' accounts that fathers' intimidation and physical abuse was fully recognised in terms of its effects on children, as seen in the following example:

> "They were all nervous wrecks basically, very introverted, very nervous, not doing well at school. He would shout at them for nothing – they were very frightened to get up and go to the toilet in the night – there was bedwetting but it got to the point when he started to hit them – that was about six months before I left, he punched my youngest daughter – she was eight and he punched her because she wouldn't go to sleep." (Margaret, describing the effect the

children's first violent father had on them when he looked
after them for one night a week)

These accounts indicate that fathers' parenting of children cannot
be disconnected from their violence and abuse directed at mothers,
since they view and treat children in a similar way, using intimidation,
cruelty and physical abuse as forms of extreme control over them, and
often regarding very young children as deliberately causing their abuse.
Furthermore, although a few fathers in retrospect recognised that they
had harmed their children, their failure to regard and value children as
human beings in their own right meant that, as Bancroft and Silverman
(2002) have noted, they were unable to empathise with children's
feelings of fear or recognise the extent of their harm to children, as
highlighted in the mothers accounts. Moreover, far from them making
them more caring or nurturing, the fathers' accounts indicated that
their increased involvement in looking after children, provided them
with further opportunities to harm very young children in their care.

Thus, as Baynes (2009) has noted, in terms of professional and child
protection practice these findings point to the need to identify and
assess violent fathers' parenting and their involvement in looking after
children when considering children's safety and wellbeing rather than
focusing only on mother's parenting practices. They also indicate that
consideration of whether children are experiencing significant harm
from such fathers should not be limited to signs of physical abuse but
should recognise that intimidatory parenting involving threats and
emotionally and psychological cruelty can be equally as harmful. This
is discussed further below in terms of violent fathers' contact with
children post-separation.

Fathers' views on contact post-separation

In common with other separated fathers (Smart and Neale, 1999),
most men in this study viewed contact within a discourse of fathers'
rights. They argued that they had a legal entitlement to see their
children, usually regardless of children's feelings or wishes or any
acknowledgement that their contact might be inappropriate because of
their prior violence towards the mothers and their abuse of the children.
Within this discourse of legal entitlement, there was also a sense of legal
ownership of children. For example, Rob, who had earlier admitted
to a conviction for physically abusing his disabled child and had stated
that he felt the only way to control children was 'to hit them', said
"No one is going to come between me and my children, because they

are mine." Worryingly, as highlighted in other research (Humphreys and Thiara, 2002), Rob also related that although social workers had been involved in the child abuse investigation when he was still living with the family, they had shown no interest in whether or not he had contact with his children after he separated from his partner.

A few fathers acknowledged that contact might need to be restricted or prevented where children had been 'seriously abused', but rarely viewed their own behaviour as falling into this category. This is illustrated in Jeremy's account, where he begins by acknowledging that unsupervised contact may not be appropriate where there is child abuse, but then goes on to qualify this, perhaps because he realised that his own violent behaviour might be construed as abuse:

> Q: "What are your views about violent fathers having contact?"

> J: "It depends if the father has been involved in child abuse [pause] – in extreme abuse – physical torture and burning or sexual molestation."

Bill, who had earlier acknowledged that he had been cruel towards his children, also saw sexual abuse as one circumstance where contact might be supervised, but he did not view it as a reason for a complete denial of fathers' rights:

> "If there's genuine feeling there and the father wants to see them and they haven't been a child molester or something like that – but I would be loathe to see a father denied the right to see his children – possibly with a third party or something."

A few of these fathers acknowledged that children should be given a choice about whether they wanted contact, but only when they were teenagers and not when they were younger.

Responsible fatherhood

Some fathers drew on a discourse of 'responsible fatherhood,' arguing that they were being 'good and responsible fathers' by seeking contact and failing to acknowledge that they had already demonstrated their 'irresponsibility' through their violence and abuse, and that children might have their own views in this matter. Few fathers elaborated on the notion of responsibility, however, with some simply echoing the common discourse promoted in family law, as in Pete's account that a 'child needs both parents'. Pete also stressed that it was a father's right to choose not to see the children:

> "The father may decide he doesn't want to see his children. That is one thing. I think it's the child's right to see their father. I also think it's the father's right to see the child."

Jeremy, drawing on the discourse of fathers as role models, argued that fathers' contact was necessary, because children needed to learn about the 'differences between men and women' and, in a bizarre ironic twist, he suggested that his two teenage daughters had benefited from living with his violence towards their mother because they had 'learnt that there is violence in the world.'

In the name of love

As with non-violent fathers, discourses of love and the idealisation of children's love were significant to violent fathers as reasons for wanting contact (Lupton and Barclay, 1997). Yet for these fathers, such discourses had very different meanings from what might be conventionally understood as an unselfish emotional commitment to children's wellbeing. For instance, while some stated that they wanted contact because of children's love for them, it did not seem to occur to them that children's own feelings might have been affected by their violence and abuse and that they might not want to see them because of this.

Several fathers also regarded children's love as being 'unconditional'. As Bill put it, "It's about love – you can't get love like that from anyone else," and Dave said, "It's because of the unconditional love they give you, it's one of the most important things in life." Yet both these fathers had indicated in their accounts that they regarded the children as a nuisance prior to separation. Dave, for example, had admitted that he had physically abused one of the children and had preferred to work on the garden rather than be with his three-year-old daughter and seven-year-old stepson. Furthermore, although he admitted that they were reluctant to come for contact and 'cried and screamed' at contact handover, he preferred to explain this in terms of 'the manipulations' of his ex-partner and her 'insecurity' and 'jealousy'.

Other fathers such as Matt and Jeremy felt that a father's love for the children cancelled out any violence and abuse they might be responsible for and that such love justified contact with the children.

But, as Bancroft and Silverman (2002) have noted, in both these types of discourse children are perceived as some kind of emotional property that exists only for fathers' emotional benefit and fathers' love is a form of power over children. The fathers' perceptions of a child's love may also be used as a form of power against mothers and some fathers' accounts in the current study suggested that the children loved them more than their mothers and regarded themselves as in competition with mothers for children's love.

Only one father in this study, John, acknowledged that his violent and abusive behaviour had destroyed any affectionate relationship with his children and he understood why they did not want to have contact with him. In talking about his then 15-year-old daughter, for example, he said, "I think it was because I hurt her so much and because of the violence and what happened between me and her Mum."

However, another father, Max, admitted that his relationship with his older children from his first family had been affected by his further violence towards his second partner, when he threatened to stab her with a knife and throw her out of the house:

> "Well the upshot of this is that my children [from his first family] got to hear that I'd actually assaulted [X]. I had told them we'd split up – I hadn't told them that I'd assaulted her. My daughter [aged 11] was very quiet but my son [aged 15] wouldn't come out with me – he went down to the bottom of the garden and started smashing things up."

Most fathers, however, dismissed children's fears of them while promoting their own sense entitlement to contact, even when, in Simon's case, his four-year-old daughter asked him if he was going to kill her mother during her first contact visit. Other fathers described children's reluctance to have contact with them as being caused by mothers' undue influence, rather than recognising it as the consequence of their own behaviour.

Fathers' abusive care in contact situations

At the time of interviews, fathers had various forms of contact. Some fathers stated that because the children were of an age when they could choose whether or not they wanted contact (usually when they were 11 or older), they saw the children infrequently. In the case of fathers with much younger children, it was clear that initial contact had been limited and often informally supervised, particularly where child abuse had been identified by child protection agencies. Some of these fathers were still having limited contact, which could take place at the mother's or grandparents' home, although this did not necessarily mean that these children were safe from abuse and some had clearly witnessed further violence towards their mothers during this contact as indicated in the father's accounts. In a few of these cases, however, fathers' contact had progressed to having children to visit their homes or to stay overnight, and in these situations children could be still perceived as provoking fathers' abuse.

Tom, for example, initially described how he had intimidated his children because they were constantly badgering him for attention and had indicated that one of his daughters had had 'catatonic states' as a direct consequence of his behaviour. However, although the children had only just started staying overnight, he still found himself 'losing patience' and 'the same patterns of abuse coming back' when the children woke up too early and made demands on him. At the same time, he justified his ongoing contact with them on the grounds that he was 'entitled to put himself right'. Dave also described continuing difficulties looking after his two children for five hours a week: "When a child is crying and you have a short fuse like I have, what do you do?"

Using children as weapons against mothers

Despite acknowledging that he had difficulties in controlling his abuse, Dave stated that he had told the children that he wanted more contact and he would have their mother sent to prison unless she agreed to overnight visits. Dave seemed totally unconcerned about the impact of such a threat on his two young children and this is best illustrated in a mother's account:

> "Coming back from contact they are very quiet – they don't speak. It was after a few days they started saying he's told them mummy will go to prison if they don't go – Since they've known they are going for staying contact, Jane [the older child] has asked me what should they do when they wake up – should they stay in the bedroom? I say she should ask him and she says, 'I'm too frightened, I'm too scared to ask him.' He's not hitting them – he's a control freak – he doesn't have to say anything – he only has to look and it's the tone of his voice – he knows they are terrified of him – Jane is now crying all the time and abusing herself, she rubs herself and is very sore and won't sleep. I stay up till

11 or 12 o'clock reading to her because she won't sleep."
(Tina, describing the impact of continuing emotional abuse
on her seven-year-old daughter)

Other fathers described deliberately insulting mothers in front of the
children during contact visits in order to get back at them, without
any consideration of how this might be perceived by the children
themselves. Collin even dismissed the idea that such behaviour could
have an impact on his children, aged four and seven:

> Q: "Have you said things to the children about their
> mother?"
>
> C: "Yeah – I've said she's no good; that she's got other
> boyfriends."
>
> Q: "How do you think they feel about that?"
>
> C: "They don't know the truth, do they? They're just
> listening to me spouting rubbish from their point of view
> – they're just thinking I'm not a nice person saying things
> about their mum – you see I'll say anything because I know
> I can get back at her."

There were many examples of this type of emotional abuse of children
and its impact is illustrated in the mothers' accounts, where women
described their concerns about children having contact with violent
fathers. Pat recounted the severe effect on her five-year-old son of the
father's emotional abuse during 18 months of regular staying contact,
which led to a child psychologist being appointed by the child's school
to assess his difficulties. The psychologist diagnosed the child as being
depressed and having various behavioural and stress-related problems,
including constant bedwetting and attention deficit disorder, as a direct
result of what his father was telling him when he went for weekly
overnight staying contact. The child also regularly kicked and hurt
other children at school. Pat said:

> "He was telling him, mummy's a liar and don't believe a
> thing she says – she's a thief and she stole your Christmas
> stocking and daddy's house is better than mummy's and
> you're going to live at daddy's soon anyway – because
> when you lose a mummy it's not so bad, because sometimes

mummies die. And you can misbehave here and what you do here you can do at your mum's house and kick your friends."

Fathers' 'needs' and neglect of children during contact

Fathers' focus on contact as a means to meet their own needs rather than those of their children and to get back at their partners was apparent when they were asked what they felt they had to offer children during contact visits. Some of those who had had contact for short periods of time and were seeking more contact said they had never really thought about it, but for most, this question was met with silence. This was further illustrated by Collin, who was in the process of applying for contact through the family courts, after his ex-partner had stopped the current contact arrangement, because of his further violence towards her.

> Q: "What does being a father mean to you?"

> C: "Satisfaction, happiness, security, wellbeing, I feel good, I feel proud, I feel I can do anything in the world."

> Q: "So the kids give *you* security?"

> C: "Yes, I feel I can do anything in the world and land on top – it would benefit the whole family."

> Q: "So what will you do with the children when they come for contact?"

> C: [Silence]

Only one father, Max, said that he tried to address the interests of his older children, aged 11 and 13, during contact visits, although his arrangements were compromised by his continuing violence.

Unsurprisingly, mothers' accounts were far more explicit about how children's needs and interests were neglected during contact visits, as they had to deal with the consequences when the children were returned. As in earlier research (Radford et al, 1999), mothers described babies and toddlers as having their basic physical care needs neglected, with infants being returned in unchanged nappies and in soiled clothes covered in excrement. One mother, Fiona, related how, until contact was stopped by the family courts, her ex-partner used to take her two daughters to the pub all day and returned them crying and vomiting because their father was driving dangerously drunk. Tina described how her young children, aged four and seven, were sat in front in the television for five hours and told not to move while their father went to sleep on the sofa. Since the children were extremely afraid of their father, they were too frightened to move or to wake him up.

Susan related how her ex-partner refused to take her two sons to their football activities despite this being a condition of the contact order. At the same time, he continued to intimidate and humiliate all three children in different ways. This behaviour had such serious effects on the children over a period of two years that at the time of interview their contact was being reassessed by social services. The youngest child, then aged nine, was also being psychologically assessed because he was still soiling and wetting himself and was too frightened to sleep on his own. He was refusing to eat as a consequence of repeatedly being told by his father that he was too fat (a form of humiliation that had also been persistently used against his mother). The oldest child, a daughter then aged 15, whom the mother suspected was being sexually abused by her father, was described as having uncontrollable rages and had physically attacked the mother with a pair of scissors and was repeatedly violent to the other children. The middle child, then aged 11, had written a letter to the social worker that was shown to the author during the research. It stated: "I get scared when my dad gets angry, because I know what he has done to me and my mum, when he gets angry."

Margaret described the long-term effects on her 19-year-old daughter of several years' contact with her controlling and aggressive father. The daughter was significantly 'depressed' and on anti-depressants as a result of her father's abuse. Margaret talked of the father's behaviour in the following terms:

> "His view of being a father is telling everyone what to do and a father hits everyone if they don't do what they are told – a father has control of everyone and who they can and can't be friends with and what they can do with their lives and what they can't do with their lives and far as he is concerned his word is law."

Mothers' struggle for recognition of ongoing harm to children during child contact

In contrast to the fathers' accounts, which emphasised how the family courts had supported them in obtaining contact, mothers' accounts illustrated how they struggled to get the courts and child contact centres to address their concerns when it became clear that children were continuing to be harmed during contact with fathers. Most mothers had initially agreed to contact and like some professionals 'hoped' that fathers would become better parents because of this. As Susan stated:

> "When I first filed for divorce I thought my ex-partner would become a normal parent and we could discuss contact between us and he would have regular contact with the children. It was only afterwards I knew that this could not happen and that contact with the children was traumatic for them."

Other mothers related how they tried to be supportive of contact, despite having some concerns about what was happening to their children. Pat, for example, in describing her first son's initial contact, said:

> "I had hoped that at least his father would have to get to know him. John didn't want to go at first. He used to scream and run into other people's houses when his dad's car arrived outside. He would say, 'I don't want to go mummy – I don't want to go.' I didn't realise at the time, but I used to put him the car and say, 'Have a nice time. You'll have a great time at daddy's.'"

Where contact took place at contact centres and mothers raised concerns about children being harmed, centre workers preferred to believe fathers' accounts, as has been seen in other research (Aris et al, 2002; Harrison, 2006). One mother, Aisha, who had described to a centre worker how the father had snatched her two-year-son away from her and just driven off, received the response 'Oh, you just don't want him to have contact.' She was only taken seriously later when the father had been directly violent and threatening towards the worker herself.

Mothers described judges as being particularly reluctant to change fathers' contact orders, even where there was substantial evidence of direct harm to children from independent psychologists' reports and where the child welfare report recommended no contact. In Pat's case, where the child psychologist had found substantial harm to her five-year-old son as a result of the father's continuing emotional abuse, the judge merely told the father not to make inappropriate comments to the child and allowed contact to continue as before. Even where courts had accepted that contact needed to be supervised because of a serious risk of sexual abuse, or, as in Aisha's case, because the father's continued and extreme controlling behaviour was deemed to be harmful to the two-year-old child, judges were only prepared to stop contact after considerable periods of observed supervised contact during which these very young children continued to be harmed. In the case of Aisha's child, it was only after the father had attended a perpetrator programme and the programme leader gave a report to the court about the father's unwillingness to change that contact was stopped. In another case, Jean's three-year-old daughter experienced two years of sexual grooming at a supervised contact centre by the violent father before the judge finally made a finding of fact of sexual abuse and limited contact to twice a year under heavy supervision, which the father chose not to take up. She stated:

> "Throughout this time the father was observed by contact centre workers as engaging in sexual 'grooming' behaviour with the child, when he played with her. [I was told] he was being very 'physical' with her and getting her to jump on top of him and lie on top of him. He would also hold her between her legs. One time when they were in the garden he had her head on his groin and her legs in his face and he was always trying to play with her where the other workers couldn't see what he was doing – the workers who were observing him recorded details and also this was observed by several court welfare officers. My court welfare officer said in court that this was typical grooming behaviour by abusers and [it] concerned them greatly."

Conclusion

One of the arguments for children's continued contact with fathers in psychological discourses is that children need a fathers' love and that this is important to children's emotional development, particularly when the children are very young (Sturge and Glaser, 2000). Yet, as the accounts of these violent fathers illustrate, although they may have desired a loving relationship with their children (see Perel and Peled, 2008) for the most part their concepts of love were bound up with their own needs, rights and privileges as fathers and a failure to prioritise children's feelings and needs, leading to further harm. Moreover, because some fathers regarded children as their possessions, it did not matter that children were fearful of them or that they continued to abuse them during contact visits. It was also clear that in many cases fathers' reasons for having contact were connected with their desire to get revenge on the mothers and they were prepared to use and abuse the children in this process, as illustrated in the mothers' accounts.

Mothers' accounts also indicated that regular ongoing contact with their children did not serve to improve violent fathers' parenting but provided a context where children continued to experience prolonged abuse that could have long-term effects on their wellbeing. Yet when they took steps to try to safeguard their children and reported continuing harm, professionals often preferred to believe fathers rather than mothers. This suggests that fathers' views are more valued than those of mothers in social and legal discourses, as indicated in earlier research (Cavanagh et al, 2001; Radford and Hester, 2006).

Note

[1] A short description of the methods can be found in Appendix 1. For a fuller description of the methodology, see Harne (2005).

FIVE

Rehabilitating violent fathers

Introduction

As seen in Chapter Three, perpetrator programmes for domestically violent men in the UK have regarded increasing children's safety as one of the aims of their work (Respect, 2004) and this was the case in relation to the programmes the fathers were attending in this study. This chapter therefore discusses the approaches of these projects in addressing children's safety in their interventions with violent fathers. It also looks at how far these informed fathers' views of change in their parenting practices in the context of their violence and abuse.

This is not, however, an evaluation of how effective the different programmes were in addressing violent fathering and children's safety overall, as this would have required different research methods[1]; rather, the research findings discuss the impact of the programmes on the fathers' accounts and raise a number of questions and issues in this regard.

Background to the programmes

The four programmes involved in the study comprised two voluntary sector programmes (V1 and V2) and two probation-led programmes (P1 and P2). The main difference between these two types of programme were the conditions of admittance, with the probation-led programmes usually only admitting men who had been convicted by a criminal court, or men who had come out of prison on licence. All four projects had forms of pre-assessment where the men were expected to acknowledge some level of wrongdoing and willingness to change before being accepted on a programme. In the case of men on probation, the assessment was carried out at pre-sentence report stage, but as one probation-led project manager (N1) emphasised, 'realistically this was often at a minimum level'.

Programmes approaches

A major part of the programmes' work was addressing men's violence towards partners/ex-partners, with the aim of reducing or preventing further physical violence in the early stages of attendance. One programme (V1) also stated that it was important to address sexual violence at this stage. In the later stages, the programmes aimed to address controlling behaviour and other forms of abuse. All four programmes took a similar approach to addressing men's violence through the use of cognitive-behavioural group work, overlaid with a gendered analysis addressing perpetrators' assumptions of dominance over women and attitudes of entitlement. Within this work, the aims were to use cognitive restructuring to broaden the participants' definitions of what constitutes violence and enable them to take responsibility and recognise the intentionality of their violence, as well as to develop empathy for partners' feelings and perspectives. Thus, programme materials indicated that work with the men in the early stages focused on getting them to expand their definitions of what counts as violence and looking closely at how they made decisions to be violent. Such learning often took place through re-enactments that were videoed and played back to the course participants for discussion. This could include addressing certain situations that might be perceived by the men as acting as 'triggers' for their violence and using behavioural techniques from social learning approaches such as 'time outs' when they felt they were about use violence.

The two voluntary sector programmes also included some individual counselling with perpetrators, with one programme (V2) providing extensive counselling from a psychodynamic perspective over an eight- to 12-week period before the group-work programme started. Commenting on this in his interview, the programme leader stated that in his view the men needed to 'connect with their underlying feelings and emotions before they could develop empathy for victims and change their attitudes'.

Another variation was in programme length. Three programmes involved two stages, the first to address the physical violence and the second to focus on other forms of abuse and control. The programmes lasted 26 weeks, 32 weeks and 56 weeks, respectively (the latter being the psychodynamic programme, which included the eight individual counselling sessions). The fourth, probation-led, project lasted only 10 weeks. This was in the process of being extended to 20 weeks, as it was recognised that 10 weeks was too short to address aspects of perpetrators' abusive and controlling behaviour over and beyond their physical violence.

All the programmes stated that their priority was the safety of women and children, and for this reason they all aimed to provide a support service for mothers and to offer the women information on the men's progress. However, only the two voluntary-sector programmes sought feedback from mothers and emphasised that they assessed whether a perpetrator's attendance on the programme would increase safety risks, with one programme saying that it was in contact with 90 per cent of women partners. Nevertheless, in the second programme (V2), the women's support service was not functioning at the time of interview.

One of the probation-led programmes (P1) was in the process of trying to improve its support service for women and its exchange of information about perpetrators, and the other, most recently established, programme had not yet established its women's support service.

Children's safety

All four programmes saw addressing men's violence towards mothers as an important factor in increasing children's safety. However, they also aimed to address children's safety specifically, usually through sessions on how fathers' violence affected children and in some cases through separate sessions on parenting. The way the programmes dealt with fathers' contact with children post-separation was one indication of how far they prioritised the safety of children. At the time that this research took place, none of the programmes said that participants had been referred from child protection services, although the two voluntary sector programmes stated that they were beginning to change their practice in this area. The two voluntary sector programmes indicated that they specifically admitted men referred to them from the family courts in child contact cases, and would undertake risk assessments for the courts regardless of whether a perpetrator attended a programme. However, it was apparent that these two projects took very different approaches to the issue of contact in their risk assessments. In the case of V2, the project leader stated that the programme would generally recommend supervised contact where there were concerns about children's safety, while in the case of V1, contact would not be supported if there were safety risks and programme workers would take on board mothers' views about this:

> "Clearly we would say that child contact would be inappropriate if it is unsafe for the child and the mother

and our point of view would be that safety overrides the rights of the child for contact. We would also question the usefulness of contact in these situations. Any risk assessment we do is on a very objective basis where safety comes over and above contact – we have protocols around that. If we are in contact with the mother and she is opposing contact on the grounds of safety, we would write a report for her about her partner's history of violence for the court." (Programme worker, V1)

The work the programmes did with fathers on child contact was also approached differently, with one recognising that violent fathers' motivation for contact could be harmful for children and abusive when fathers were unable to prioritise children's needs:

"We look at how men may use children on separation and in relation to contact, and the appropriateness of chasing contact. We work with men to stop seeking contact where their motivation is about control. If men already have contact we get them to look at doing it less abusively and more positively – so that they can separate their own needs from those of the child." (Programme leader, V1)

The other voluntary sector programme supported violent fathers seeking contact through a discourse of responsible fatherhood, although it was recognised that contact should be supervised if there were significant child protection concerns. In this approach, the focus was on fathers being responsible for children and an assumption of optimism that they would be prepared to prioritise children's needs. Fathers were viewed as needing to make reparation to children and take responsibility by supporting their ex-partners in their mothering role.

"Our position would be that the safety of the mother and children is the priority and the men recognise as far as the children are concerned that they are responsible for the children and not the other way round ... and that's very effective because other men really support that ... and there's a very strong sense that you are there for your children and it's not okay to use your children to even actually see your partner, that's quite a strong position. I think the group is very valuable on that, because they reinforce that that's the way it should be." (Programme worker, V2)

However, there appeared to be a lack of recognition in the programme's approach that children who had lived with their fathers' violence and abuse might not have loving feelings towards them, and a minimisation of children's safety in their approach to child contact, as seen in the following quote.

> "The other thing we put emphasis on though, is that from the child's point of view both parents are *lovable,* so it's not very good for the child, if he's being at all negative about his partner – the child already has to deal with his behaviour, but some of his reparation is to start to recognise that – so whatever relationship he formally has with the child he is supporting the child's mum – and the need to recognise that the mum is liable [for the child] and the father is supporting that too – so we put that very much in the frame." (Programme worker, V2)

The probation-led programmes stated that they did not carry out formal risk assessments in relation to child contact, but the leader for one programme (P1) indicated that they did do reports for the family courts, if requested, after or during a father's attendance on a programme. Several of these had recommended that the fathers concerned were not yet ready for contact.

Parenting

All the programmes undertook some group work with the perpetrators on parenting, with the shortest probation-led programme (P2) devoting one session to the impact of domestic violence on children, during which it showed a video on children's perspectives. The other probation-led programme (P1) put considerable emphasis on parenting issues, and ran five sessions in conjunction with a voluntary sector children's agency, four in the first and one in the second stage of the programme. Topics covered in these sessions included looking at children's experiences of domestic violence; looking at specific offences where children had been involved; looking at what children need; the negative experiences that perpetrators had brought into their lives and how they can improve; and how children are affected by violence at different stages of childhood including pre-birth. The sessions also involved role-play exercises on 'responsible parenting', where the violent fathers acted out various common scenarios based on children's own perspectives. These exercises could cover scenarios such as 'Sometimes when daddy comes home, I am afraid for mummy and for myself' and 'When my dad takes me out, he will talk about mummy and is not interested in me.'

One of the voluntary sector programmes (V1) ran three separate sessions on parenting in the second stage of its programme. These addressed men's direct physical abuse of children in the context of 'discipline' and parenting and childcare issues more broadly. This was the only programme that stated that it dealt with violent fathers' possible sexual abuse of children. The other voluntary programme (V2) did not run separate sessions on parenting but integrated parenting issues throughout, in line with the 'responsible fathering' approach indicated above. The programme worker interviewed stated that a number of participants had been violent towards their children 'often in the context of discipline' and that this was therefore an issue that was addressed specifically:

> "We talk about why it doesn't work and connect it to what they are doing to their partners; that works very well – as a group they are very receptive, because for a lot of them it's a struggle about 'How do I deal with this – how do I deal with this without hitting them, what can I do?' so it has a very practical application."

These programmes therefore presented a mixed picture of practices relating to children's safety where violent fathers were concerned. There were differences in priorities in relation to children's safety in the child contact context and how far the programmes understood the impact of fathers' violence in relation to children's fears and fathers' unwillingness to separate their own needs from those of children. In this regard, two programmes referred to 'responsible father' approaches, but the meanings given to these were very different, with one programme (P1) aiming to enable violent fathers to recognise children's feelings and views and the other (V2) regarding 'responsible fatherhood' as fathers making reparation through having or seeking contact, supporting mothers and assuming that children would still have 'lovable' feelings towards them. This programme also appeared to take an over-optimistic view of violent fathers being able to prioritise children's needs and not using the children as weapons against mothers. This is discussed in more depth below.

There was also some recognition that violent fathers may abuse children directly, although this was largely limited to physical abuse within a discourse of fathers' responsibility for discipline. Yet many of the fathers' accounts in this research indicated that, rather than abuse being about 'discipline' per se, abusive behaviour occurred when fathers were looking after children and the children 'provoked' them. There was also far less recognition of harmful and abusive parenting more broadly when fathers were caring for very young children, particularly in relation to direct emotional cruelty and abuse, and neglect and failure to prioritise children's needs. Moreover, only one programme (V1) recognised the interconnections between a father's domestic violence and possible sexual abuse of children.

Programme effectiveness: monitoring and evaluation

Projects monitored perpetrators' violence towards women throughout their attendance on programmes, using tools such as perpetrators' self-reports, although, as recognised in Chapter Three, these are not particularly reliable in monitoring or assessing actual change. Those programmes that had contact with partners and ex-partners included feedback from them in their monitoring of the men's behaviour.

Since in their interviews eight fathers had admitted to intimidating and being 'seriously' physically violent towards partners or ex-partners while attending their programme, programme workers were asked what happened when this occurred. This varied from project to project and depended on the type of offence. One probation project worker (P1) stated that men would be retained in the programme, unless they had been remanded in custody. In one of the voluntary sector projects (V2), the programme leader said that men who had not been ordered by the courts to attend the programme would be retained as long as they had been 'engaging' with the work of the project and 'recognised what they had done', subject to certain conditions like 'staying away' from their (ex-)partner. Some fathers would also have to repeat the programme. In this project, women might be supported to take out a civil injunction or to make a complaint to the police, but it was emphasised that at that time the response of local criminal courts was poor and perpetrators might only receive a fine in these circumstances, so women often saw little benefit in pursuing criminal charges even where there was sufficient evidence to prosecute.

It was less clear how far children's safety was being specifically monitored, or if it was being monitored at all, particularly in relation to harmful parenting practices where fathers were still living, or had contact, with children. This was an issue that was raised by the researcher with the relevant programmes and there was an acknowledgement that there was a need for an improved focus on children's safety in this area.

Two programmes (V1 and P1) had also undertaken, or were in the process of undertaking, long-term evaluations with men who had completed programmes. These evaluations focused on assessing any reduction in violence towards women and although they also encompassed children's safety in cases where they were being exposed to violence, they did not address children's safety in relation to changes in harmful and abusive parenting. Further, V1 was the only programme to have instigated an evaluation by external assessors where women's views on the reduction of violence had been sought. In P1, the evaluation was an internal one, looking at reoffending rates in terms of the reporting of further violence. The leader of this programme acknowledged that this was not a reliable measure of change, because domestic violence offending is considerably under-reported by victims.

The recently established probation-led programme (P2) had not yet considered long-term evaluation. The other voluntary sector programme (V2) raised issues concerning problems with evaluating and measuring 'success', particularly in terms of considering in isolation the reduction of physical violence towards women. It described the biggest difficulty as being able to develop fathers' empathy for their victims. In talking about this the programme worker said:

> C: "It depends what you mean by success. I would certainly say the men change for the better – whether they change enough for the better, without more in-depth research is unanswerable. But across the spectrum from the guys who are really quite domineering and chauvinistic to the guys who aren't generally that way but are still violent and abusive, even [they] have little sense of who she [the partner/ ex-partner] is as a person in her own right. She's important to them only in terms of what they can get from her – so the idea of her existing as a person with feelings and how she might feel is surprisingly absent."

> L: "That's interesting because a lot of them talk about children in those terms as well."

> C. "Yes – children aren't there for you, you're there for them. You might get things from them - that's secondary, that's by the bye."

This extract illustrates the unwillingness of violent fathers to consider the feelings, needs and interests of significant others that has been highlighted in the practice literature. It also pinpoints the difficulties for programmes in achieving changes in attitudes that are highly significant in relation to increasing the safety and wellbeing of both children and mothers.

Violent fathers' accounts of change

One of the problems in analysing the impact of interventional programmes on violent fathers is that their own accounts are very unreliable as indicators of any real change in their views and perceptions, let alone changes in their actual behaviour. The contradictory nature of their accounts also makes it difficult to analyse any change. This study attempted to assess the impact of the programmes on the fathers' views and perceptions by analysing their accounts to try to gain a picture of change and what this might mean for children's safety. It found that fathers' views were not homogenous, and this did not appear to relate to how long fathers had been on the programmes, but rather to their own personal insights and how they had interpreted the programme content, as well as their own personal circumstances and willingness to change.

Resentment and rejection of programme content

Four fathers expressed extreme resentment about being on a programme. These were all fathers who had been mandated by the criminal courts and were participating in probation-led projects, although other fathers who had also been mandated did not express such views. The resentful fathers frequently argued that they had been wrongfully convicted or that their violence towards mothers was so minor it was not significant enough to require them to attend a programme. As a consequence, their resentment appeared to fuel wholesale rejection of the programme content. For example, one father, Geoff, who had been attending a programme for 32 weeks, said he did not understand why he was on it. When asked if he had learnt anything, he replied: "All I've ever done is love, care and provide for the whole family and if that's wrong then I'm guilty."

Collin, who had been attending a programme for 24 weeks and was on a further charge for assaulting his ex-partner at the time of interview, responded by stating what he had learnt about other men's violence:

> "My problem is more – it's nothing to do with actually beating her up – mine is down to verbal more than anything.

> So I've come here and had my eyes opened about what does happen in relationships and other people's convictions far worse than mine. I know mine sounds worse, but it's just the tip of iceberg compared to other people's."

These responses raised questions about whether the programmes were having any impact on these fathers in terms of changing their attitudes and behaviour.

Changed understandings or 'talking the talk'

In looking at whether fathers' understandings had changed in a positive sense as a consequence of programme intervention, one of the main problems for the researcher was assessing whether fathers were just using the language and concepts they had learnt – in other words, 'talking the talk' or 'spinning' different stories about their behaviour. As seen in Chapter Four, some of these fathers were able to use techniques learnt on programmes, such as conceptualising their violence as part of an overall pattern of 'controlling behaviour', but, while using the language they had learnt, they might also resist acknowledging such control through the use of justifications. This was illustrated in Brian's account of his violence where he talked about having a 'controlling problem' but went on to justify his control anyway, because his partner was not doing enough housework and childcare.

On the other hand, some fathers talked in a more self-reflective way about the impact of their violence. Jeremy, for example, who had been attending a programme for about eight months, talked about his violence towards his partner and his 'dominant' behaviour in the family home in the following terms:

> "I thought the only thing she had to be afraid of before was the violence, but I understand now, it's not just the violence, it was the domination and control and not having the freedom to make her own mind up."

However, this understanding did not extend to why his partner and children were still frightened of him when they initially fled the family home. He seemed to be more focused on his own needs and feelings:

> "I hadn't been violent for a long time [this later turned out to be a few weeks], but she wouldn't let me in and the girls were screaming upstairs. That really hurt me. I don't

understand why she wouldn't let me in and she won't discuss it."

Similarly, Matt, who was one of two fathers who had returned to live with his partner, felt that being on a programme for 24 weeks had lessened his physical violence towards the mother of his two young daughters. But he also seemed unaware how he was shifting his abuse to more emotional forms with no thought about how this might affect the children, as illustrated in the following extract:

> "If it wasn't for this programme. I would be getting done for domestic violence ... she's moaning [his partner] and she's tired from getting up in the morning with the kids and I'm not sleeping and it does get my back up and I count to 10 and it doesn't work and I count to 10 again and I make a joke with the baby [aged three], *I say, 'She* [the mother] *is going round the twist."* [his emphasis]

Violence and its impact on children

Eight fathers stated that the programmes had made them aware or more aware of the impact of their violence on children. However, as seen in the previous chapter, the men frequently minimised the impacts and gave them little significance. Jeremy was one of a very few fathers who said that the programme had helped him acknowledge the extent of his children's fears:

> "They were frightened – frightened for their mother and for themselves. I feel sick about that now. I'm hoping it won't have a lasting effect. I'm hoping because they've seen that and learnt that there is violence in the world, but that they can see a change over the last few months."

Another father, Simon, who acknowledged that his violence had been so serious that he would have gone to prison if he had not agreed to attend a programme (P2), described how a particular session where participants had seen a video on children's perceptions of witnessing domestic violence had made him think about how his three children, who were all under five, must see it. This had made him 'more cautious' about what he said to the children about their mother when he had contact with them. On the other hand, he also minimised his four-year-old daughter's fears that he was going to 'kill her mother' when she saw him on one contact visit and felt that she would soon get over this.

Significantly, a few fathers attributed changed understandings, not only to the programmes but also to hearing the views of young people themselves. Bill, for example, said he had recently met up with his now adult daughter from his first marriage and she had told him how good she felt when he had left the family home and how it was 'the best thing that had ever happened'. Three other fathers with older children from first families stated that it was the children's refusal to see them that had made them think about the consequences of their behaviour, although contradictorily this understanding did not apply to second families.

Understandings of the impact of directly abusive parenting

Other fathers said they had become more aware of the impact of directly abusive behaviour towards children as a consequence of being on a programme, but still found it very difficult to change their behaviour. Tom, for example, who acknowledged that one of his very young daughters had been seriously affected and still had 'catatonic states', said that although he had 'learnt' that he should not shout at or intimidate his two young daughters, he still found himself 'doing it again' when they came for overnight staying contact.

Max talked about how the programme had made him question smacking his stepson in his second family, but his understanding seemed ambiguous to say the least:

> "I struggle with how hard to do it – am I going to really hurt him – am I going to break a limb? I would never use a weapon like my mum did with me, but then I laughed at her .... but I've come to a grey area now – because of the work I'm doing here – I don't think it's right, am I just teaching a child that I'm bigger and stronger than him?"

Four fathers described some change as a consequence of what they had learnt on the programme, such as not losing their tempers so much and not 'shouting' at children when they were in their presence or came on contact visits. Like Tom, however, they also talked about how 'difficult' they found it to stop this intimidatory behaviour. Three of these fathers talked about how the programme had challenged their own views that they 'were always right' and that, as a result, they sometimes allowed older children to have their own opinions (something they never would have allowed in the past). For example, Bill, who had stated that he believed that 'children should be seen and not heard', later said that he had realised that he needed to try to 'communicate with the children more' rather than just telling them to 'get out' of the room when they annoyed him during contact visits.

On the other hand, Dave, who had been on his programme for nine months and had admitted that his very young children were reluctant to have contact with him, argued that it was more a matter of being educated about children than of changing his own attitudes. He had also told the children that he would have their mother sent to prison if they did not allow more contact. Although he stopped making such threats when the programme leader told him 'it was not a good idea', there appeared to be no understanding of how these threats would be received by the children.

While these views indicated some limited changes in fathers' understandings as a consequence of being on a programme, they need to be seen in the context of their accounts as a whole, where, for the most part, fathers continued to blame both mothers and children for provoking abuse and demonstrated that they had given little thought to how the children might feel. These accounts therefore raised questions about whether the men had changed enough to have safe contact and whether the children themselves were gaining any benefit from such visits.

Contradictory programmes effects

Responsible fatherhood, reparation and child contact

The issue of children's safety and wellbeing and whether it was sufficiently addressed in the study programmes was particularly relevant to the programme V2, which viewed violent fathers' contact as a means of making reparation to children and supporting the mother's parenting. The fathers interviewed on this programme seemed to be far more focused on their own needs than on those of their children. Tom, for example, while admitting to behaviour that was harmful to his two very young daughters, still felt he should be allowed to 'make amends', despite his awareness that he was continuing to use harmful behaviour towards them. He said, "The violent partner needs to be given a chance to make amends and to put himself right ... just because he's made some mistakes he can still perform the role of the responsible and loving father."

Max was the only one who specifically dissociated himself from other fathers on this programme who appeared to be intent on using contact with the children against their mothers:

> "In our group meetings what's come across from the other guys is that their contact is mixed up with the issues they have with their partners, but that's not the issue for me. For me, my kids are the issue – it's my relationship with them, regardless of how their mum [his first partner] and me are getting on."

Resistance to change: violent fathers as victims

The lack of focus on children's own fears and feelings was also illustrated by several fathers who perceived themselves as 'the victims who needed help'. These were all fathers who were attending the programme which included a psychodynamic approach (V2).

Two of these fathers said that they had learnt that domestic violence was 'a cry for help' and both felt that if their own older daughters got together with violent partners, their main advice would be 'to get the violent partner to seek help' rather than report them to the police or seek other protection. Another father, Phil, illustrated the 'perpetrator as victim' discourse in relation to child contact, as seen in the following extract:

> Q: "Do you think there any circumstances when fathers shouldn't have contact?"
>
> P: "If there's been sexual abuse – but then from the work we have done here, which is teaching us not to be judgemental and to view perpetrators of that sort of abuse as victims as well who need help, I would say no, I can't think of any circumstances."

While the programme worker for this project stated that the programme did not support child contact where there had been sexual abuse, this father's view does raise concerns about the mixed messages that may be conveyed when programmes encourage perpetrators to focus on their 'own pain'. Although the stated aim of this approach is to enable perpetrators to develop empathy for their victims, the opposite seemed to be the case for some of these fathers.

On a more general level, as others have noted (Adams, 1988; Hearn, 1998a), such programmes may be regarded as support groups for violent men and may enable them to resist change through shared discourses of their own psychological victimisation. These discourses allow perpetrators to deny the intentionality of their violence and represent it as beyond their control by attributing it to some underlying emotional trauma. This was the explanation used by Pete, who had been attending a programme for more than six months:

> "It's such a relief to sit in a group of men that have experienced loss of ... [control] – for so many years I thought I was the only bloke who couldn't control his rage – I didn't see myself as psychotic or stupid, but my violence comes from moments of extreme emotional distress."

However, as seen in Chapter Four, discourses of victimisation through partner blame were common among the violent fathers and were one of the key means by which they resisted change, particularly to their own sense of dominance and entitlement to having their needs met by partners and children. Tony, who had been on his programme for 11 months, argued early on in his account that he was violent towards his partner because she had become pregnant when he did not want to be a father. He acknowledged that the programme had had some benefits for him but still blamed his partner for the violence because she would not live with him, saying:

> "It's teaching me a lot of things, like why I'm so frustrated with myself, like booze and drugs, don't help but I am still not there yet. But I want S [ex-partner] to live with me. I can't accept that she is not living with me. I resent her living on her own and being independent. She's very strong and I'm not included. She doesn't see us as a family – she sees the baby as hers."

In this extract, Tony not only fails to recognise the contradictory nature of his wish to be included in a family, when according to him not wanting to be a father had been the main reason for his violence, but also demonstrates a continuing focus on his own needs being met rather than on those of the mother and child.

Conclusion

These findings indicate that fathers have diverse responses to the content of perpetrator programmes and that they cannot be seen as a panacea in effecting change. All but two of the fathers (who had been on the shortest 10-week programme) had been attending programmes for six months or more and their accounts suggest that even where they may develop some limited understandings of the impact of their behaviour, it may take a very long time to ensure they are no longer a risk to children.

The fathers' accounts as a whole raised questions about programme content and particularly how far the programmes were able sufficiently to address harmful, abusive and neglectful parenting, and to what extent they recognised that perpetrators' sense of entitlement to having their own needs met often extended to their own children and integrally informed their own parenting practices, including using the children as objects to get back at mothers (Bancroft and Silverman, 2002). Thus, as noted in the literature on Caring Dads (Scott, 2004), violent fathering is not in the first instance about 'poor parenting' or violent fathers lacking 'parenting skills' on how to 'discipline' children without using physical abuse, but rather about their own attitudes towards children and failure to see them as persons in their own right with their own feelings and needs.

Individual programme approaches also raised questions about whether programmes were primarily considering children's safety. This was particularly so in those programmes where violent fathers were seen 'responsible' in seeking contact with their children, and where fathers' own parenting practices and their attitudes towards their children were not being adequately assessed and children's own fears and views of their fathers not taken into account. This is discussed further in Chapter Six.

Note
[1] This would require seeking the views of mothers and children, as well as making a comparison between fathers attending programmes and those not participating in such interventional projects.

SIX

The need for change

Although there is beginning to be some policy recognition of the problem of violent fathering, it is frequently in conflict with policies that promote the involvement of fathers in children's lives. Too often such policies are focused on fathers' needs rather than those of children. There is therefore an urgent requirement for change more broadly and at a number of different levels. This includes primary preventative measures, which in an era of social welfare cutbacks are likely to be more effective than those that aim to deal with harm to children after it has happened.

Children's welfare and safeguarding

First, at a very basic level there needs to be policy recognition that a significant minority of fathers may harm the children in their care and that far from benefiting them, some may have a detrimental effect on children's long-term welfare. This includes fathers who are domestically violent as well as substance abusers and those who engage in other forms of abuse. Rather than continuing with the current split constructions between fathers and domestically violent perpetrators, social policies need to name domestically violent men as fathers and acknowledge their harmful parenting practices. While there is a common understanding that some mothers may harm children, this recognition needs to be extended to fathers and take into account the fact that in the context of domestic violence fathers are more likely to pose the greatest risk, not only to mothers' parenting, but also to children themselves, as evidenced by the research discussed in this book. Therefore, instead of viewing domestic violence as a mutual problem between parents, its gendered power dynamics need to be recognised and violent fathers as primary perpetrators of harm to children identified. Too often policies in this area have reflected a gendered double standard of parenting, where abused mothers are blamed and violent fathers' parenting escapes scrutiny.

Social justice for children and their mothers

The empirical research discussed in this book indicates that violent fathers' sense of masculine privilege and entitlement to have their own needs met by children leads to abusive parenting and a failure to prioritise the needs of the child. These findings are in direct contradiction to policy claims that despite their violence towards mothers, violent fathers can still be good enough parents and that continuing relationships with them are essential to children's development. In this context, current psychological discourses of 'attachment' that argue that children need to have an emotional bond with a father can be dangerous when they are used to override the risks such fathers can pose to children's safety and welfare. This is particularly the case in terms of babies and very young children, who are at greatest risk of harm from abusive parenting by violent fathers. Research into older children's experiences demonstrates that many do not want ongoing relationships with these men and that coercing them into such relationships may compound their experiences of harm.

Such policies also raise crucial questions of ethics and social justice towards children and their mothers when violent fathers are rewarded for harming children and undermining mothers' parenting through being allowed child contact and shared parenting or, following their violence towards mothers during pregnancy, they are encouraged to engage in the birth and care of a newborn child. They convey strong cultural messages that men can continue to use violence against women with impunity, and contradict other preventative discourses that aim to challenge dominant and violent masculinities. Finally, the considerable cost of providing services to mothers, children and young people as a consequence of abuse by violent fathers should inform changes in policies to prevent these fathers having access to children in a number of different contexts.

Family law policies

Private family law policy and practice has been one of the key areas where mothers and children have suffered because of the presumption that contact with a non-residential father is nearly always in the child's best interests. It is underlined by assumptions that violent fathers can be safe as parents and that violence against mothers ceases on separation. However, legislative measures (2002 and 2006 Children and Adoption Acts) and practice directives have brought about some limited improvements, introducing screening for domestic violence with the police and social services and risk identification and assessment by family court advisers where such cases come before the courts. Nevertheless, it is often difficult for abused mothers to 'prove' that domestic violence has occurred unless the father has been convicted. Moreover, more weight may be given to fathers' statements when they deny that domestic violence has occurred or make counter-allegations of abuse against mothers. In these circumstances, there may be no welfare report and thus no opportunity for children's views to be heard or violent fathers' own parenting capacities to be assessed (Harne, 2009).

Yet even these limited safeguarding measures are being bypassed by the pressure, through massive cuts in the legal aid budget, to get parents to agree to arrangements for children without going to court. This has meant that many mothers and children experiencing domestic violence are unable to obtain legal advice to assist them in gaining safety. In addition, there have been huge cutbacks to the family court child welfare service Cafcass, affecting its ability to provide a safeguarding service to children (Guardian, 2010). Such developments have put mothers and children at increased risk and limited their access to social justice.

Current government proposals to enforce mediation on all separated parents to settle arrangements for children 'providing it is safe', following similar policy changes in Australia based on the demands of fathers' rights groups, are likely to further exacerbate the problem and redirect the costs to mediation services (DCSF, 2010). Compulsory mediation is also likely to remove opportunities for children's voices to be heard and their safety assessed.

In this context a change in policy to a legal presumption against violent fathers having contact or residence of their children could be a great improvement in safeguarding children and protecting their long-term welfare. It would also send a key message to violent fathers that their behaviour will be penalised. The New Zealand family law legislation, which has a presumption against unsupervised contact in the context of domestic violence and provides for a statutory assessment of risk, is perceived as providing greater protection for children at risk than the English law system, although it has encountered opposition, particularly from fathers' rights groups (Chetwin et al, 1999; Perry, 2006).

Nevertheless, the practice of supervised contact does not necessarily guarantee safety for children or their mothers, either when contact is taking place or in the long term, because violent fathers do not necessarily change their abusive parenting behaviour. Supervised contact as well as indirect contact by telephone or email may continue to allow for the continuing manipulation and emotional abuse of children by violent fathers, undermining their relationships with mothers, as well as in some cases grooming children for sexual abuse. A presumption against any contact in cases where fathers have been shown to be violent is therefore likely to provide much greater protection.

In the absence of this, assessing violent fathers' parenting becomes crucial in determining the risks to children and such assessments need to give sufficient weight to the views of children as well as those of abused mothers. This would require much greater investment in Cafcass as the family court's safeguarding service for both private and public law cases. Government should also provide a free legal advice service to abused parents and their children, so that they are aware of their rights to safety in family law policies.

Criminal justice and policing policy and practice

Although the number of policies that criminalise domestic violence has increased, they have not always improved safety for mothers and children in practice. While there has been some increase in the conviction rates, particularly where agencies work together in specialist domestic violence courts, sentencing policies and practices frequently convey messages that domestic violence is only a very minor offence, usually resulting at worst in a small fine and at best a possible requirement to attend a perpetrator programme. Where the violence is regarded as so serious as to require a custodial sentence, this can be reduced where the perpetrator/father claims his relationships with his children would be disrupted. Even where the violence perpetrated is such that fathers are sent to prison, contact with children is encouraged on the grounds that this meets fathers' needs. Overall, criminal justice should focus much more on prioritising children's and mothers' safety, both in sentencing and prison policy and practice, than excusing fathers' violence.

Problems have also been identified in policing practices, where some frontline police engage in advising victim/mothers and perpetrator/fathers at domestic violence incidents about children's 'rights' to contact, rather than considering the risks to children from perpetrators'/fathers' violence. In effect, such practices tend towards meeting the needs of perpetrators/fathers and may deter mothers from reporting domestic violence, because doing so can seem pointless if they do not obtain the appropriate protection for themselves and their children.

At the same time, when attending incidents of domestic violence the police are expected to undertake victim risk assessment and identify a primary perpetrator (ACPO, 2006, 2008). As a safeguarding agency, they must notify local authority children's social care services when children have been present at a domestic violence incident, and refer cases where the risk to children is identified as high.

Recent research, however, has indicated that children and young people are often ignored by frontline police officers at domestic violence incidents and are not perceived as victims in their own right. It identified a need for the police to give children information about what was happening and work more closely with other safeguarding agencies to identify specific risks to children (Stanley et al, 2009).

Child protection and safeguarding practices

There is a need for all safeguarding agencies to acknowledge that violent fathering poses considerable risks to children in its own right, since it is a form of emotional abuse of the child and leads to other aspects of fathers' abusive parenting. It also has the potential to undermine parenting by mothers. Repeated violence by fathers has a corrosive impact on children, leading to long-term harm, as highlighted in the Edlington case review in Chapter Two. At the same time, children can be traumatised through witnessing single events of severe physical or sexual violence or through the constant humiliation and emotional abuse of their mothers. In addition, ongoing violence is a key risk factor for other forms of harm to children, including physical and/ or sexual abuse. However, the focus of family system approaches on holding 'families' rather than individual parents responsible for harm to children can obscure individual violent fathers' responsibility for harm.

Maternity services and teenage pregnancy

There is an urgent need to change current maternity policies that encourage fathers in heterosexual relationships to participate in the prenatal care of the unborn child before mothers have been consulted about any experiences of domestic violence and/or other forms of risk from fathers such as substance abuse. This is essential in the case of teenage putative mothers, since young violent fathers pose the highest risk to unborn and newborn children (Ferguson, 2009). Enabling mothers to disclose incidents of domestic violence, however, requires understanding of its gendered power dynamics. In order to be effective and promote disclosure, screening needs to be undertaken in such a way that putative mothers are not blamed for the violence. A number of tools can be used for screening purposes, such as the power and control wheel highlighted in Chapter One and checklists of abusive behaviour (see Appendix 2), but a major priority is to train healthcare professionals in understanding men's abuse of women in intimate and familial relationships and its impact on children.

Those fathers identified through screening procedures as violent should be prevented from attending prenatal sessions and attending the child's birth, and should not be encouraged to participate in the baby's care. Assumptions that they can still be good enough parents, despite their violent behaviour towards mothers, only put both mother and child at much greater risk of harm. Children's centres should follow similar procedures.

Children's social care

As seen in Chapter Two, although children's social care has key responsibility for safeguarding children, child protection practices are highly variable in relation to violent fathering, characterised in some local authorities by a lack of assessment of fathers' parenting capacities and a failure to undertake basic screening checks with police or other services. Serious case reviews have repeatedly highlighted how the failure to identify violent fathers as primary abusers and assess their parenting has led to the physical abuse and neglect of children, resulting all too often in serious injury or death, or the killing of children during child contact. Assumptions that violent fathers are safe as parents just because children have not directly witnessed their violence or are too young to notice are no longer tenable in the face of such evidence and there is an urgent need for changes in training and practice in this area.

At the same time, a progress report by Lord Laming has identified that frontline social worker services are at breaking point, with 'low staff morale, poor supervision, high case loads and inadequate training' (Lord Laming, 2009, p 44). The children's social care profession therefore can no longer be treated as a 'Cinderella' service. There is a need for adequate investment in service provision and social work training, specifically in the area of gendered dynamics of domestic violence, in understanding the corrosive impacts a pattern of violence and coercive control can have on children and in understanding and identifying the role violent fathering plays in causing significant harm to children.

Risk identification and assessment

Risk identification and assessment of fathers' violence and coercive control is a useful tool in a variety of safeguarding and child welfare settings for identifying and informing professional judgements and actions necessary to safeguard children and mothers from immediate harm. Nevertheless they are no substitute for more comprehensive assessments of children's safety and welfare needs and should not be used as a means of directing resources only to those identified as very high risk. They are not accurate predictors of risk, but may inform the nature of danger to mothers and children based on past behaviour.

In identifying risks from violent fathers more broadly, a number of precautionary factors needs to be borne in mind. The following list of typical behaviours has been developed from the literature on violent fathers and the author's own research discussed earlier in the book:

- violent fathers tend to deny, minimise and justify their violent behaviour, or state that it is all in the past and that they have changed;
- they may be serial abusers, who have been violent in previous relationships;
- they may be highly manipulative and charming towards professionals;
- they frequently deflect blame by making counter-allegations of violence or abuse of children against mothers; blaming harm to children on mother's own behaviour and parenting; blaming mothers for provoking violence; or arguing that very young children have provoked abusive parenting practices by their own unreasonable behaviour;
- they frequently state that they love their children, are very proud of them and would never harm them;
- they may have learnt to 'talk the talk' while attending perpetrator or parenting programmes but do not necessarily show any change in their actual behaviour. Simple statements of a willingness to change are not sufficient to ensure that children will be safe in their care.

These behaviours indicate that violent fathers' accounts are unreliable indicators of the risk they pose to children or their parenting ability and that in carrying out risk assessments information must be taken from other sources, primarily mothers and children where appropriate. In seeking such information, it needs to be recognised that mothers often do not report fathers' violence to the police for a variety of reasons and where they do so, it is usually only after a large number of violent incidents or because they have been physically injured (Walby and Allen, 2004). Thus, although screening information from the police and police notifications may provide warning signs of serious and chronic violence, they exclude the majority of cases where violence has not been reported and give no indication of the level of risk or the extent of a father's *coercive control*. Furthermore, where mothers do disclose domestic violence, they are more likely to do so to other agencies such as health professionals or women's support services (Walby and Allen, 2004). In addition, professionals themselves need to guard against viewing fathers' accounts as more credible than those of mothers and/ or children on the spurious grounds that the latter are more likely to lie about abusive experiences Brown et al, 2000; Brown 2006).

Children's needs and parenting assessments

The types of assessment discussed above address the extent of fathers' violence and coercive control towards mothers and the immediate safety risks to mothers and children. They do not, however, address other parenting risks or the suitability of violent fathers as carers of children. These need to be assessed separately and can inform the long-term effects of harm. However, general assessments of parental capacity are not sufficient in assessing violent fathering, since they do not address violent men's own attitudes as parents and the way they view children. These attitudes are outlined in Chapter Three, but can be summarised as follows:

- a sense of entitlement to have their own needs met by the children;
- a lack of consideration for children's feelings and a tendency to dismiss children's own fears and the impact of their violence on them;
- a tendency to undermine the mother in front of the children and use them as weapon against her;
- a lack of consideration of children's own needs, including their basic care and welfare needs;
- a sense of ownership of the children, leading to risks of child abduction;
- excessive control of children, involving authoritarian and intimidatory parenting and neglect of developmental needs;
- emotional and psychological cruelty towards children;
- the overall risks of neglect, physical or sexual abuse and grooming of children.

It should also be recognised that babies, very young children and disabled children are at particular risk of harm from violent fathers and any consideration of fathers' contact in these circumstances should be weighed against these risks.

Since violent fathers frequently perform well during interviews, under observation and during supervised contact, their behaviour should not be assessed in this way. Information from mothers and significantly children themselves may be a better guide for assessment purposes, although it needs to be recognised that some children will be too fearful to disclose abusive parenting behaviour and some mothers may not be aware of fathers' directly abusive behaviour until separation.

The rehabilitative discourse and perpetrator programmes

A number of policy and practice discourses assume that the risks posed to children by violent fathers can be reduced or eliminated through identifying men's willingness to change and using rehabilitative measures to effect such changes. These measures include referrals to psychiatric services and anger management or perpetrator programmes. Expressing a commitment to change, however, does not mean that violent fathers will change or will be able to change enough to be safe with children, even where they attend a perpetrator programme (see Chapter Five).

Perpetrator programmes for domestically violent men are frequently seen as an all-embracing solution to rehabilitating violent fathers and making them safe to be with children. Yet the evidence is that over 50 per cent of perpetrators referred to programmes will drop out of or never attend them (Gondolf, 2004; Williamson and Hester, 2009). Those that do attend often demonstrate a sense of entitlement to have their own needs met and a failure to change sufficiently to prioritise children's needs and feelings, throwing into question their capabilities as parents and fitness to keep children safe (see Chapters Four and Five).

One of the key findings of the author's empirical research was fathers' persistent disregard of children's own fears of their violent behaviour while emphasising their own rights to contact, even though many acknowledged that their children were terrified of them. Further, even where fathers admitted that their own parenting behaviour was continuing to harm children, they still regarded their perceived rights or the need to make reparation as more important than children's rights to be free from harm.

The empirical research highlighted that perpetrator programmes can take very different approaches to fathering and children's safety and that children's safety is equally important as mothers' safety. While the programmes recognised that children's and mothers' safety are interconnected and that children experience harm when their mothers are harmed, in some programmes there was little acknowledgement that men's parenting practices can harm children directly and that these need to be monitored and assessed.

Although all of the programmes addressed aspects of parenting to some extent, they tended to focus on fathers' role in disciplining children rather than recognising that many fathers now engage in other aspects of childcare, thus providing further opportunities for abusive parenting through neglect, mental cruelty and sexual abuse (including grooming and exposure to pornography). These risks may be heightened in the context of child contact visits, where violent fathers are frequently the sole carers of children. Where programmes promoted discourses of responsible fatherhood whereby violent fathers should seek contact with children and make reparation, the focus was clearly on the emotional needs of the father rather than the emotional and safety needs of the child. It was also apparent that some violent fathers were manipulating group-work processes to resist change and were using children to get revenge on their mothers during contact visits by conveying abusive verbal messages about mothers to the children or threatening the children and it was unclear how far such behaviour was being addressed on the programmes.

The recently established Caring Dads programmes in a few areas of the country obviously focus on children's needs much more widely and in greater depth. But as with more generalist programmes, the question remains as to whether Caring Dads are able to change violent fathers enough to be safe to look after children in their care and promote their own development and wellbeing.

This research indicates that achieving such change depends as much on the motivations and individual insights and circumstances of different perpetrator fathers as on programme content and length. Change for those who have long histories of violence and abuse towards mothers and children can be very difficult, since their abusive behaviour towards partners and children has become a way of life and cannot be ignored or treated as irrelevant to the current situation. This book therefore makes the following recommendations in relation to perpetrator programmes, while recognising that some of these issues are already addressed in the national standards set by Respect (2010):

- Perpetrator and Caring Dads programmes should not be viewed by family courts or child protection agencies as a definitive solution to making violent fathers safe enough to parent, or have contact with, children.
- Assessment of violent fathers' parenting capacity should be added to risk assessments and assessments of violent fathers' capacity to change where requested by the family courts in relation to private law proceedings or by child protection agencies. Such assessments

should be independent of those relating to programme attendance and should include the views of children and those of abused mothers (where appropriate).

- Pre-attendance assessments of risk should include parenting assessments in order to take account of any direct risks to children.
- Contact with children should not be supported as part of a responsible father approach. Instead, programmes should discourage fathers from seeking contact until they have demonstrated through end-of-programme assessments that they are safe to see the children and that the children wish to see them.
- Children's safety must be given equal priority to that of mothers.

Whether this is done through existing generalist programmes addressing violent fathers' abusive parenting more comprehensively, or through Caring Dads schemes alongside or following programmes that address violence towards women, is a matter for further discussion and debate.

Conclusions

This chapter has summarised a number of policy and practice recommendations towards violent fathering based on the research and policy evidence discussed in this book with the aim of increasing the safety and wellbeing of children and recognise their own human rights to be protected from maltreatment by their parents and rights to be heard. Some of these proposals will be seen as controversial, as they impinge on perceived fathers' rights and challenge notions of equality in the 'new family', where parenting should purportedly be shared. However, as the empirical research in this book has shown, equality is about more than the sexual division of labour in parenting and fathers' increased involvement in caring for children, since where fathers are violent and abusive towards mothers such equality is impossible.

Moreover, violent fathers' behaviour carries over into their parenting and attitudes towards children, rather than being a separate issue from violence towards mothers. Because of this, their increased involvement in children's care needs to be recognised as putting children at increased risk from abusive parenting practices. Far more research is needed in this area on diverse groups of domestically violent fathers and on their capacity to change. In the meantime children's safety and wellbeing should not be compromised to the shared parenting ideal.

References

Abbott, P. and Wallace, C. (1992) *The Family and the New Right*, London: Pluto.

Abrahams, C. (1994) *The Hidden Victims: Children and Domestic Violence*, London: NCH Action for Children.

ACPO (Association of Chief Police Officers)/Home Office (2006) *Lessons Learnt from the Domestic Violence Enforcement Campaign*, London: Police and Crime Standards Directorate, Home Office.

Adams, D. (1988) 'Treatment models of men who batter: a pro-feminist analysis', in K. Yllo and M. Bograd (eds) *Feminist Perspectives on Wife Abuse*, Newbury Park, CA: Sage Publications.

Alder, C.M. and Polk, K. (1996) 'Masculinity and child homicide', *British Journal of Criminology*, vol 36, no 3, pp 396-411.

Aris, R and Harrison, C. (2007) *Domestic Violence and the Supplemental Information Form C1A*, Ministry of Justice Research Series No 17/07 London: Ministry of Justice.

Aris, R., Harrison, C. and Humphreys, C. (2002) *Safety and Child Contact: An Analysis of the Role of Child Contact Centres in the Context of Domestic Violence and Child Welfare Concerns*, London: Lord Chancellor's Department.

Babcock, J.C. and La Taillade, J.J. (2000) 'Evaluating interventions for men who batter', in J.P. Vincent and E.N. Jouriles (eds) *Domestic Violence Guidelines for Research Informed Practice*, London: Jessica Kingsley.

Backett, K. (1987) 'The negotiation of fatherhood', in C. Lewis and M. O'Brien (eds) *Reassessing Fatherhood: New Observations on Fathers and the Modern Family*, London: Sage Publications.

Bainham, A. (1990) *Children and the New Law: The Children Act 1989*, Bristol: Family Law.

Bancroft, L. and Silverman, J.G. (2002) *The Batterer as Parent: Addressing the Impact of Domestic Violence on Family Dynamics*, Thousand Oaks, CA: Sage Publications.

Barclay, G. and Tavares, C. (2003) *International Comparisons of Criminal Justice Statistics, Issue 12/03*, London: The Stationery Office.

Barnett, A. (2009a) 'The welfare of the child re-visited: in whose best interests? Part I', *Family Law*, vol 39, www.lexisnexis.com/uk.

Barnett, A. (2009b) 'The welfare of the child re-visited: in whose best interests? Part II', *Family Law*, vol 39, www.lexisnexis.com/uk

Barron, J. (1990) *Not Worth the Paper? The Effectiveness of Legal Protection for Women and Children Experiencing Domestic Violence*, Bristol: Women's Aid Federation, England.

Barter, C., McCarry, M., Berridge, D. and Evens, K. (2009) 'Partner exploitation and violence in teenage intimate relationships. Executive summary', www.nspcc.org.uk/inform

Baynes, P. (2009) 'Social work with violent men: what has changed?', Paper presented to Cafcass Research Conference, Birmingham, 27 February.

Beck, U. (1992) *Risk Society: Towards a New Modernity*, London: Sage Publications.

Beail, N. (1982) 'Role of the father during pregnancy and childbirth', in N. Beail and J. Mcguire (eds) *Fathers: Psychological Perspectives*, London: Junction Books.

Beail, N. and Mcguire, J. (eds) (1982) *Fathers: Psychological Perspectives*, London: Junction Books.

Bell, M. (2007) *Barnardos Multi-agency Domestic Violence Risk Identification Threshold Scales*, Northern Ireland: Barnardos.

Bent-Goodley, T. and Williams, O. (2007) 'Fathers' voices on parenting and violence', in J. Edleson and O. Williams (eds) *Parenting by Men who Batter: New Directions for Assessment and Intervention*, Oxford, New York, NY: Oxford University Press.

Bentovim, A. (1987) 'Breakdown of parenting function in abusing families: how can professionals think about these issues and be helpful?', in P. Maher (ed) *Child Abuse – The Educational Perspective*. Oxford, Blackwells.

Bertoia, C.E. and Drakitch, J. (1995) 'The fathers' rights movement: contradictions in rhetoric and practice', in W. Marsiglio (ed) *Fatherhood, Contemporary Theory, Research and Social Policy*, Thousand Oaks, CA: Sage Publications.

Blackstone, W. (1825 [1765]) *Commentaries on the Laws of England*, Reproduced in Clark, NJ, Lawbook Exchange, 1825, www.lonang.com/exlibris/blackstone/bla-003.htm

BMA (British Medical Association) (1997) *Domestic Violence: A Healthcare Issue*, London: BMA.

Bowlby, J. (1953) *Childcare and the Growth of Love*, Harmondsworth: Penguin.

Bradshaw, J., Stimson, C., Skinner, C. and Williams, J. (1999) *Absent Fathers?*, London: Routledge.

Brandon, M. and Lewis, A. (1995) 'Significant harm and children's experiences of domestic violence', *Child and Family Social Work*, vol 1, pp 33-42.

Brandon, M., Belderson, P., Warren, C., Howe, D., Gardner, R., Dodsworth, J. and Black, J. (2006) *Analysing Child Deaths and Serious Injury through Abuse and Neglect: What can we Learn? A Biennial Analysis of Serious Case Reviews 2003-2005*, London: Department for Children, Schools and Families.

Brannen, J. and Moss, P. (1987) 'Fathers in dual-earner households – through mothers' eyes', in C. Lewis, and M. O'Brien *Reassessing Fatherhood: New Observations on Fathers and the Modern Family*, London: Sage Publications.

Bretherton, H. (2002) '"Because it's me the decisions are about" – children's experiences of private family law proceedings', *Family Law*, vol 32, pp 450-5.

Brophy, J. (1985) 'Childcare and the growth of power: the status of mothers in custody disputes', in J. Brophy and C. Smart (eds) *Women in Law: Explorations in Law, Family and Sexuality*, London: Routledge and Kegan Paul.

Brown, T (2006) 'Child abuse and domestic violence in the context of parental separation and divorce: new models of intervention', in C. Humphreys and N. Stanley (eds) *Domestic Violence and Children Protection: Directions for Good Practice,* London: Jessica Kingsley.

Brown, T., Frederico, M., Hewitt, L. and Sheehan, R. (2000) 'Revealing the existence of child abuse in the context of marital breakdown and custody and access disputes', *Child Abuse and Neglect*, vol 24, no 6, pp 849-59.

BSA (British Sociological Association) (2002) 'Statement of ethical practice', www.britsoc.co.uk/library/ethicsguidelines2002.doc?

Burgess, A. (1997) *Fatherhood Reclaimed*, London: Vermilion.

Burgess, A. and Ruxton, S. (1996) *Men and their Children: Proposals for Public Policy*, London: Institute for Public Policy Research.

Burghes, L., Clarke, L. and Cronin, N. (1997) *Fathers and Fatherhood in Britain*, York: Joseph Rowntree Foundation.

Burton, S., Regan, L. and Kelly, L. (1998) *Supporting Women and Challenging Men: Lessons from the Domestic Violence Intervention Project*, Bristol: The Policy Press.

Cafcass (Children and Family Court Advisory and Support Service) (2007) 'Safeguarding framework', www.cafcass.gsi.gov.uk/publications/policies

Campbell, J. (1995) 'Prediction of homicide of and by battered women', in J. Campbell (ed) *Assessing the Risk of Dangerousness: Potential for Further Violence of Sexual Offenders, Batterers and Child Abusers*, Newbury Park, CA: Sage Publications.

Calder, M. (2008) 'Professional dangerousness: causes and contemporary features', in M. Calder (ed) *Contemporary Risk Assessment in Safeguarding Children*, Lyme Regis: Russell House Publishing.

Cavanagh, K., Dobash, R.E. and Dobash, R.P. (2005) 'Men who murder children inside and outside the family,' *British Journal of Social Work*, 35, pp 667–88.

Cavanagh, K., Dobash, R.E. and Dobash, R.P. (2007) 'The murder of children by fathers in the context of child abuse', *Child Abuse and Neglect*, vol 31, no 7, pp 731–46.

Cavanagh, K., Dobash, R.E., Dobash, R.P. and Lewis, R. (2001) 'Remedial work: men's strategic responses to their violence against intimate female partners', *Sociology*, vol 35, no 3, pp 695–714.

Cawson, P., Wattam, C., Brooker, G. and Kelly, G. (2000) *Child Maltreatment in the United Kingdom*, London: National Society for the Prevention of Cruelty to Children.

Chant, S. (1997) *Women-Headed Households*, London: Routledge.

Chetwin, A., Knaggs, T. and Te Wairere Ahiahi Young, P. (1999) *The Domestic Violence Legislation and Child Access in New Zealand*, Aukland: Ministry of Justice.

Children Act Sub-Committee (CASC) (2000) *A report to the Lord Chancellor on the Question of parental Contact in cases where there is domestic violence*, London: Lord Chancellor's Department.

Church, J. (1984) *Violence against Wives: Its Causes and Effects*, Christchurch, New Zealand: John Church.

Cobbe. F.P (1868) Criminals, Idiots, Women and Minors. Is the Classification Sound? *Frasers Magazine,* December, 380–367

Cobbe, F.P (1878) 'Wife torture in England', *Contemporary Review* (April), partially reprinted in J. Radford and D. Russell (eds) (1992) *Femicide: The Politics of Woman Killing*, New York, NY: Macmillan.

Coid, J. (2000) *Conference Report: Domestic Violence, A Health Response, Working in a Wider Partnership*, London: Department of Health.

Collier, R. (1995) *Masculinity, Law and the Family*, London: Routledge.

Collier, R .(2005) 'Fathers 4 Justice, law and the new politics of fatherhood', *Child and Family Law Quarterly*, vol 17, no 4, www.lexisnexis.com/uk

Collier, R. and Sheldon, S. (2008) *Fragmenting Fatherhood: A Socio-legal Study*, Oxford: Hart Publishing.

Cook, D., Burton, M., Robinson, A. and Vallely, A. (2004) *Evaluation of Specialist Domestic Violent Courts/Fast Track Systems*, London: Crown Prosecution Service Policy Directorate.

Connell, R.W. (1987) *Gender and Power*, Sydney: Allen and Unwin.

Connell, R.W. (1995) *Masculinities*, Cambridge: Polity Press.

Connell, R.W. (2002) 'On hegemonic masculinity and violence: response to Jefferson and Hall', *Theoretical Criminology*, vol 16, no 1, pp 89-99.

Connell, R.W and Messerschmidt, J. (2005) 'Hegemonic masculinity: rethinking the concept,' *Gender and Society*, vol 19, no 6, pp 829-59.

Dale, P., Davies, M., Morrison, T., and Waters, J. (1986) *Dangerous Families*, London: Tavistock.

Daniel, B. and Taylor, J. (2006) 'Gender and child neglect: theory, research and policy', *Critical Social Policy*, vol 26, p 426.

Davidoff, L., Doolittle, M., Fink, J. and Holden, K. (1999) *The Family Story: Blood, Contract and Intimacy, 1830-1960*, London: Longman.

Dennis, N. and Erdos, G. (1992) *Families without Fatherhood*, London: Institute of Economic Affairs.

DCSF (Department for Children, Schools and Families) (2009) *Working Together to Safeguard Children*, London: DCSF.

DCSF (2010) *Support for All*, London: DCSF.

DCSF and DH (Department of Health) (2009) *Getting Services Right for Pregnant Teenagers and Young Fathers*, London: DCSF/DH.

DfES (Department for Education and Skills) (2003) *Every Child Matters*, London: HMSO.

DfES (2004) *Parental Separation: Children's Needs and Parental Responsibilities*, London: DfES.

DfES (2005) *Parental Separation: Children's Needs and Parental Responsibilities. Next Steps: Report of the Responses to Consultation and Agenda for Action*, London: DfES.

DfES (2006) *Working Together to Safeguard Children*, London, DfES

DfES (2007a) Department for Education and Skills recognises 'Every Parent Matters', 15 March, http://webarchive.nationalarchives.gov.uk/+/www.direct.gov.uk/en/Nl1/Newsroom/DG_066880

DfES, (2007b) Every Parent Matters. London:Dfes.

DH (Department of Health) (1999) *Working Together to Safeguard Children*, London: DH.

DH (2002) *Women's Mental Health: Into the Mainstream. Strategic Development of Mental Health Care for Women*, London: DH.

DH (2004) *National Service Framework for Children, Young People and Maternity Services*, London: DH.

Dingwall, R., Eekelaar, J. and Murray, T. (1983) *The Protection of Children: State Intervention and Family Life,* Oxford: Blackwell.

Dobash, R.E. and Dobash, R.P. (1992) *Women, Violence and Social Change*, London: Routledge.

Dobash, R.E. and Dobash, R.P. (1998) 'Violent men and violent contexts', in R.E. Dobash and R.P. Dobash (eds) *Rethinking Violence Against Women*, London: Sage Publications.

Dobash, R.E., Dobash, R.P., Cavanagh, K. and Medina-Ariza, J. (2007) 'Lethal and nonlethal violence against an intimate female partner: comparing male murderers to nonlethal abusers', *Violence against Women*, vol 13, pp 329-53.

Dobash, R.P., Dobash, R.E., Cavanagh, K. and Lewis, R. (1996) *Research Evaluation of Programmes for Violent Men*, Edinburgh: The Scottish Office.

Doncaster Safeguarding Children Board (2010) *A Serious Case Review: 'J' Children. The Executive Summary*, Doncaster: Doncaster Safeguarding Children Board.

Dunn, J. (2003) 'Contact and children's perspectives on parental relationships', in A. Bainham, B. Lindley, R. Richards and L. Trinder (eds) *Children and their Families: Contact, Rights and Welfare*, Oxford: Hart Publishing.

Eadley, N. and Wetherell, M. (1996) 'Masculinity, power and identity', in M. Mac An Ghaill (ed) *Understanding Masculinities*, Buckingham: Open University Press.

Edleson, J. (1999) 'Children's witnessing of adult violence', *Journal of Interpersonal Violence*, 14, pp 839-70.

Eekelaar, J. and Clive, E. (1977) *Custody after Divorce*, Oxford: Centre for Socio-Legal Studies, Oxford University.

Epstein, C. and Keep, G. (1995) 'What children tell ChildLine about domestic violence', in A. Saunders with C. Epstein, G. Keep and T. Debbonaire *'It Hurts Me Too': Children's Experiences of Domestic Violence and Refuge Life*, Bristol: Women's Aid Federation of England/ChildLine/National Institute for Social Work.

Eriksson, M. and Nasman, E. (2008) 'Participation in family law proceedings for children whose father is violent to their mother', *Childhood*, vol 15, p 259.

Family Justice Council (2006) *Report to the President of the Family Division on the approach to be adopted by the Court when asked to make a contact order by consent, where domestic violence has been an issue in the case*, London: Family Justice Council.

Farmer, E. (2006) 'Using research to develop practice in child protection and child care', in C. Humphreys and N. Stanley (eds) *Domestic Violence and Child Protection: Directions for Good Practice*, London: Jessica Kingsley.

Farmer, E. and Owen, M. (1995) *Child Protection Practice: Private Risks and Public Remedies. Messages from Research*, London: HMSO.

Farmer, E. and Pollock, S. (1998) *Substitute Care for Sexually Abused and Abusing Children*, Chichester: John Wiley and Sons.

Featherstone, B. (2000) Big daddy, big brother: New Labour and the politics of fatherhood', Paper presented to Social Policy Association Annual Conference, Roehampton, 18-20 July.

Featherstone, B. (2003) 'Taking fathers seriously', *British Journal of Social Work*, 33, pp 239-54.

Featherstone, B. and Peckover, S. (2007) 'Letting them get away with it: fathers, domestic violence and child welfare', *Critical Social Policy*, vol 27, pp 181-200.

Feder, L. and Forde, D.R. (2000) *A Test of the Efficacy of Court-Mandated Counselling for Domestic Violence Offenders: The Broward Experiment*, Washington, DC: National Institute of Justice.

Ferguson, L. (1999) 'Dispatches: child contact and domestic violence', London: Channel Four.

Ferguson, L. (2009) 'Dispatches child homicide study: main findings', www.channel4.com/dispatches_downloads/dispatches_child_homicide_research.pdf

Ferri, E. and Smith, K. (1996) *Parenting in the 1990s*, York: Joseph Rowntree Foundation.

Flouri, E. (2005) *Fathering and Child Outcomes*, Chichester: John Wiley and Sons.

FNF (Families Need Fathers) (2008) 'Parental alienation report', www.fnf.org.uk/parental_alienation_report.pdf

FNF (2009a) 'Aims of families need fathers', www.fnf.org.uk/about-us/aims-and-objectives/news-and-events/family-justice-council-initiative

FNF (2009b) 'Guidance for Cafcass case officers on shared parenting', www.fnf.org.uk/publications-and-resources

Forman, J (1995) *Is There a Correlation between Child Sexual Abuse and Domestic Violence? An Exploratory Study of the Links between Child Sexual Abuse and Domestic Violence in a Sample of Intrafamilial Child Sexual Abuse Cases*, Glasgow: Women's Support Project.

Fox, G. and Benson, M. (2004) 'Violent men, bad dads? Fathering profiles of men involved in intimate partner violence', in R. Day and M. Lamb (eds) *Conceptualising and Measuring Father Involvement*, Mahwah, NJ. Lawrence Eribaum.

Fox, G., Sayers, J. and Bruce, C. (2001) 'Beyond bravado: fatherhood as a resource for rehabilitation of men who batter', *Marriage and Family Review*, vol 30, pp 137-63.

Gavanas, A. (2002) 'The fatherhood responsibility movement: the centrality of marriage, work and male sexuality in reconstructions of masculinity and fatherhood', in B. Hobson (ed) *Making Men into Fathers: Men, Masculinities and the Social Politics of Fatherhood*, Cambridge: Cambridge University Press.

Gelles, R.J. (1983) 'An exchange/social control theory of family violence', in D. Finkelor, R.J. Gelles, G.T. Hotaling and M.A. Straus (eds) *The Dark Side of Families: Current Family Research*, Beverly Hills, CA: Sage Publications.

Giddens, A. (1984) *The Constitution of Society: Outline of the Theory of Structuration*, Berkerley, CA: University of California Press.

Giddens, A. (1998) *The Third Way: The Renewal of Social Democracy*, Cambridge: Polity Press.

Gilbert, L.A. (1993) *Two Careers / One Family*, London: Sage Publications.

Gittins, D. (1985) *The Family in Question: Changing Households and Familiar Ideologies*, Basingstoke: Macmillan.

Goldstein, J., Freud. A. and Solnit, A. (1979) *Beyond the Best Interests of the Child* (2nd edn), New York, NY: Free Press.

Gondolf, E. (1998) 'A 30-month follow-up of court-referred batterers in four cities', Paper presented at Program Evaluation and Family Research: An International Conference, Durham, DA.

Gondolf, E. (1999) 'A comparison of four batterer intervention systems: do court referral, program length and services matter?', *Journal of Interpersonal Violence*, vol 14, pp 41-61.

Gondolf, E. (2004) 'Evaluating batterer counselling programs: a difficult task showing some effects and implications', *Aggression and Violent Behaviour*, vol 9, pp 605-31.

Gordon, L. (1988) 'The politics of child sexual abuse', *Feminist Review*, 28, pp: 56-74.

Graycar, R. (1989) 'Equal rights versus fathers' rights: the child custody debate in Australia', in C. Smart and S. Sevenhuijsen (eds) *Child Custody and the Politics of Gender*, London: Routledge.

Gregory, C. and Erez, E. (2002) 'The effects of batterer intervention programs: the battered women's perspective', *Violence against Women*, vol 8, pp 206-36.

Guardian, The (2001) 'Fathers picket judges over child contact', 30 October, www.guardian.co.uk

Hague, J. and Wilson, C. (1996) *The Silenced Pain*, Bristol: The Policy Press.

Hague, G., Kelly, L., Malos, E. and Mullender, A. with Debonnaire, T. (1996) *Children, Domestic Violence and Refuges: A Study of Needs and Responses*, Bristol: Women's Aid Federation of England.

Hall, E. and Guy, J. (2009) *The 'Baby Peter Effect' and the Increase in S.31 Care Applications*, London: Cafcass, www.cafcass.gsi.gov.uk/publications

Hammerton, J. (1992) *Cruelty and Companionship: Conflict in Nineteenth Century Married Life*, London: Routledge.

Hanmer, J. (1998) 'Out of control: men, violence and family life', in J. Popay, J. Hearn and J. Edwards (eds) *Men, Gender Divisions and Welfare*, London: Routledge.

Harne, L. (2004) *Violence, power and the meanings of fatherhood in issues of child contact*, PhD thesis, Bristol: University of Bristol.

Harne, L. (2005) 'Researching violent fathers', in T. Skinner, M. Hester and E Malos (eds) *Researching Gender Violence: Feminist Methodology in Action*, Cullompton: Willan Publishing.

Harne, L. (2009) 'Domestic violence and safeguarding children: the use of systematic risk identification and assessment in private law proceedings by family court advisors: a pilot study', www.bristol.ac.uk/sps/research

Harne, L. and Radford, J. (1994) 'Reinstating patriarchy: the politics of the family and the new legislation', in A. Mullender and R. Morley (eds) *Children Living with Domestic Violence: Putting Men's Abuse of Children on the Child Care Agenda*, London: Whiting and Birch.

Harne, L. and Radford, J. (2008) *Tackling Domestic Violence: Theories, Policies and Practice*, Maidenhead: Open University Press.

Harne, L. and Rights of Women (1997) *Valued Families: Lesbian Mothers' Legal Handbook*, London: The Women's Press.

Harold, G. and Murch, M. (2005) 'Inter-parental conflict and children's adaptation to separation and divorce: theory, research and implications for family law, practice and policy', *Child and Family Law Quarterly*, vol 17, no 2, p 185.

Harrison, C. (2006) 'Damned if you do and damned if you don't: the contradictions of public and private law', in C. Humphreys and N. Stanley (eds) *Domestic Violence and Child Protection: Directions for Good Practice*, London: Jessica Kingsley.

Hart, B. (1988) 'Beyond the "duty to warn": a therapist's "duty to protect" battered women and children', in J.C. Campbell (ed) *Assessing Dangerousness: Violence by Sexual Offenders, Batterers, and Child Abusers*, Newbury Park, CA: Sage Publications.

Hawkins, A.J. and Dollahite, D.C. (1997) 'Beyond the role – inadequacy perspective of fathering', in A.J. Hawkins and D.C. Dollahite (eds) *Generative Fathering*, London: Sage Publications.

Hearn, J. (1998a) *The Violences of Men: How Men Talk About and How Agencies Respond to Men's Violence to Women*, London: Sage Publications.

Hearn, J. (1998b) 'Men will be men: the ambiguity of men's support for men who have been violent to known women', in J. Popay, J. Hearn and J. Edwards (eds) *Men, Gender Divisions and Welfare*, London: Routledge.

Hearn, J. (2001) 'Nation, state and welfare: the cases of Finland and the UK', in B. Pease and K. Pringle (eds) *A Man's World: Changing Men's Practices in a Globalised World*, London: Zed Books.

Hearn, J. and Pringle, K. (2006) 'Men, masculinities and children: some European perspectives,' *Critical Social Policy*, vol, 26, pp 365-89.

Hester, M. (2009) *Who does What to Whom? Gender and Domestic Violence Perpetrators*, Bristol: Bristol University in association with Northern Rock, www.bristol.ac.uk/sps/research

Hester, M. and Pearson, C. (1998) *From Periphery to Centre: Domestic Violence in Work with Abused Children*, Bristol: The Policy Press.

Hester, M. and Radford, L. (1996) *Domestic Violence and Child Contact Arrangements in England and Denmark*, Bristol: The Policy Press.

Hester, M and Scott, J (2000) *Women in Abusive Relationships: Group Work and Agency Support*, London: Barnardos.

Hester, M., Hanmer, J., Coulson, S., Moriahan, M. and Razak, A. (2003) *Domestic Violence: Making it through the Criminal Justice System*, Sunderland: Northern Rock Building Society in association with the University of Sunderland.

Hester, M., Pearson, C., Harwin, N. and Abrahams, H. (2007) *Making an Impact: Children and Domestic Violence, A Reader* (2nd edn), London: Jessica Kingsley.

Higgins, G. (1994) 'Children's accounts', in A. Mullender and R. Morley (eds) *Children Living with Domestic Violence: Putting Men's Abuse of Women on the Child Care Agenda*, London: Whiting and Birch.

HMICA (HM Inspection of Court Administration) (2005) 'Domestic violence, safety and family proceedings', www.hmica.gov.uk/files/HMICA_Domestic_violence_linked1.pdf

Holcombe, L (1983) *Wives and Property*, Toronto: Toronto University Press.

Holden, G. and Ritchie, K. (1991) 'Linking extreme marital discord, child rearing and child behaviour problems: evidence from battered women', *Child Development*, 62, pp 311-27.

Home Affairs Committee (1993) *Domestic Violence. Vol II Memoranda of Evidence, Minutes of Evidence and Appendices*, London: HMSO.

Home Office (1998) *Supporting Families*, London: Home Office.

Home Office (2003) *Safety and Justice: The Government Proposals on Domestic Violence*, London: Home Office.

Home Office (2009) What is domestic violence?, www.homeoffice.gov.uk/rds/violencewomen.htm

Home Office (2010) National Domestic Violence Delivery Report 2008-9. London: Home Office

Humphreys, C. (1997) 'Child sexual abuse allegations in the context of divorce: issues for mothers', *British Journal of Social Work*, vol 27, pp 529-44.

Humphreys, C. (2000) *Social Work, Domestic Violence and Child Protection: Challenging Practice*, Bristol: The Policy Press.

Humphreys, C. (2006) 'Relevant evidence for practice', in C. Humphreys and N. Stanley (eds) *Domestic Violence and Child Protection: Directions for Good Practice*, London: Jessica Kingsley.

Humphreys, C. (2007) 'Domestic violence and child protection: exploring the role of perpetrator risk assessments,' *Child and Family Social Work*, 12, pp 360-9.

Humphreys, C. and Thiara, R. (2002) *Routes to Safety: Protection Issues Facing Abused Women and Children and the Role of Outreach Services*, Bristol: Women's Aid Federation of England.

Hunt, J. and Roberts, C. (2004) *Child Contact with Non-resident Parents*, Family Policy Briefing 3, Oxford: Centre for Family Law and Policy, University of Oxford.

Include (2006) *Teenage Mothers' Experiences of Domestic Violence: Identifying Good Practice for Support Workers*, Leeds: Include.

Izzidien, S. (2008) '*I Can't Tell People What is Happening at Home.' Domestic Abuse within South Asian Communities: The Specific Needs of Women, Children and Young People*, London: NSPCC.

Jaffe, P.G., Wolfe, D.A. and Wilson, S.K. (1990) *Children of Battered Women*, Thousand Oaks, CA: Sage Publications.

Jaffe, P.G., Lemon, K.D. and Poisson, S.E. (2003) *Child Custody and Domestic Violence: A Call for Safety and Accountability*, Thousand Oaks, CA: Sage Publications.

James, A. and Prout, A. (1990) *Constructing and Reconstructing Childhood*, London: Falmer.

Jeffreys, S. (1985) *The Spinster and her Enemies: Feminism and Sexuality 1880-1930*, London: Pandora.

Justice for Women (2006) 'Men, women and murder', *Summer Newsletter*, www.Justiceforwomen.org.uk

Kaye, M. (1996) 'Domestic violence, residence and contact', *Child and Family Law Quarterly*, vol 8, no 3, pp 50-7.

Kaye, M. and Tolmie, J. (1999) 'Discoursing dads: the rhetorical devices of fathers' rights groups', *Melbourne University Law Review*, 22, p 162.

Kaganas, F. and Day Sclater, S. (2004) 'Contact disputes: narrative constructions of "good parents"', *Feminist Legal Studies*, vol 12, p 1.

Kelly, L. (1994) 'The interconnectedness of domestic violence and child abuse: challenges for research, policy and practice', in A. Mullender and R. Morley (eds) *Children Living with Domestic Violence: Putting Men's Abuse of Women on the Child Care Agenda*, London: Whiting and Birch.

Kelly, L. (1999) *Domestic Violence Matters: An Evaluation of a Development Project. Home Office Study 188*, London: The Stationery Office.

Kitzmann, K. Gaylord, N., Holt, A. and Kenny, E. (2003) 'Child witnesses to domestic violence: a meta-analytic review', *Journal of Consulting and Clinical Psychology*, vol 71, no 2, pp 339-52.

Kolbo, J., Blakely, E. and Engleman, D. (1996) 'Children who witness domestic violence: a review of empirical literature', *Journal of Interpersonal Violence*, vol 11, no 2, pp 281-93.

Kropp, P.R. (2004) 'Some questions regarding spousal assault risk assessment', *Violence against Women*, vol 10, pp 676-97.

Lamb, M.E. (1997) *The Role of the Father in Child Development* (3rd edn), New York, NY: John Wiley and Sons.

Laws, S. (1996) 'The 'single' mothers' debate: a children's rights perspective', in J. Holland and L. Adkins (eds) *Sex, Sensibility and the Gendered Body*, Basingstoke: Macmillan.

Lewis, C. (1982) 'The observation of father–infant relationships: an attachment to outmoded concepts', in L. McKee and M. O'Brien (eds) *The Father* Figure, London: Tavistock Publications.

Lewis, J. (2002) 'The problem of fathers: policy and behaviour in Britain', in B. Hobson (ed) *Making Men into Fathers*, Cambridge, Cambridge University Press.

Lewis, C. and O'Brien, M. (1987) *Reassessing Fatherhood: New Observations on Fathers and the Modern Family*, London: Sage Publications.

Lewis, G. and Drife, J. (2001) *Confidential Inquiry into Maternal Deaths 1996-1999*, London: Department of Health.

Littlechild, B. and Bourke, C. (2006) 'Men's use of violence and intimidation against family members and child protection workers', in C. Humphreys and N. Stanley (eds) *Domestic Violence and Child Protection: Directions for Good Practice*, London: Jessica Kingsley.

London Safeguarding Children Board (2008) 'Safeguarding children abused through domestic violence', www.londonscb.gov.uk

Lord Laming (2009) *The Protection of Children in England: A Progress Report*, London: The Stationary Office.

Lundgren, E. (1995) *Feminist theory and Violent Empiricism*, Aldershot: Avebury.

Lupton, D. and Barclay, L. (1997) *Constructing Fatherhood: Discourses and Experiences*, London: Sage Publications.

Macdonald, G. (2009) 'Domestic violence, children's voices and child contact: an examination of section 7 Cafcass reports (England)', Unpublished PhD thesis, School for Policy Studies, University of Bristol.

Maclean, M. and Eekelaar, J. (1997) *The Parental Obligation: A Study of Parenthood across Households*, Oxford: Hart Publishing.

Mann, C. (1996) 'Girls' own story: the search for a sexual identity in times of family change', in J. Holland and L. Adkins (eds) *Sex, Sensibility and the Gendered Body*, Basingstoke: Macmillan.

Marsiglio, W. (1995) 'Fatherhood scholarship: an overview and agenda for the future', in W. Marsiglio (ed) *Reassessing Fatherhood: Contemporary Theory, Research and Social Policy*, Thousand Oaks, CA: Sage Publications.

Masson, J. (2006)' Consent orders in contact cases: a survey of resolution members', *Family Law*, vol, 36, pp 1041-3.

Mathews, D. (1995) 'Parenting groups for men who batter', in E. Peled, P. Jaffe and J. Edleson (eds) *Ending the Cycle of Violence: Community Responses to Children of Battered Women*, Thousand Oaks, CA: Sage Publications.

McGee, C. (2000) *Childhood Experiences of Domestic Violence*, London: Jessica Kingsley.

McKee, L. and O'Brien, M. (1982) *The Father Figure*, London: Tavistock Publications.

McWilliams, M. and McKiernan, J. (1993) *Bringing it Out in the Open: Domestic Violence in Northern Ireland*, Belfast: HMSO.

Mertin, P. (1995) 'A follow-up study of children from domestic violence', *Australian Journal of Family Law*, vol 9, pp 76-85.

Messerschmidt, J. (1993) *Masculinities and Crime*, Langham, MD: Rowland and Littlefield.

Mezey, G. and Bewley, S. (1997) 'Domestic violence and pregnancy', *British Journal of Obstetrics and Gynaecology*, 104, pp 528-31.

Mirrlees-Black, C. (1999) *Domestic Violence: Findings from a new British Crime Survey Self-completion Questionnaire*, Home Office Research Study 191, London: Home Office.

Mirror (2004) 'Unmasked', 28 October, www.mirror.co.uk

Mooney, A. Oliver, C. and Smith, M. (2009) *Impact of Family Breakdown on Children's Well-Being. Evidence Review*, London: Thomas Coram Unit, Institute of Education, London University.

Mott, F.L. (1993) *Absent Fathers and Child Development: Emotional and Cognitive Development at Ages Five to Nine. Report for National Institute of Child Health and Development*, Columbus, OH: Centre for Human Resources Research, Ohio State University.

Mullender. A., Hague, G., Imam, U., Kelly, L., Malos, E. and Regan, L. (2002) *Children's Perspectives on Domestic Violence*, London: Sage Publications.

Munroe, E. (1999) 'Common errors of reasoning in child protection work', *Child Abuse and Neglect*, vol 23, no 8, p 744.

Murray, C. (1990) *The Emerging British Underclass*, London: Institute of Economic Affairs Health and Welfare Unit.

NACPO (National Association of Probation Officers) (2002) *Contact, Separation and the Work of Family Court Staff*, London: NACPO.

Nazroo, J. (1995) 'Uncovering gender differences in the use of marital violence: the effect of methodology', *Sociology*, vol 29, pp 475-95.

Neale, B. and Smart, C. (1998) *Agents or Dependents?: Struggling to Listen to Children in Family Law and Family Research*, Working Paper 3, Leeds: Centre for Research on Family, Kinship and Childhood, University of Leeds.

Neale, B., Flowerdew, J. and Smart, C. (2003) 'Drifting towards Shared Residence,' *Family Law,* vol 33, p 904.

Oakley, A. (1976) *Housewife*, Harmondsworth: Penguin.

O'Hara, M. (1994) 'Child deaths in the context of domestic violence: implications for professional practice', in A. Mullender and R. Morley (eds) *Children Living with Domestic Violence: Putting Men's Abuse of Women on the Child Care Agenda*, London: Whiting and Birch.

Parsloe, P. (1999) 'Introduction', in P. Parsloe (ed) *Risk Assessment in Social Care and Social Work*, London: Jessica Kinglsey.

Parsons, T. (1951) *The Social System*, New York: Free Press.

Parton, J. (1998) The Joint Residence Issue, *Family Law,* vol 27, p 775.

Peled, E. (2000) 'The parenting of men who abuse women: issues and dilemmas', *British Journal of Social Work*, vol 30, pp 25-36.

Pence, E. (1987) *In our Best Interest: A Process for Personal and Social Change*, Facilitator Handbook, Deluth, MN: Minnesota Programme Development Inc.

Pence, E. and Paymar, M. (1993) *Education Groups for Men who Batter*, New York, NY: Springer.

Perel, G and Peled, E (2008) 'The fathering of violent men: constriction and yearning', *Violence against Women*, vol 14, no 4, pp 457-82.

Perry, A. (2006) 'Safety first? Contact and family violence in New Zealand: an evaluation of the presumption against unsupervised contact,' *Child and Family Law Quarterly*, vol 18, no 1, p 1.

President of the Family Division (2008/9) 'Practice direction: residence and contact orders: domestic violence and harm', www.hmcourts-services.gov.uk/cms/files

Pringle, K. (1998) 'Men and childcare: policy and practice', in J. Popay, J. Hearn, and J. Edwards (eds) *Men, Gender Divisions and Welfare*, London: Routledge.

Ptacek, J. (1988) 'Why do men batter their wives?', in K. Yllo and M. Bograd (eds) *Feminist Perspectives on Wife Abuse*, London: Sage Publications.

Quinlivan, J. and Evans, S. (2001) 'A prospective cohort study of the impact of domestic violence on young teenage pregnancy outcomes,' *Journal of Paediatric and Adolescent Gynaecology*, 14, pp 17-23

Quortrup, J., Bardy, M., Sgritta, G. and Wintersberger, H. (eds) (1994) *Childhood Matters*, Aldershot: Avebury.

Radford, J. (2001) 'Professionalising responses to domestic violence: definitional difficulties', Paper presented at Social Policy Association conference, Belfast, 24-26 July.

Radford, J. and Russell, D. (eds) (1992) *Femicide: The Politics of Woman Killing*, New York, NY: Macmillan.

Radford, J., Harne, L. and Friedberg, M. (2000) 'Introduction', in J. Radford, M. Friedberg and L. Harne (eds) *Women, Violence and Strategies for Action*, Buckingham: Open University Press.

Radford, L. and Hester, M. (2006) *Mothering through Domestic Violence*, London: Jessica Kinglsey.

Radford, L., Blacklock, N. and Iwi, K. (2006) 'Domestic abuse risk assessment and safety planning in child protection: assessing perpetrators', in C. Humphreys and N. Stanley (eds) *Domestic Violence and Child Protection: Directions for Good Practice*, London: Jessica Kingsley.

Radford, L., Sayer, S. and AMICA (1999) *Unreasonable Fears? Child Contact in the Context of Domestic Violence: A Survey of Mothers' Perceptions of Harm*, Bristol: Women's Aid Federation of England.

Reece, H. (2006) 'UK women's groups' child contact campaign: "so long as it is safe"', *Child and Family Law Quarterly*, vol 18, no 4, p 538.

Regan, L., Kelly, L., Morris, A. and Dibb, R. (2007) *'If Only we'd Known': An Exploratory Study of Seven Intimate Partner Homicides in Engleshire*, London: Child and Woman Abuse Studies Unit, London Metropolitan University.

Respect (2004/2008/2010) *Statement of Principles and Minimum Standards of Practice*, London: Respect.

Rich, A. (1977) *Of Woman Born: Motherhood as Experience and Institution*, London: Virago.

Richards, M. (1982) 'Foreword', in N. Beail and J. Mcguire (eds) *Fathers: Psychological Perspectives*, London: Junction Books.

Richards, M. (1999) 'The interests of children on divorce', in G. Allan (ed) *The Sociology of the Family: A Reader*, Oxford: Blackwell.

Rights of Women (1984) *Lesbian Mothers on Trial*, London: Rights of Women.

Rittmeester, T. (1993) 'Batterers' programs, battered women's movement and issues of accountability', in E. Pence and M. Paymar (eds) *Education Groups for Men who Batter*, New York, NY: Springer.

Robinson, A. (2004) *Domestic Violence MARACS (Multi-Agency Risk Assessment Conferences) for Very High Risk Victims in Cardiff, Wales: A Process and Outcome Evaluation*, Cardiff, Cardiff University.

Robinson, A. and Tregidga, J. (2005) *Domestic Violence MARACS (Multi-Agency Risk Assessment Conferences) for Very High Risk Victims: Views from the Victims*, Cardiff: Cardiff University.

Rodgers, B. and Pryor, J. (2001) *Children in Changing Families: Life after Parental Separation*, Oxford: Blackwell.

Rodgers, B. and Pryor, J. (1998) *Divorce and Separation: Outcomes for Children*, York: Joseph Rowntree Foundation.

Rosen, L., Dragiewiez, M. and Gibbs, J. (2009) 'Fathers' rights groups: demographic correlates and impact on custody policy,' *Violence against Women*, vol 15, no 5, pp 513-31.

Ross, S. (1996) 'Risk of physical abuse to children of spouse abusing parents', *Child Abuse and Neglect*, vol 20, no 7, pp 589-98.

Rossman, B. (1998) 'Descartes's error and post-traumatic stress disorder: cognition and emotion in children who are exposed to domestic violence to parental violence', in W. Holden, R. Geffner and E. Jouriles (eds) *Children Exposed to Domestic Violence*, Washington, DC: American Psychological Association.

Rossman, B. (2001) 'Longer term effects of children's exposure to domestic violence', in S. Graham-Burton and J. Edlesson (eds) *Domestic violence in the lives of children: The future of research, intervention and social policy*, Washington DC: American Psychological Association.

Rothman, E., Mandel, D. and Silverman, J. (2007) 'Abusers' perceptions of the effect of their intimate partner violence on children', *Violence against Women*, vol, 13, pp 1179-91.

Rutherford, J. (1988) 'Who's that man?', in R. Chapman and J. Rutherford (eds) *Unwrapping Masculinity*, London: Lawrence and Wishart.

Saunders, D.G. (1995) 'Prediction of wife assault', in J.C. Campbell (ed) *Assessing Dangerousness: Violence by Sexual Offenders, Batterers, and Child Abusers*, Thousand Oaks, CA: Sage Publications.

Saunders, H. (2001) *Making Contact Worse. A Report of a National Survey into the Enforcement of Contact Orders*, Bristol: Women's Aid Federation of England.

Saunders, H. (2003a) *Failure to Protect? Domestic Violence and the Experiences of Abused Women and Children in the Family Courts*, Bristol: Women's Aid Federation of England.

Saunders, H. (2003b) 'Child homicide cases in cases of child contact', www.womensaid.org.uk/dv/childhomicidecases.htm

Saunders, H. (2004) *Twenty-nine Homicides: Lessons still to be Learnt on Domestic Violence and Child Protection*, Bristol: Women's Aid Federation of England.

Scott, K. (2004) *Final Report: Pilot Implementation of the Caring Dads Program for Abusive and At-risk Fathers*, London, Ontario: Centre for Research on Violence against Women and Children, University of Ontario.

Scott, K. (2006) *Caring Dads. Helping Fathers Value their Children. Program workbook*, www.caringdadsprogram.com/homeworkbook.pdf

Scott, K , Francis, K, Crooks, C, Paddon, M and Wolfe, D (2007) Guidelines for Interventions with Abusive Fathers in Edleson, J and Williams, O (eds) *Parenting by men who Batter*. New York: Oxford University Press.

Scourfield, J. and Drakeford, M. (2002) 'New Labour and the problem of men', *Critical Social Policy*, vol 22, p 619-40.

Sentencing Guidelines Council (2006) *Sentencing Guidelines on Domestic Violence*, London: Sentencing Guidelines Council.

Sharpe, S. (1994) *Fathers and Daughters*, London: Routledge.

Smart, C. (1989) 'Power and the politics of child custody', in C. Smart and S. Sevenhuijsen (eds) *Child Custody and the Politics of Gender*, London: Routledge.

Smart, C. (2004) 'Equal shares: rights for fathers or recognition for children', *Critical Social Policy*, vol 24, pp 484-503.

Smart, C. and Neale, B. (1997) 'Arguments against virtue: must contact be enforced?', *Family Law*, vol 27, pp 332-6.

Smart, C. and Neale, B. (1999) *Family Fragments?*, Cambridge: Polity Press.

Smart, C. and Sevenhuijsen, S. (eds) (1989) *Child Custody and the Politics of Gender*, London: Routledge.

Smith, L. (1989) *Domestic Violence: An Overview of the Literature*, Home Office Research Study 107, London: HMSO.

Smith, M., Robertson, J., Dixon, J., Quigley, M. and Whitehead, Z. (2001) *A Study of Stepchildren and Step-parenting*, London: Thomas Coram Research Unit, London University

Stanko, E.A. (1994) 'Challenging the problem of men's individual violence', in T. Newburn and E.A. Stanko (eds) *Just Boys Doing Business: Men, Masculinities and Crime*, London: Routledge.

Stanley, N., Miller, P., Richardson Foster, M. and Thomson, G. (2009) *Children and Families Experiencing Domestic Violence: Police and Children's Services' Responses. Executive Summary*, London: NSPCC.

Stark, E. (2002) 'Assessing risk', in A.R. Roberts (ed) *Handbook of Domestic Violence Intervention Strategies*, Cary, NC: Oxford University Press.

Stark, E. (2007) *Coercive Control. How Men Entrap Women in Personal Life*, New York, NY: Oxford University Press.

Stark, E. and Flitcraft, A. (1996) *Women at Risk: Domestic Violence and Women's Health*, London: Sage Publications.

Straus, M.A and Gelles, R.J. (1986) 'Societal change and change in family violence from 1975 to 1985 as revealed by two national surveys', *Journal of Marriage and the Family*, vol 48, no 3, pp 465-79.

Straus, M.A., Gelles, R.J. and Steinmetz S.K. (1980) *Behind Closed Doors: Violence in the American Family*, New York, NY: Anchor Press/Doubleday.

Sturge, C. and Glaser, D. (2000) 'Contact and domestic violence – the experts' court report', *Family Law*, vol 30, pp 615-29.

Sudermann, M. and Jaffe, P. (1999) *A Handbook for Health and Social Service Providers and Educators Exposed to Woman Abuse*, Ottawa: Minister of Public Works and Government Services.

Tasker, F. and Golombok, S. (1997) *Growing up in a Lesbian Family: Effects on Child Development*, London: Guildford Press.

Thiara, R. (2010) 'Continuing control: child contact and post-separation violence', in R. Thiara and A. Gill (eds) *Violence against Women in South Asian Communities: Issues for Policy and Practice*, London: Jessica Kingsley.

Tolman, R. and Bennett, L. (1990) 'A review of qualitative research on men who batter,' *Journal of Interpersonal Violence*, 5, pp 177-90.

Tosch, J. (1999) *A Man's Place: Masculinity and the Middleclass Home in Victorian England*, New Haven, CT: Yale University Press.

Trinder, L., Connelly, J., Kellet, J., Nortley, C. and Swift, L. (2006) *Making Contact Happen or Making Contact Work*, London: Department of Constitutional Affairs.

Turney, D. and Tanner, K. (2005) *Understanding and Working with Neglect. Research in Practice: Every Child Matters Research Briefings 10*, London, DfES, pp 1-8.

Walby, S. and Allen, J (2004) *Domestic Violence, Sexual Assault and Stalking: Findings from the British Crime Survey*, Home Office Research Study 276, London: Home Office.

Walker, L. (2009) '"My son gave birth to me": offending fathers – generative, reflexive and risky?', *British Journal of Social Work*, Vol, 40 pp 1402-1418

Wall, L.J. (2006) *A Report to the President of the Family Division on the Publication by the Women's Aid Federation of England entitled Twenty-Nine Homicides: Lessons still to be Learnt on Domestic Violence and Child Protection with Particular Reference to the Five Cases in which there was Judicial Involvement*, London: Royal Courts of Justice.

Wallerstein, J.S. and Kelly, J.B. (1980) *Surviving the Breakup*, London: Grant McIntyre.

Warin, J., Solomon, Y., Lewis, C. and Langford, W. (1999) *Fathers, Work and Family Life*, London: Family Policy Studies Centre.

Warwick, M. (2006) *Domestic Violence and Teenage Pregnancy: Making the Links and Making a Difference*, Bristol: Government Office of the South West.

Weinehall, K. (2005) '"Take my father away from home": children growing up in the proximity of violence', in M. Eriksson, M. Hester, M. Keskinen and K. Pringle (eds) *Tackling Men's Violence in Families: Nordic Issues and Dilemmas*, Bristol: The Policy Press.

Weisz, A.N., Tolman, R.M. and Saunders, D.G (2000) 'Assessing risk of severe domestic violence: the importance of survivor predictions', in *Journal of Interpersonal Violence*, vol 15, no 1, pp 75-89.

Welsh Assembly Government (2005) *Tackling Domestic Abuse: The All Wales Strategy: A Joint-agency Approach*, Cardiff: Welsh Assembly Government.

Wiggins, M. and Rosato, M. (2005) *Sure Start Plus National Evaluation. Final Report*, London: Social Science Research Unit, Institute of Education, University of London.

Williams, F. (1989) *Social Policy: A Critical Introduction*, Cambridge: Polity Press.

Williams, F. (1998) 'Troubled masculinities in social policy discourses: fatherhood', in J. Popay, J. Hearn and J. Edwards (eds) *Men, Gender Divisions and Welfare*, London: Routledge.

Williamson, E. and Hester, M. (2009) 'Evaluation of the South Tyneside domestic abuse perpetrator programme: final report', www.bristol. ac.uk/sps/research

Wilson, M. (1996) 'Working with the Change Men's programme', in K. Cavanagh and V.E. Gree (eds) *Working with Men: Feminism and Social Work*, London: Routledge.

Wilson, M. and Daly, M. (1998) 'Lethal and nonlethal violence against wives and the evolutionary psychology of male sexual proprietariness', in R.E. Dobash and R.P. Dobash (eds) *Rethinking Violence Against Women*, London: Sage Publications.

Women's Aid Federation of England (2007) What is domestic violence? www.womensaid.org.uk/domestic-violence-articles.asp.?

Brief methodological note on the empirical research

A full account of the methods used in this research can be found elsewhere (see Harne, 2005). This appendix highlights some key points that inform the research findings and may be of interest to readers and other researchers.

Sampling strategy with violent fathers

Finding a sample of violent fathers willing to be interviewed about their parenting is no easy task. Most are aware that aspects of their behaviour are criminal or at least socially unacceptable to legal and child welfare agencies and will therefore deny or minimise their behaviour to professionals, as seen in more general research on fathering in specific contexts (Smart and Neale, 1999). Since fathers' contact with children post-separation was also a key aspect of this research, the task of finding such fathers was even more difficult. Initially, participants were sought through family law solicitors, but concerns about confidentiality and how fathers' contact with children might be affected contributed to the failure to find any volunteers by this means. Some child protection agencies working with violent fathers agreed to provide access, but again no volunteers came forward. It is not surprising, therefore, that as with other research on violent men as fathers (see for example, Perel and Peled, 2008) perpetrator programmes became the means of finding fathers willing to participate. Some interested programmes that specifically addressed violent fathers' parenting provided access to fathers who were either attending or had recently completed a programme. The empirical research in this book therefore reflects this specific context.

The mothers' sample

The original intention was to interview mothers who were ex-partners of fathers attending the programmes, but, as in earlier studies in this area, most of the fathers interviewed were separated from first partners and their children, and some were no longer living in the same locality, making it difficult to gain access to them (Dobash et al, 1996; Gondolf, 2004). In addition, the research process itself raised confidentiality and safety concerns for women ex-partners and their children of the fathers interviewed, which might have put them at risk (for more detail see Harne, 2004). Moreover, although a few fathers were still living with second partners and children, continuing safety and ethical concerns for these mothers and their children led to a decision to find a separate sample of mothers who could be interviewed about their ex-partners' parenting (see also Hester and Radford, 1996; Smart and Neale, 1999) This involved seeking access to mothers attending support groups provided by perpetrator programmes for women whose partners or ex-partners were attending programmes. Some programmes, however were unwilling to provide access because of safety and ethical concerns, and eventually the mothers' sample was recruited from a variety of support groups for separated, abused mothers, in the knowledge that participants would have access to other supports once the interviews were completed.

Interviewing strategies

The research involved one-off 'snap-shot' qualitative interviews with both fathers and mothers and as such reflects views held in one particular time frame. Although all of the interviews focused on specific topics, they were open-ended and lasted between an hour and two hours, depending on how much the participants had to say, and returned to particular topics throughout. As Cavanagh and Lewis (1996) have highlighted, there were strong 'gendered differences' in the motivations of the men and women to participate in the research and the interviewing strategies therefore varied[1].

When interviewing the violent fathers, it was necessary to establish some rapport and retain a non-judgemental stance while focusing on the men's violent and abusive behaviour and its impact on children. In practice, although most of the fathers initially denied or minimised their behaviour and were anxious to demonstrate what good fathers they were, as the interviews progressed, and since 'it is difficult to conceal one's views and experiences in conversation over a period of time', some were eventually prepared to discuss these areas with 'seeming frankness' and in doing so contradicted earlier assertions (Harne, 2005, p 178). However, none acknowledged the full extent of his violence and abuse or directly intimidatory parenting practices when interviewed, and, as discussed in Chapter Four, the checklists were often more revealing (see Appendix 2). A few fathers found any questioning about their violent and abusive behaviour threatening and in two cases fathers became so angry and aggressive that the interviews had to be terminated. Nevertheless, these interviewing strategies indicate the advantages of open-ended interviewing over more standardised, closed, forms in obtaining a more credible picture of violent fathers' views and motivations.

Confidentiality with violent fathers

Standard confidentiality principles become more complex for researchers when they are interviewing powerful, dominant or criminal groups, particularly where the safety and welfare of children and mothers are concerned and there is potential for continuing harm (BSA, 2002). At the same time, without some guarantee of confidentiality, research participants are likely to be inhibited when discussing criminal or abusive behaviour and this may defeat the purposes of the research (Hearn, 1998a). Hearn resolved this dilemma in his research with violent men by applying the confidentiality principle to any disclosures 'within the law'. In the current research, confidentiality was not guaranteed to violent fathers where they talked about harm that was clearly ongoing or where they indicated a potential for future harm. This included ongoing directly abusive behaviour towards children that the fathers themselves did not define as harmful. Any such disclosures were discussed with programme workers.

Note

[1] For a fuller account of methods used when interviewing the mothers, see Harne (2004)

Men's abuse checklist

Many men regret hurting their loved ones and want to stop, but they find it too difficult to admit what they have done, and so only reveal a fraction of their violence. The following categories represent some of the behaviours men report using against their partners/ex-partners and children. Please read the categories carefully and put a tick if you have acted in that particular way within the past two years of your most recent relationship.

Physical abuse

Spit at her___
Poke or prod ___
Push, pull or trip___
Hold, grab or shake_
Pin her to wall or floor___
Slap or hit___
Pull her hair___
Sit or stand on her___
Punch with fist___
Kick or knee her___
Burn or scald___
Twist her arm or leg___
Bang her head or body___
Head-butt___
Choke or strangle___
Smother mouth___
Cut or slash with knife___
Violent sex/rape___
Throw things at her ___
Use a weapon or object___
Violence to pets___
Tie or lock her up___
Throw her around___
Hold her under water___

Intimidation

Use aggressive looks gestures___
Swear, shout and scream___
Make her do degrading things___
Harass her by spying, stalking___
Checking up on her___
Threaten to hurt her___
Threaten harm to other family members____
Threaten to harm the children___
Threaten with weapon or object___
Rip her clothes___
Pound your fists or punch the wall___
Throw food, objects around ___
Smash possessions___
Not leave when asked___
Stand over her___
Prevent her from leaving___
Threaten to kill her___

Sexual abuse

Get angry if you don't have sex___
Touch her sexually without consent___
Use pressure or threats to get sex___
Make her perform sex acts against her will___
Force her to have sex___
Make fun of her sexually___
Treat her as a sex object___
Forced use of pornography___
Forced prostitution___
Physically attack sexual parts of her body___

Financial abuse

You decide on family spending___
Make her beg for money___
Make her account for every penny___
Sabotage her paid work___
Withhold money___
Be secretive with money___

Psychological abuse

Criticise her or call her names__
Make her out to be stupid/mad__
Make fun of or humiliate her__
Blame her, make her feel guilty__
Twist her words__
Threaten to commit suicide__
Accuse her of having affairs__
Deprive her of food or sleep__
Listen to her phone calls__
Open her mail__
Force her to do housework to your standards__
Threat her as a servant, act as lord of the manor__
Interrupt her or not let her speak__
Ignore her, blank her, refuse to listen__
Threaten to involve social services__
Tell her what to wear__
Ogle at other women, threaten affairs__
Prevent her contact with friends and family__
Make her account for every moment of her time__
Not let her go where/when she wants__

Abuse towards children

Psychological/emotional abuse

Manipulate children to take sides__
Shout at or swear at children__
Frighten, threaten children__
Threaten to harm mother__
Damage children's possessions__
Threaten to put children into care__
Threaten children's pets__
Tell children they aren't loved__
Force them into criminal activities__
Force children to keep secrets__
Regularly criticise children__
Humiliate children__
Harm mother in front of children__
Never allow them to see friends__
Not allow children to go outside__

Force children outside of house__
Ignore children__
Humiliate mother in front of children__

Physical abuse or neglect

Hit or slap children hard__
Slam or throw objects to frighten__
Leave young children unsupervised__
Lock them in room in house__
Fail to feed children__
Deprive them of medical care__
Threaten to kill them__
Try to strangle or suffocate them__
Threaten them with sharp weapon__
Use children to attack mother__
Shake children__
Deprive them of clothes__
Threaten to hurt them__
Throw them across room/downstairs__
Pull their hair__
Punch, kick them__
Throw a heavy object at them__
Intentionally burn/scald them__
Beat them with strap or other instrument__

Index

Note: The letter n following a page number indicates an endnote